THE POWER OF
PRESIDENTIAL IDEOLOGIES

THE POWER OF PRESIDENTIAL IDEOLOGIES

Dennis Florig

PRAEGER

Westport, Connecticut
London

Library of Congress Cataloging-in-Publication Data

Florig, Dennis.
    The power of presidential ideologies / Dennis Florig.
       p.   cm.
    Includes bibliographical references.
    ISBN 0-275-94304-6 (alk. paper)
    1. Presidents—United States—History—20th century. 2. Political
leadership—United States—History—20th century. 3. Ideology—
History—20th century. 4. United States—Politics and
government—1981-1989—Decision making. 5. United States—Politics
and government—1989—Decision making.   I. Title.
JK518.F58   1992
324.6'3'0973—dc20   92-14726

British Library Cataloguing in Publication Data is available.

Library of Congress Catalog Card Number: 92-14726
ISBN: 0-275-94304-6

First published in 1992

Praeger Publishers, 88 Post Road West, Westport, CT 06881
An imprint of Greenwood Publishing Group, Inc.

Printed in the United States of America

The paper used in this book complies with the
Permanent Paper Standard issued by the National
Information Standards Organization (Z39.48-1984).

10 9 8 7 6 5 4 3 2 1

To Bob, a friend in need.

CONTENTS

Contents

TABLES AND FIGURES

TABLES

FIGURES

INTRODUCTION

Consider two similar cases in foreign policy facing American presidents. In both cases the key actor is a middle-sized third world nation with a military-dominated government financed by oil exports. The government has one of the largest militaries in the region, built up through massive supplies of arms from Western nations, paid for by oil revenues. In the past decade the United States and its Western allies have backed the government as a force for regional stabilization. The West has continued to aid the government as a check against regimes more hostile to the West, despite its brutal repression of domestic opponents and even charges of genocide against its own people.

Then suddenly the government launches a massive invasion of a much smaller and weaker neighbor. It occupies the smaller country and attempts to incorporate the formerly independent nation into its own territory. It kills thousands, probably tens of thousands, of resisters in a massive campaign of terror.

In the first of these two cases the president acts decisively against the aggressor. He repeatedly uses the news media to denounce the invasion as a blow against international peace, a threat to small nations everywhere, and an offense against world order. He gathers the support of U.S. allies and even some of its former enemies for United Nations votes for an economic boycott and other international sanctions against the aggressor. He personally takes the lead in assembling a coalition of Western and regional forces, sending half a million U.S. troops to the war theater.

When economic sanctions and military threats do not quickly convince the aggressor to withdraw, the president authorizes a massive bombing campaign to destroy its economic capacity. Millions are glued to their televisions sets, anxiously following America's first war since the disaster in Vietnam. When, after a month of massive bombing, the opponent will not capitulate, the president launches a ground attack, putting tens of thousands of U.S. soldiers at risk. The ground fighting is surprisingly brief, with few United States or allied casualties. However, the military campaign inflicts tens of thousands of casualties on the enemy, who is chased out of occupied territory. The old government is restored. The president proclaims that the peace has been protected and small nations everywhere can rest secure that they will be protected from more powerful aggressors.

In the other case, the administration tries to hide the act of aggression from public view. The president is silent on the issue, and the government tries to divert world attention from the situation. The media are discouraged from even mentioning the story, and in private administration officials downplay the significance of the event. The United States keeps the issue from coming to a vote in the United Nations, implicitly threatening to use its veto power or to withhold financial support from the United Nations if action is taken. The administration tries to quiet those in allied and nonaligned governments who are concerned about the massive human suffering and the dangerous international precedent that is being set.

The aggression is successful. The tiny neighbor disappears from the political map. After a brief slap on the wrist, U.S. arms shipments to the aggressor government resume, despite the fact that these arms are being used in violation of both U.S. and international law. The aggressor pays no significant costs for its action and is today a respected member of the world community, considered by American presidents as part of the "free world." The case is not even a footnote in contemporary or historical assessments of the president's administration.

Virtually all Americans will recognize the first case as the Bush administration's response to Iraq's invasion of Kuwait. But what is the second case? It is not a hypothetical example of how a weak-kneed, liberal Democratic president would have handled the Persian Gulf crisis. It is a real case from recent history. Not one in a thousand Americans could recognize the second case as U.S. ally Indonesia's invasion of the nation of East Timor during the Ford administration.

Such is the power of presidential ideologies. In the case of the Persian Gulf, President Bush made the liberation of Kuwait a personal and a national crusade. Not a day went by that the media and the American people's attention were not pointed toward the Persian Gulf by the administration. However, President Ford and his advisers chose to ignore the plight of East Timor. Without presidential attention, the media, which at first gave some coverage to the story, soon lost interest. The American people never had their attention engaged, and most were never aware that a nation had been erased from the face of the earth.

What can explain the different standards that were applied to Iraqi and Indonesian aggression? Certainly no simple-minded notion of liberalism versus conservatism can explain the differences in presidential response to these acts of aggression. Both President Ford and President Bush are moderately conservative Republicans. By conventional measures of ideology they are virtual twins; in fact, George Bush was an important member of the Ford administration. But despite the obvious similarities of the cases of Kuwait and East Timor, these two philosophically similar presidents applied very different principles to the practice of foreign policy-making.

Clearly the principal reason President Bush stated for intervening in the Persian Gulf also applied in the case of East Timor. In both cases a bigger nation was guilty of unprovoked aggression against a smaller neighbor. If it is a threat to world peace for a stronger nation to gobble up a weaker nation, then the action of Indonesia against East Timor was as much a threat to world peace as Iraq's action against Kuwait. The difference in responses in these two cases indicates that there is more to presidential ideologies than meets the eye.

Actually, any thoughtful explanation of the difference in presidential policy in these two cases would be fairly complex. My purpose in raising this contradiction here is not to provide a simple solution to the puzzle. Rather, it is to show that presidents have a powerful impact in shaping the way we perceive the world. The Iraqi invasion of Kuwait dominated American public life for the better part of a year. The Indonesian invasion of East Timor never even entered the consciousness of most Americans.

The way presidents characterize world events deeply affects our lives. The words and ideas of presidents matter.

PART I

PRESIDENTIAL IDEOLOGIES

1

THE PRESIDENT AS IDEOLOGICAL LEADER

THE PRESIDENT AS MEDIA POLITICIAN AND POLICYMAKER

Every four years the American people participate in the strange and wonderful rite of selecting the leader of the nation. If one judged from the sound and fury of the candidates' campaigns, there would be no doubt that the future well-being and even the existence of the nation are riding on the selection the people make. But many citizens are not so sure. Nearly half of them do not vote, and many of those who do vote see their choice as between the lesser of two evils. Voters see the gap between promise and performance, between rhetoric and reality, and wonder if in the long run their choice has any meaningful impact on their lives.

That is what this book is about—what kind of substantive difference it makes who is president. It will begin by examining the roles of the president as media politician, as policymaker, and as shaper of the public philosophy.

The President as Media Politician

In the late twentieth century we live in the media age, and our politics are increasingly media politics. Most citizens get most of their political information from watching television. Politicians, aware of this fact of political life, shape their campaigns for office and their actions in office to make the TV cameras work for them rather than against them. More and more our political system seems to operate on the adage that if it wasn't seen on TV, it didn't happen. In the age of media politics, the president is the premier media politician. He is simultaneously the symbolic embodiment of the nation and the most powerful figure in the political system. He is "what's happening," he "is" news. The president personalizes the political process for people. No other political leader so often comes directly into people's living rooms to make public statements and appeals. No one else becomes so widely recognized as a personality. At least some of Ronald Reagan's success as "the great communicator" was based on his unique ability to influence people through television, since he was an actor and a television pitchman for a major corporation before he was a politician.

The presidency provides the incumbent with a set of impressive stages from which to deliver his messages. The president speaks before the assembled Congress when he delivers the annual State of the Union address and special crisis messages. He travels around the world to scenic vistas for summits with foreign leaders. He entertains politicians, personalities, and foreign visitors at picturesque locales. The president can appear at colorful mass rallies of cheering supporters, or before carefully chosen audiences of concerned citizens, settings that amplify the impact of his remarks. He can commandeer the airwaves for televised messages that literally reach citizens where they live.

The President as Policymaker

The media, obsessed with the aura of power and mindful that the symbolic trappings of the chief of state make for good pictures, give disproportionate attention to the presidency. The presidency has very real powers, but it projects an appearance of power that is larger than real life. Decisions made in the bowels of the bureaucracy or in the working out of legislation in Congress often have as much influence on the actions of government and the lives of the people as presidential decisions. But these forms of power do not make good television. They usually do not make good pictures, and they are too complicated to explain in a 30-second spot on the evening news. The president, on the other hand, personalizes politics. Whether they see him as a hero, a villain, or just an ordinary guy, TV viewers can relate to an individual in a way that is more visceral than that of comprehending a complex system.

The president is more than just a person, however. As a policymaker he must make decisions. He must make a series of choices as he responds to the economic, social, and international problems of the nation. If the economy falters, or if a foreign hot spot erupts, the president is expected to act to protect and further the interests of the nation. When foreign militants seize American hostages, the president is expected to respond. When inflation mounts or a recession strikes, the president is expected to know what to do. In such circumstances he must choose between different sets of options for action offered by his advisers. In these policy choices, the president is actually selecting among different expectations about what government is supposed to do. He is acting on some philosophy about the legitimate role of government.

The focus of this book is on the president's role as a policymaker and an ideologue. The media are obsessed with the president as a personality, with polls on the current popularity of the man. This is one measure of the president's ability to influence policy and the public philosophy. Unpopular presidents generally have less influence than popular presidents. But to fully understand the president as policymaker, one must move beyond the cult of personality and the media images to examine an administration's real impact on issues that affect the lives of citizens. Presidential personality cults can obscure the negative impacts of presidential policies or the lack of any sustained substantive impact on policy problems. On the other hand, presidents may lose popularity by making controversial decisions that are later proven to be effective policies. There is more to the presidency than media politics.

WHAT DIFFERENCE DOES IDEOLOGY MAKE?

The President as Ideologue

At the intersection of the president's roles as media politician and as policymaker is political philosophy or ideology. The president must offer justifications for the policy actions he takes. He can use media politics to avoid difficult policy decisions and obscure the real impacts of policy choices behind reassuring photo opportunities. But ultimately the president must make policy choices and explain why he pursues the policies he has selected.

All presidents are conscious of their public policy responsibilities. Some presidents are also very self-conscious about defining a consistent public philosophy that justifies the choices they make. Other presidents are almost anti-ideological in their attempts to avoid being seen as outside the political center. Ronald Reagan and Franklin Roosevelt are examples of presidents with distinct ideologies to legitimate their policies. Roosevelt, in coping with the Great Depression crisis, had to embark on new policy directions, and he developed the philosophy of activist government to justify his new policies. Ronald Reagan, by contrast, was a spokesman for the limited state, a persistent critic of the ability of government to make people better off. Jimmy Carter and Dwight Eisenhower, on the other hand, stand out as presidents who tried to avoid ideological labels and commitments.

Ideological Symbolism as a Substitute for Policy Performance

The relationship between the symbolic politics of media appearances and the difficult substance of government is crucial to understanding the contemporary presidency. Media symbolism and public rhetoric can often substitute for effective policy action. Murray Edelman has pointed out that the dramatic projection of coping actions can create the illusion that problems are being solved, even if they are not.[1] Repeated summit meetings of U.S. and Russian leaders, complete with TV cameras whirring and personal assurances of the leaders that arms control is on the agenda, can reassure the public that relations between the great powers are being managed and arms control is continuing apace, even if no concrete agreements are reached and relations deteriorate once the leaders return home. Presidential trips to urban renewal projects and conferences with leading minority personalities seen on the evening news can project the image that race and poverty problems are being dealt with effectively, even if poverty is increasing and ghetto conditions are worsening.

This tendency of media politics to substitute for policy substance is comically illustrated in Peter Sellers' last movie, *Being There*. Sellers plays a simpleminded gardener who through a series of coincidences becomes a friend of a corporate magnate and eventually an adviser to the president. Sellers' inane utterances about gardening are taken by these powerful people as a series of metaphors about the political system. Sellers becomes a media celebrity and an administration power even though he doesn't have the least clue about the meaning of politics, much less of the subtleties and complexities of governance. But he looks and sounds good on TV.

Presidential use of words, pictures, and symbols goes deeper, however, than simply substituting the image of coping for effective policy action. Presidential ideologies are used to obscure the real motivations behind policy actions, to disguise them behind rhetoric that is out of touch with the realities of a policy. For example, the doctrine of the national security state, which has strongly influenced U.S. foreign policy since the World War II, explicitly recommends that presidents at times conceal their intentions from adversaries. Of course, adversaries can come in domestic as well as foreign forms. Richard Nixon, for example, justified the burglary of the offices of the Democratic National Committee on the phony grounds that national security was at stake.

But conscious lying is actually less important in understanding the president as ideologue than is recognition that every presidential philosophy contains some truth and some false ideas. Ronald Reagan spoke continually of the success of his administration in cutting government spending. Certainly some programs were cut. But because of the military buildup and the rising interest on debt, government spending when Reagan left office took the same percentage of resources from the economy as it did when he became president. In the same vein, Lyndon Johnson talked about a war that would eradicate poverty. The war on poverty helped many people, but it was more a skirmish than all-out war. Johnson thought it was necessary to oversell the merits of his Great Society programs to get them through Congress and get funds appropriated.

Ideology as the Basis for Policy Choice

So skepticism about the connection between media rhetoric and policies is certainly justified. But as Lincoln said, "You may fool all the people some of the time, you can even fool some of the people all of the time, but you can't fool all of the people all the time." The relationship between media symbolism and the substance of governance is more complex than simply the substitution of appearance for reality. Media symbolism and public rhetoric also spur the public's appetite for real action on policy problems. While a single summit without action may in the short term reassure the public that problems are being dealt with, repeated summits reflect the continuing public expectation that real action will be taken on arms control and other East-West issues. Repeated summits reinforce the expectation that real results will follow. At an even deeper level, presidential symbolism and rhetoric shape public and official perceptions of what are the legitimate roles of government. The public pronouncements of presidents play a major role in the justification of governmental action, particularly those made at highly charged symbolic events. Policy decisions do not occur in a vacuum; they occur in some ideological context. They must be justified by an explicit or implicit philosophy about what government should be doing.

Presidents play a crucial role in the articulation of these public philosophies. In the 1960s President Kennedy and President Johnson used their media visibility to advance the philosophy that it was the responsibility of the national government to pursue civil rights, to combat poverty, and to take an activist role in solving social problems. Their administrations not only expanded the range of concrete government programs but also expanded the perception of what roles it was legitimate for government to be playing in society—they advanced the ideology of the activist state. In the 1980s Ronald Reagan used the presidency to advance the philosophy that government itself is the problem and that it cannot offer successful solutions to social problems. While Reagan had little success in cutting overall government spending, he did create an ideological climate in which it is much more difficult for those who wish to use government to attack social problems to operate. His skillful use of the media and ideological resources of the presidency advanced the cause of the limited state.

So presidential ideologies are, in the words of the songwriter, "walking contradictions, partly truth, partly fiction." On the one hand, they can substitute convenient, simplistic media fictions for real political change. But on the other hand, the president, either consciously or by his policy actions, reveals a philosophy about what are the legitimate expectations of government in our democratic society.

IDEOLOGY IN THE 1988 ELECTION

The Reagan-Bush Strategy of Ideological Polarization

The importance of political ideology can be seen in the 1988 election. Ronald Reagan, the most conservative president in many decades, was leaving office. He had been the most successful president in turning his agenda into policy action in recent years. The first two years of the Reagan administration represent the highest tide of the conservative ideology in at least half a century. For George Bush, claiming the mantle as Reagan's successor meant proclaiming the ideology of conservatism. Bush ran as an ideological conservative, repeatedly attacking Michael Dukakis as a liberal and trying to emphasize the philosophical and policy differences between his conservatism and Dukakis' liberalism.

The strategy of polarizing the country and the electorate along conservative-liberal lines is part of a larger Republican electoral strategy, the "Sunbelt" or "southern" strategy. Historically the 11 southern states that had formed the Confederacy during the Civil War were solidly Democratic because the Republican Party was associated in the southern mind with the hated postwar Reconstruction. But in the 1960s a liberal Democratic administration oversaw the "second Reconstruction," the dismantling of official structures of racial segregation. Now the Republicans were no longer the greatest threat to white southern political power; rather, it was the Democrats, the party of civil rights. The Republican Party consciously tried to make electoral inroads in the South by emphasizing its opposition to big government in Washington in general and to the liberal agenda in particular. This ideological appeal to racially conscious white Southerners as well as genuine philosophical conservatives in the region has worked to deny the Democrats their historic southern base in presidential elections since 1968. The southern strategy had propelled the Republicans to the White House in four of the last five elections and Texan Bush hoped it could do it again in 1988.

Dukakis and the Democratic Flight from Ideology

Michael Dukakis, on the other hand, consciously tried to avoid ideological classification. He reacted to Bush's charges that he was a liberal outside the political mainstream not by defending liberalism but by treating these attacks as a form of political name-calling. He called charges of liberalism meaningless "labeling." This was no accident. Liberalism had been as popular and as much the dominant public philosophy in the 1960s as conservatism was in the 1980s. But since the late 1960s it had become associated in the popular mind with serious crises of government. In race relations liberalism was associated with minority rights, and by implication with the violence and crime of the ghettos of the inner cities. In foreign policy liberalism came to be blamed both for the

Vietnam War and for the disturbing protests against it. In the 1970s liberals also took the blame for rising budget deficits and declining economic performance.

Just as important in the decline of liberalism, proclaiming liberalism no longer fits the Democratic Party's electoral strategy. The Democratic Party has a broader and more diverse social base than the Republican Party. It is the party of both George McGovern and George Wallace. Ideological polarization tends to divide it along ethnic cleavages. Blacks are both the most consistently liberal and the most consistently Democratic voters. But northern white ethnic and southern white Protestant Democrats tend to be more politically moderate and sometimes openly antiblack and antiliberal. Yet in order to win a national election a Democratic candidate must hold together this heterogeneous set of supporters. This is one key reason why Democrats have not done well in recent presidential elections. It is also why Democratic presidential candidates from Kennedy to Carter to Dukakis have tried to avoid being labeled liberals.

PRESIDENTS AND IDEOLOGICAL CONSTRUCTION

Presidential elections play an important role in shaping the ideas that will guide public policy in the years ahead. But while a candidate campaigns for roughly a year, an administration holds power for at least four years. Presidents in office have a broader and deeper impact on the public philosophy than do candidates. Because of its media visibility the presidency is the single most important institution in the American political system for the development of ideology and particularly for ideological change. The president is literally the main communication link between the government and the people. Far more people see or hear his words directly than those of any other political figure. The ideas of presidents are carried along the airwaves into the homes of millions of citizens, countless opinion leaders, and even lesser members of the administration.

Certainly the minimum conditions for any philosophy or ideology to develop broad political support are that it be known to a large number of citizens, and that it influence the beliefs of political elites. The president is usually the only politician to command the sustained attention of both ordinary citizens and elite opinion leaders, the only one who can successfully disseminate new ideas rapidly and widely throughout the political system. Years ago Teddy Roosevelt called the presidency a "bully pulpit," and this is even more true in the media age.

The president is particularly important in the process of ideological change. Once a doctrine has become embedded in political thought, many institutions may play a role in reinforcing it. But the presidency is the only part of the political system biased toward broad-based policies and toward change. It is well known that most institutions of U.S. government are biased toward maintenance of the status quo, or only incremental change. The courts and the bureaucracy are shielded from direct popular control, and senior members are recruited from elite social strata, a combination that insulates them from many currents of change. Members of Congress are enmeshed in a web of parochial electoral demands that ties them closely to dominant economic interests. This predisposes Congress to narrow and specialized policy interests rather than large-scale political change.

The presidency, however, is different. The president must stand for election nationally, and thus must develop a broad program with truly mass appeal in order to advance his candidacy. Once in office, he is, rightly or wrongly, held responsible for major changes in national conditions—the ups and downs of the economy, the outbreak of new foreign crises, and so on. These pressures bias presidential administrations toward developing truly national programs and bold, sweeping doctrines to justify them to the people.

There is a direct link between perceptions of particular presidencies as "strong" or "weak" and their role in ideological construction. Strong presidents are remembered as much as anything for their role in developing new political ideas. Presidents must make difficult policy choices, and therefore they must develop ideologies that justify these choices. FDR is remembered as a strong president exactly because his administration decisively defeated the doctrine of strictly limited government and replaced it with the idea of activist, positive, helping government. Similarly, FDR led the United States to complete commitment to the doctrine of internationalism, and his successor, Harry Truman, developed the idea of containment to explain the new U.S. role in the world to the people.

These doctrines were not simply the empty words of self-serving politicians. Instead, they represented fundamental change in policies and practices throughout government. These doctrines did not shape policymaking just in the administrations that first enunciated them; instead they endured to shape policy-making in future generations.

Lesser, but historically significant, shifts in ideas and practice can be seen in the Johnson administration's imagery of new activism for political and economic equality, in Nixon's ideas about detente, in the movement back toward both the limited state and the cold war under Ronald Reagan, and in the concept of a new world order emerging from the Bush administration. Strong presidents are more likely to leave doctrines that survive them. Weak presidents cannot control policy discourse in their own time, much less the ideas of succeeding administrations.

Of course, new ideological doctrines are always the target of severe criticism. Strong presidents have the ability to navigate turbulent ideological waters, but weaker presidents can run aground or sink on the shoals of policy failure. When policies fail, political conflict over ideology intensifies and incumbent administrations and their doctrines are blamed. Johnson's tragic application of the cold war doctrines to Vietnam undermined not only his own administration but also political support for cold war ideology. In the same way, Herbert Hoover's clinging to the doctrine of limited government in the midst of the Depression crisis undermined not only his administration but also political support for the idea of limited government.

THE CYCLE OF IDEOLOGICAL CONSTRUCTION

Decline of the Prior Public Philosophy

The ideological role of the president can be placed in the broader context of a cycle of policy legitimation and ideological development. The process of ideological construction begins with the decay of the power of old ideas to justify government policies and practices, what can be called a decline in the prior public philosophy. The public philosophies that predominate in one historical era often prove inadequate for a changing political world. The balance of political power between different groups within the nation or between nations can shift, and with such shifts come changes in the power of the dominant ideas to influence events. As the political world evolves, the interests of political groups can alter. New groups may become politically mobilized and press for change in prevailing doctrines, or formerly well-organized and influential power blocs may lose their sway in the political process.

One case where an ideological doctrine lost some of its persuasive power because of shifting political interests is the support of business interests of the idea of limited government. The interest of nineteenth century merchants and industrialists in the doctrines and practices of limited government differed substantially from the need of late twentieth century corporations for government assistance in providing the physical, technical, and human infrastructure of a developed capitalist economy.

The decay of public philosophies can also be associated with shifting political forces and mobilizations. The Great Depression of the 1930s changed more than calculations about material interest. More important, it spurred the political mobilization of the working class as membership in trade unions swelled and citizen activism on many other fronts erupted. The philosophy and practices of limited government could not cope with this changing balance of political power between labor and capital. Another case where new political mobilizations affected the prevailing public philosophy was race relations in the 1960s. As the civil rights movement emerged and black people became politically active in ever-increasing numbers, the doctrines of segregation and national government nonintervention in local race issues were unable to withstand the new pressures.

Changes in the world balance of power affect the prevailing doctrines about foreign policy. Isolationism was an appropriate philosophy for a small, weak nation in a far corner of the world, as the United States was in its first 100 years. But as U.S. interests and influence spread beyond the North American continent in the second half of the nineteenth century, the doctrine of isolationism was no longer adequate. While isolationism survived to influence policy into the first third of the twentieth century, it was less and less relevant to the American experience. In the aftermath of World War II the United States developed the doctrines of containment of communism and the national security state to reflect its deepening involvement in global politics. But in the later twentieth century these doctrines have come increasingly under challenge. The national security state was unable to stop the growth of the Soviet Union's nuclear arsenal, which presented a real threat to the very survival of the American people. While containment produced some successes against radical forces in the Third World, it also had some spectacular failures such as Vietnam, Iran, and the Bay of Pigs. Certainly the cold war ideology could not help the United States cope with the rising competition of the Japanese and western European economies. And the national security ideology was totally unprepared for the collapse of communism in the Soviet bloc in recent years.

The Rise of Contending Doctrines

The decline of a dominant public philosophy is ultimately accompanied by the rise of contending doctrines and rising public attention to competing ideological formulations. New political ideas are always being developed by minority parties, ideological blocs in Congress, and newly emerging contenders for the presidency. But when a predominant ideology begins to falter, this process intensifies.

Minor parties are often ignored in American political analysis, but they are frequently the source of new political ideas that are later taken up by the major parties during political crises. Ideas of the Progressive and Socialist parties became part of the New Deal. Themes from the 1968 splinter candidate George Wallace have played a role in a generation of Republican presidential politics.

The major parties themselves may be taken over by presidential candidates who articulate new policy approaches, as Barry Goldwater did in 1964 and George McGovern did in 1972. In the 1988 election the primary candidacies of Jesse Jackson and Pat Robertson offered new and different ideas about how to approach problems of public policy. Failing presidential campaigns of major party candidates are particularly important sources of ideological innovation because, as both a cause and an effect of their weakness, they tend to devote more energy to long-term moral teaching than to the immediate quest for office. Even in defeat, Goldwater prefigured the ideas of the successful Nixon and Reagan candidacies. Primary campaigns can also influence future presidential philosophy, as demonstrated by the impact of the ideas of the 1968 Eugene McCarthy and Robert Kennedy campaigns on the foreign policy of presidents Nixon and Carter in the 1970s.

Congressional blocs are another source of new ideologies. James Sundquist has demonstrated how many of the ideas that ultimately became the Great Society program were incubating in liberal Democratic minorities in the Congresses of the 1950s.[2] More recently, the Kemp-Roth tax cut and supply-side economics were debated in Congress before Ronald Reagan was president.

The Critical Role of the Presidency in Ideological Change

But new ideas rarely become dominant public philosophies unless they engage the attention and action of a sitting president. Historically, movement of the preponderance of elite and mass opinion to a new set of doctrines requires engagement of the unique ideological power of the president. The president is the symbolic embodiment of the nation. He is the central figure for both elite and mass political communication.

Only the president has the capacity to sustain the attention of the political system long enough to bring about enduring change in basic political ideas. The triumph of the activist state is hard to imagine without the fireside chats of FDR that repeatedly brought these ideas into the homes of millions of citizens. It is hard to imagine the American people being willing to bear the massive human and material costs of the cold war without the repeated personal assurances of several successive presidents that these sacrifices were necessary. President Bush and his successors will have the greatest impact on defining what the catchy slogan "a new world order" actually means for U.S. foreign policy.

Success and Failure of Presidential Doctrines

However, simply because a president proclaims a new doctrine, this does not make it a dominant public philosophy. Virtually all significant ideological changes require presidential leadership. But not all attempts of presidents to exercise ideological leadership are successful. The political landscape is littered with the remnants of new ideas proclaimed by presidents that have had little effect on the political world beyond the president's most loyal followers. With ideology, as with legislation, the president proposes but other political institutions dispose. The truly historic presidential doctrines have gained deep and enduring support from other leading politicians, public officials, opinion leaders, and the public.

The presidential doctrines that matter influence Congress to pass legislation, create bureaucracies, and vote funds for programs. Cold war doctrines convinced Congress to support the necessary military, intelligence, and diplomatic programs; to create the new military planning and national security bureaucracies to implement these programs; and to vote the funds to sustain them. The doctrines of political and economic equality, infused with new power by the civil rights movement, convinced Congress to create a series of new programs aimed at using the power of government to assist people.

A key point in the historical development of a public philosophy is what Lowi calls "validation through succession."[3] When a new administration comes to power and accepts a predecessor's doctrine as a continuing guide to policy, this doctrine has passed a critical test of its power to endure. Validation through succession is particularly significant when the new president is from the opposition party, and thus demonstrates bipartisan commitment to a set of ideas. The power of the national security state was demonstrated by the series of both Republican and Democratic presidents who accepted its basic premises. The process of ideological construction is nearing completion when the prior public philosophy slowly ceases to provide the intellectual basis for opposition forces and parties. It is final when even political opponents of a president come to accept the fundamental tenets of his doctrines, and policy disputes center more and more on the inability of an administration to make policy outcomes conform to the promises of their doctrines. When in 1960 Kennedy and Nixon debated who would be the more effective cold warrior, they were indirectly demonstrating the power of national security ideology to shape public discourse.

The most successful ideologies become so deeply embedded in political thought and speech that they are no longer recognized as problematic assumptions. The most powerful ideologies are taken on faith and repeated as rote incantations ever more intensely when policy outcomes are not consistent with promises.

Ideological Restoration

Not every round of the ideological cycle is characterized by the emergence of totally new ideas. The 1980s brought a significant ideological offensive by conservative political forces inside and outside the White House. While this new generation of conservatives had some truly new ideas, the Reagan and Bush administrations can better be understood as attempting to restore the ideological power of traditional ideas that had guided government in prior eras. Even the most innovative policies of the Reagan administration derived from older ideas. "Supply-side economics" may have been a new term, but it was largely a restatement of the classic doctrine of the limited state, which argues that more wealth can be created in the private sector than through government taxing and spending. "Star Wars," the Strategic Defense Initiative, may have been a new concept in hardware, but it stemmed from the basic doctrine of arms competition and cold war confrontation with the Soviet Union.

IDEOLOGICAL CRISIS AND PRESIDENTIAL POWER

By describing the cycle of ideological construction I do not mean to imply that every time there is a decline in the power of the predominant public philosophy to cope with new policy challenges, a new public philosophy that can cope with these challenges automatically appears. When events outrun a prevailing public philosophy, contending ideologies will inevitably arise that attempt to replace the existing philosophy. But that does not mean these new ideas will be successful in gaining the political support necessary to replace the current ideology. Nor does it mean that even if such new ideas do gain the necessary political support, they will be any more successful in dealing with the policy problems which generated the crisis. Often crises linger unresolved for decades.

The interrelated crises of the urban underclass and racial tension in American society have simmered for generations without ever being decisively "solved." For most of the twentieth century the ideology of the limited state blocked any activist government attack on such social problems. The ideological shifts of the 1960s brought an activist government response, but clearly whatever the philosophies and policies adopted in the 1960s did accomplish, they did not bring an end to either the urban underclass or racial tensions.

However, when the nation faces political crises, there is a tendency to look to the president to lead the country out of the crisis. At the appearance of a new crisis the nation turns to the president to provide new ideas and new policies to cope with the crisis. But when such attention is focused on the presidency and the president is not able to deal effectively with events, then the president may be blamed for the continuing crisis, and suffer politically as a result.

FDR and his New Deal offer an example of a new president with new ideas who was politically successful in replacing the prevailing public philosophy even though he was not particularly successful in dealing with the substance of the crisis that brought him to power. In the 1930s FDR stepped into the breach when the prior public philosophy was unable to cope with the Great Depression. His philosophy of an activist state that would decisively attack the economic crisis was politically successful. Under FDR the Democratic Party created a political coalition that would hold the presidency for twenty years and control Congress for generations. FDR's administration was politically successful in part because so many people benefited from his public works and relief policies, and because, in contrast with the prior administration, the New Deal did seem to be actively combating the depression. But these activist policies did not really solve the crisis, which was ended only by the military spending that followed from U.S. entry into World War II. Many students of the era argue that the U.S. victory in the war, not his New Deal policies, cemented FDR's reputation in history as a great president.

The responses of other administrations to policy crises will be dealt with in later chapters. The point here is that the inability of the current public philosophy to cope effectively with new policy problems leads to intensified ideological conflict. New crises may lead to the emergence of a newly dominant public policy, but this is not necessarily the case. Instead, prolonged periods of ideological crisis may ensue.

Presidents who successfully cope with policy crises and articulate a new public philosophy to guide public policy are remembered as great presidents. Presidents who are unable to master the currents of ideological conflict and crisis are likely to leave little lasting legacy in policy or philosophy.

NOTES

1. Murray Edelman, *The Symbolic Uses of Politics* (Urbana: University of Illinois Press, 1964).

2. James Sundquist, *Politics and Policy* (Washington, DC: Brookings Institution, 1968).

3. Theodore Lowi, *The End of Liberalism* (New York: Norton, 1979).

2

THE AMERICAN
IDEOLOGICAL SPECTRUM

BEYOND LIBERALISM AND CONSERVATISM

The Limits of Liberalism versus Conservatism

In order to understand ideological dynamics in any particular presidency, it is necessary to set them in the context of the general ideological conflicts within the U.S. political system. Yet the problem of characterizing the range of political ideologies has perplexed students of American politics for a long time. The idea of an ideological spectrum makes sense on one level, but when one moves from the general concept to actually characterizing political views, the task becomes difficult. For example, many politicians, pundits, and even political scientists use the concepts of conservatism and liberalism to characterize the policies of administrations. In this way the actions of the Reagan administration are explained in light of his conservative political philosophy, as the policies of FDR and LBJ are attributed to their liberal philosophy. However, the concepts of conservatism and liberalism will carry one only so far.

The basic problem in thinking about the ideological spectrum is the problem of multidimensionality. There are always many active political issues, and philosophical agreement on one issue or even one set of issues does not guarantee philosophical agreement on others. For example, most conservatives believe in limiting government and maximizing individual choice on economic issues like regulation, government spending, and taxation. Yet in the area of social issues like abortion, sexual behavior, women's roles, and alcohol and drug usage, many who call themselves conservatives favor traditional values over individual choice. Yet others who think of themselves as conservatives, particularly younger people, believe in the primacy of individual choice in these areas as well. When one factors in other clusters of issues, such as foreign policy, the waters become even more muddied.

The problem is further compounded by changes in what is considered liberal or conservative over historical time. From the 1930s into the 1950s, conservatives tended to be isolationist and to oppose U.S. involvement in foreign conflicts. In this period it was liberals who tended to support intervention abroad. Yet by the 1970s and 1980s the picture was different. Conservatives were the strongest supporters of interventions overseas, while liberals had become more skeptical of foreign military actions. Another problem with the liberal-conservative dichotomy is the pervasive tendency of American politics to be "centrist." Many successful presidential candidates are not too closely identified with either liberalism or conservatism. It is no accident that presidents recycle lines from past presidents from the opposing party who sought to blur ideological distinctions. Thus Jimmy Carter repeated Eisenhower's phrase that he was "a conservative on economic issues, but a liberal on social issues." Ronald Reagan used John Kennedy's line muting conflict over economic ideology, "A rising tide lifts all boats." Even presidents who come to office strongly associated with one doctrine, such as FDR or Reagan, tend to move to the center over time.

But perhaps the most serious problem with using the ideas of conservatism and liberalism to characterize presidential administrations is that these labels do little to illuminate the actual policies pursued by either Republican or Democratic administrations. Theodore Lowi argues that while the public debate between the parties emphasizes a conflict between the "liberal" philosophy of using the activist state to help the disadvantaged and the "conservative" philosophy of the limited state, neither party lives up to its rhetoric in practice.[1] Despite their rhetoric, conservative Republican presidents do not shrink the size of government; they only slow the rate of growth of government programs, and sometimes they change the forms of government spending. Similarly, the official liberal ideology is the use the activist state to help the disadvantaged members of society, while in practice the programs that liberals put in place more often serve powerful interest group oligarchies. According to Lowi, Republican and Democratic administrations' rhetoric is still fixed on an issue that was settled in the 1930s—whether government is to play an activist role in society.

However, the very fact that pundits continually try to label various administrations and the actions of these administrations as liberal or conservative attests to the necessity for some way of characterizing ideological variation. Sometimes these terms are a convenient shorthand way of locating presidents on the ideological spectrum and describing movements of political philosophy between and within administrations.

Ideological Poles and the Political Center

But the twofold liberal-conservative typology, or even a threefold liberal-moderate-conservative typology, is not adequate to deal with the complexity of the issues. Nor can any one typology cover all the different kinds of issues the nation faces. But at the risk of repeating all of the mistakes I have just alluded to, I would like to suggest a set of typologies that put current and recent ideological conflict into better perspective.

These typologies begin with recognition that ideological conflict is characterized by simultaneous tendencies toward centrist politics and toward ideological polarization. Therefore, each party is cross-pressured by its centrist wing and its ideological wing. The obvious similarities between the parties is the result of their striving for the elusive political center. The differences in rhetoric and policy between the parties is the result of the different political and ideological groups that are part of the party coalition. The picture is further complicated by the fact that the center is continuously in flux—what is perceived as the ideological center changes significantly over time, largely as a result of the differing forces exerted by the ideological poles. In the 1950s and 1960s, it was a centrist position to conduct a cold war with the Soviet Union. But by the late 1980s it was centrist to support arms reduction treaties and a more flexible approach to the Soviet Union.

The relationship between the polar and centrist tendencies of the parties can be represented by aligning them on a spectrum of political philosophy as shown in Figure 2.1. To begin, let us use the conventional terminology "liberalism" and "conservatism." By breaking the ideological spectrum into four categories, we can represent the political center as opposed to the ideological poles of thought. We can also show that each party has an ideological wing and is uncomfortably located between its ideological wing and the centrist wing of the opposing party.

Figure 2.1
Political Parties and the Ideological Spectrum

Ideological (Democratic) Left	Democratic Center	Republican Center	Ideological (Republican) Right
or	or	or	or
Very Liberal	Moderately Liberal	Moderately Conservative	Very Conservative

[Range of Probable Behavior
of Democratic Administrations]

[Range of Probable Behavior of
Republican Administrations]

But the picture is still not complete. In order to understand the policy maneuvers of presidents of either party, we need to know more about the substantive differences between the expectations of the political center and of each party's ideological wing. The rest of this chapter and Chapter 3 describe the different ideas about public policy and the role of government that have held the political center or emerged on the ideological wings to challenge the center.

The Concept of the State

The typologies of political philosophy and public policy introduced in this chapter often use the term "state," so it is useful to make clear how the concept of the state is being used in this book. The term as it is being used here has four dimensions: (1) a set of similar public policies, (2) a set of ideas that justify these policies, (3) a set of institutions and government agencies that carry out these policies, and (4) a set of political and power relationships that supports these policies, ideas, and institutions—a social bloc that sustains these philosophies and practices.

For example, I have used the term "national security state" to label the institutions, ideas, and practices that dominated U.S. foreign policy-making in the 1950s and 1960s at the height of the cold war and that still play a large role in shaping U.S. foreign policy. The national security state pursued a clearly definable set of policies toward the Soviet Union and the rest of the world. These policies were justified by a series of ideas about the roles of the United States and the Soviet Union in the world and how the United States could be safe in world of hostile forces. The national security state has also been a series of government and nongovernment institutions, most notably those established by the National Security Act of 1947, at the beginning of the cold war. And finally, the national security state has been a set of powerful political actors who push to maintain the ideas, practices, and institutions that pursue the ends they seek.

The discussions of these clusters of policies in this chapter are necessarily relatively brief and sketchy. The details of these philosophies and how they have been put into practice over the years will be covered in much more detail in later chapters. The purpose here is simply to introduce the framework that structures analysis in succeeding chapters.

IDEOLOGIES ABOUT ECONOMIC POLICY

Presidential economic policy-making ultimately rests on some theory about the role of the state in a capitalist economy. Most of the range of American political thought about the proper role of government in the economic system can be captured by the following categories aligned on a continuum from ideological left to ideological right, as represented in the following schematic:

SOCIAL DEMOCRACY	SOCIAL SECURITY STATE	LIMITED INTEREST STATE	LAISSEZ-FAIRE

Laissez-Faire

Laissez-faire was the dominant public philosophy of the late nineteenth century, and still exerts considerable influence on political rhetoric, if not on government budgets. At the heart of the laissez-faire philosophy is the separation of the public and private spheres of society. Government, or the state, is defined as the realm of coercion, and the private sector as the realm of freedom and prosperity. According to laissez-faire philosophy, the smaller the coercive state, the greater the private realm of freedom. The greater the realm of freedom, the better the life of the people. The laissez-faire philosophy believes in a state that is strictly limited in its size and scope. As Thomas Jefferson put it, "The government that governs least, governs best." The laissez-faire philosophy does prescribe certain appropriate roles for the state. It is legitimate for government to defend against foreign enemies, to maintain law and order, and to set some basic rules for the conduct of commerce. But the emphasis in laissez-faire philosophy is on the protection of individual rights. The legitimate roles of the state derive only from protecting individual rights against those, foreign and domestic, who would violate them. The metaphor which is often used to describe the ideal state is that of a nightwatchman, whose role it is to protect property but not to interfere unless that property is threatened.

Laissez-faire philosophy still influences the political rhetoric of presidents. In preparing for his 1964 campaign as Republican presidential nominee, Barry Goldwater gave a succinct statement of the laissez-faire philosophy:

Throughout history, government has proved to be the chief instrument for thwarting man's liberty. Government represents power in the hands of some men to control and regulate the lives of other men. And power, as Lord Acton said, corrupts men.[2]

More recently, some of Ronald Reagan's most famous lines appealed to laissez-faire principles. When Reagan spoke of "getting government off the backs of the people" or when he argued that "government is the problem, not the solution," he was expressing laissez-faire sentiments. But, as we shall see in later chapters, the policies pursued by the Reagan administration cannot really be understood as being driven by an authentic laissez-faire philosophy.

In the late nineteenth century laissez-faire was the predominant philosophy that guided American government, though not without challenges. During the Theodore Roosevelt and Woodrow Wilson presidencies in the first two decades of the twentieth century, the hold of laissez-faire weakened as the principle that government has an important role in regulating economic markets was established. But with the "return to normalcy" after World War I and the conservative Republican administrations of the 1920s, laissez-faire once again asserted its primacy.

The Social Security State

The FDR administration was the final turning point. The horrors of the Great Depression led the mass public, and ultimately political elites, to demand a newly activist role for government in economic and social affairs. The growing role of the state was reinforced by the international undertakings of the United States from World War II on. The laissez-faire philosophy still has its authentic advocates. However, today what is crucial in interpreting American public policy is the significant differences in what those who advocate an activist state want to do with that state. Let me begin describing these differences by characterizing what I call the social security state. I deliberately chose this label that connotes the single largest domestic program.

The Social Security program is based on a general set of beliefs about modern government. The Social Security program protects citizens from the inability to maintain their earnings in old age through a system of government insurance. Roughly 40 million Americans currently collect benefits. In the same manner, the social security state protects a wide range of economic and social groups from interruptions of their income or from competition that they cannot effectively meet. It provides not only insurance but also subsidies, regulation, trade protection, and other government benefits to political groups that are organized to obtain them. As with the Social Security program and the elderly, the effect, if not the rhetoric, of the social security state is maintenance of the income of politically organized groups.

FDR captured the essence of the social security philosophy when he reviewed the achievements of his first term.

> Democratic government has [the] innate capacity to protect its people against disasters once considered inevitable, to solve problems once considered unsolvable. We would not admit that we could not find a way to master economic epidemics just as, after centuries of fatalistic suffering, we had found a way to master epidemics of disease. We refused to leave the problems of our common welfare to be solved by the winds of chance and the hurricanes of disaster.[3]

FDR was talking about the Great Depression, but the philosophy of government action to provide security to those who experience economic distress has since been generalized to cover a much wider range of economic pressures on ever-increasing segments of American society.

The Limited Interest State

In our time, the key question is not whether to have an activist state, but what kind of activist state we should have. The social security state defines a different set of roles for government than either the limited interest state or the social democratic state. The limited interest state retains much of the rhetoric of the laissez-faire philosophy while at the same time accepting a wider range of roles for the state than true laissez-faire philosophy prescribes. This seeming contradiction is not simply an irrational residue of old ideas in a new age.

Rather, it reflects the fact that some of the most powerful groups in American society, particularly corporations and upper-income groups, favor an activist state when it works to serve their interests and oppose too broad a definition of the roles of an activist state when that works against their interests. Corporate executives may oppose social programs on the grounds that they create dependency on the state at the same time they are getting most of their revenue from military contracts. Farmers may support their subsidies at the same time they oppose aid to the cities, just as big city mayors may call for more urban aid while opposing farm subsidies.

The key distinctions between the social security state and the limited interest state are in (1) the range of government activism they support, (2) the relationship between government and economic markets, and (3) the political forces that support these philosophies. Advocates of the limited interest state retain much of the rhetoric of the laissez-faire philosophy precisely because they, too, favor restricting the scope of state activity in society. While the limited interest state accepts a much wider set of roles for government than does authentic laissez-faire philosophy, it still has a more restrictive view of legitimate government action than does the social security state. Only some interests deserve protection, not all who demand it.

Both the limited interest state and the social security state are committed to maintaining a market society. But their rhetorical emphasis on the relationship between government and markets is different. The limited interest state extols the virtues of market competition even as it provides selective protection from the effects of market competition to a limited range of interests. But in order to justify the denial of benefits to excluded groups, the limited interest state relies on market philosophy. A caricature of the limited interest position would be "Markets for you, protection for me." On the other hand, while accepting the essentials of a market society, the social security state is more broadly committed to mitigating the effects of markets when they threaten established social institutions or organized political groups. The social security philosophy consciously endorses the role of the state in providing a wide range of tangible and intangible public goods and services, in correcting social inequities, and, in certain circumstances, asserting the primacy of political values over market outcomes. The caricature of the social security position might be "Some protection for everybody."

The difference in the range of state activity sanctioned by the limited interest state versus the social security state reflects the differences in the electoral coalitions of the major parties. The Republican coalition, based largely on corporate organizations, upper-income groups, and white Protestant communities, simultaneously seeks to use government to benefit these groups and to limit the claims of other social groups to government assistance. The Democratic coalition, on the other hand, with its base in lower-income groups, unions, ethnic minorities, and feminist organizations, represents a broader diversity of interests. To the extent that this coalition can be held together at all, it is on the basis of a common commitment to a state that not only serves narrow particular interests but also is philosophically committed to a broad involvement in many sectors of society.

Social Democracy

The differences between the laissez-faire philosophy and the limited interest state pinpoint the fundamental differences between the pure economic ideology of the American right and the more centrist practices of Republican administrations that accept the existence of the activist state. In the same manner, the left of the American political spectrum can be divided between those who have very different images of the purposes and institutions of the programs of the activist state.

The left pole of the ideological spectrum demands more of the activist state. than protection of well-organized political interests. The social democratic philosophy envisions a government that goes beyond ameliorating the worst excesses of market society and becomes an agent of social transformation. The basic purposes of government in the social security philosophy are to maintain the income shares of organized social groups and to supplement private markets with public goods. However, the social democratic philosophy defines the role of government as being an active agent of historical change. Government is seen as the means by which the lives of ordinary citizens, poor and middle class alike, can be significantly improved.

In European democracies this image of the state gets most of its support from trade unions and their political parties, but in the United States it is the civil rights, women's, environmental, and peace movements that have most recently made these kinds of demands on government. The government envisioned in Martin Luther King's dream is a force for massive social change, not one that ensures the maintenance of the status quo.

Just as there is an echo of laissez-faire philosophy in the rhetoric of conservative Republican presidents, so there is a trace of social democratic philosophy in the rhetoric of liberal Democratic presidents. In 1965, in the midst of the civil rights struggle, the image of social transformation was strong in the inaugural address of Lyndon Johnson:

Justice was the promise that all . . . would share in the fruits of the land. In a land of great wealth, families must not live in hopeless poverty. In a land rich in harvest, children just must not go hungry. . . . In a land of healing miracles, neighbors must not suffer and die unattended. In a great land of learning and scholars, young people must be taught to read and write. . . . Before this generation of Americans is finished, this enemy will not only retreat—it will be conquered.[4]

The social democratic view of government is more than a maximal interest group coalition. Social democracy seeks a significant redistribution of income and power. It expands the role of government not so much in the number of sectors of society it regulates as in the kinds of goals it seeks to achieve.

Corporate Planning

One final component of some philosophies of the activist state bears mentioning: the concept of corporate planning. Throughout the twentieth century many of the advocates of activist government have called for government, business, and other sectors of society to join in cooperative planning to guide the direction of the U.S. economy toward desired goals. Corporate planning was a central element of the early New Deal attempts to resuscitate the economy during the Great Depression. Today many Democrats call for corporate planning and industrial policy to meet the trade challenges of Japan and other competitors in the new international economy.

However, the political meaning of corporate planning is difficult to characterize because different forms of corporate planning can have very different effects on society. The concept of corporate planning directly conflicts with the right-wing laissez-faire philosophy of letting markets operate without government interference. Indeed, the idea of corporate planning has often been associated in the United States and around the world with left-wing political forces that seek to use such planning to empower groups previously excluded from economic decision making. But when business groups dominate the planning process, corporate planning can serve very conservative business interests, as the cases of Japan and France show. In these countries corporate planning has not worked against business interests but, rather, has entrenched their power in politics and society. Along with the issue of who participates in and controls the process, another key issue is whether corporate planning is designed to be broad industrial policy or is limited to rationalization of particular sectors of the economy. Sectoral planning is limited to one set of economic activities, such as agriculture or energy. The U.S. government has long engaged in sectoral planning in agriculture and military production. Such planning usually works as a form of cartelization, where producers band together to keep price levels high.

Industrial policy plans more broadly, trying to steer the overall development of the economy and make choices about which sectors of the economy to target for investment. Such broad industrial policy was tried during World War I, the early New Deal, and most extensively during World War II. However, it has been largely abandoned in the second half of the twentieth century. Today some Democrats advocate such a broad industrial policy as a response to the chronic trade imbalance the United States runs with the rest of the world. They argue that targeting key growth industries for public and private investment and correcting crucial deficiencies in the skills of the work force could make the United States much more competitive in the world economy. The idea of a corporate planning state has not yet had much impact on the actual practices of contemporary American government. If a future Democratic administration were to adopt an industrial policy, the key questions would be what groups participate in the process and what the goals are. Different forms of corporate planning can have very different outcomes, and thus the concept of planning itself does not fit easily on the ideological spectrum.

The Political Bases of Ideologies About the State

Each ideology about the role of government has disproportionate strength in particular sectors of society. The rise of laissez-faire philosophy was associated with the rise of the modern American industrial corporation in the nineteenth century. But the Great Depression and then World War II broke the commitment of most industrial and finance capital to a minimal state. Alarmed by the ever more severe economic cycle, lured by the guaranteed profits of the military-industrial complex, and eager for government assistance in opening up foreign markets, corporate capitalism came to accept and even to advocate certain new roles for the state. Today most elements of corporate capitalism are committed to many forms of the activist state, as long as this state is limited to a set of prescribed roles that protect corporate interests and markets.

Today authentic laissez-faire views are more associated with small businesses and certain professions that are disproportionately burdened by the activist state, elements of southern and western capital that never accepted the commitment of the "eastern establishment" to an activist state, and traditionalist Christian groups that take laissez-faire tenets more as a part of the revealed legacy of their forefathers than as political theory.

The social security state draws its support from organized groups who seek a broader definition of the roles of activist government so they can gain the benefits that flow from government programs. While the advocates of the limited interest state seek to limit government to forms that benefit them, the political forces which press for social security state programs are held together by their shared interest in a more activist state. All the partners in the social security coalition recognize that the philosophy of a limited state is a key impediment to realization of their group interests. This is the ideological glue of the New Deal coalition and the contemporary Democratic Party.

Social democratic forces in the U.S. political system can be traced back at least as far as the populist, progressive, and socialist movements during the era of laissez-faire hegemony. In the FDR years, social democrats were major organizers of the trade unions and the source of the bolder programs and rhetoric of the FDR administration. The civil rights movement further added to the belief that the state could and should be an agent of social transformation, and spurred the expansive programs and rhetoric of LBJ's Great Society. The civil rights movement was a model for the emergent antiwar, women's, and environmental movements. In the wake of the Vietnam War and the nuclear arms race, mass movements for social transformation also increasingly focused on change in the U.S. role in the world as well as at home.

Just as the limited interest state subordinates an impulse toward laissez-faire to organized economic and political interests that benefit from government programs, so the social security philosophy subordinates a vision of a state that transforms economic and social relations to more tangible economic and political interests. The difference between the social democratic and social security philosophies can be seen in the evolution of the politics of the trade unions. Once the pillar of institutional support for social democracy, the trade unions have evolved into the largest single force in the social security coalition.   In   the Great Depression, the philosophy of most of those who organized the unions encompassed more than simply increasing the paychecks of their members. Those who built the trade unions had a broad agenda of changing the relationship between owner and worker. During the Depression crisis it was evident to workers that their fates were interdependent and that change in larger political-economic relations was necessary to improve their situation.

But today trade unions rarely articulate much more than the immediate, narrow interest of their members, or at most support for government programs that disproportionately benefit their members. The unions have largely abandoned any quest for social democracy, although they are still a potent force in protecting the access of their members to selective government benefits.

SOCIAL ISSUES AND THE CULTURAL DIMENSIONS OF IDEOLOGY

Ideology, Interests, and Identity

As can be seen from the foregoing, ideology has much to do with the representation of economic interests and the translation of their demands and desires into public policy. Ideology shapes which economic interests will be served by public policy and which will not.

But politics is more than representation of economic interests, and so are political ideologies. Political ideologies are also about issues of identity. Individual citizens feel they are members of certain social groups, and their political loyalties are shaped by which groups they feel kinship with. For example, take the feeling of national identity. Today the former Soviet Union is undergoing massive transformation because many people in the republics feel stronger bonds with their historic national identities as Lithuanians, Latvians, Estonians, Moldavians, Georgians, or Ukrainians than with the Soviet Union. Kurds battle Iraqis (and Turks and Iranians) for national autonomy, Palestinians fight Israelis, and Northern Irish Catholics battle the British, to name just a small handful of such conflicts over national identity.

In the United States there are no serious secessionist movements, but there are serious political cleavages between ethnic groups. Certain black and Hispanic groups assert their special historical identities and demand public policies that recognize their status. Other ethnic groups that in the past felt excluded from mainstream American society, such as Irish, Italians, Poles, and other immigrants from southern and eastern Europe, now tend to feel greater identification with mainstream culture and less identification with currently subordinated groups such as blacks and Hispanics. Religion is another social identity that can have political implications. Earlier in American history, tensions between Protestant and Catholic groups were high, and they persist today. But many religious groups share common positions on many issues of public policy in opposition to more secular political forces. Abortion is one particularly contentious issue, but there are many more.

Individuals belong to more than one social group, and thus their group loyalties can conflict. Individuals are simultaneously members of ethnic groups, religious groups, economic groups, and other groups. Therefore, it is crucial which group loyalties are stronger. A woman of the Catholic faith may feel torn between her sense of her rights as a woman and the expectations of her church. A worker in a company may someday have to choose between a sense of shared interests with other workers and a sense of loyalty to the company. In such cases the individual's sense of social identity is the key to how he or she chooses to act when group loyalties conflict. Therefore, it is a naive view of politics that takes economic interests as easily defined or as the only determinant of political action. It is too simplistic to see politics as just conflict between static groups whose identities are clearly defined. Ideology is crucial in defining which groups individuals identify with, and the sense of political identity is as central to understanding the politics of public policy as is economic interest.

Feelings of social identity interact with public policy in what have come to be called social issues. For example, in the 1960s a plethora of new political groups raising new issues in public policy emerged—black and other ethnic identity movements, the women's movement, the peace movement, the environmental movement. In the last generation another new set of groups has mobilized to seek restoration of more traditional social values, the "new right" or "Christian right." Cultural conflicts are certainly not new to U.S. politics. The struggles between WASPs and earlier immigrant groups in the late nineteenth and early twentieth centuries were at least as bitter as today's conflicts over social issues.

But the emergence of these new groups has given new form to these struggles. The contemporary ideological spectrum on social issues can be broken down into the following categories:

COUNTERCULTURAL LEFT	CULTURAL PLURALISM	CULTURAL MONISM	CHRISTIAN RIGHT

The Christian Right

One of the most striking developments of the 1980s was the reemergence of evangelical Christians as a potent political force. Members of the Christian right are committed to restoring traditional, biblical values to a position of primacy in American society. They are distressed by many of the effects of the sexual revolution on individual behavior and the family unit. They are concerned about increases in abortion, homosexuality, sexual promiscuity, illegitimate births, and the divorce rate, and the rise of AIDs and other sexually transmitted diseases. They are opposed to the redefinition of women's roles in the family, the economy, and the society. They are unhappy with rising crime rates and the increase in drug use. They are opposed to affirmative action for minorities and women, and uncomfortable with the attention these groups get from the political system.

The Christian right attributes much of the growth of these trends to stimulation from the media. Even more fundamentally, they trace the rise of these trends to the decline of Christian values and the rise of secular values. They believe the only cure for these social ills is a return to traditional values, and to a society and a legal system that are based on biblical principles.

Presidents Reagan and Bush have given symbolic, if not always material, support to the agenda of the Christian right. In a speech before evangelical ministers, Reagan equated the health of the political system with the health of religion: "Freedom prospers when religion is vibrant and the rule of law under God is acknowledged." He went on to argue that recent Supreme Court decisions regarding the separation of church and state ignore American values and history.

The Declaration of Independence mentions the Supreme Being no less than four times. "In God We Trust" is engraved on our coinage. The Supreme Court opens its proceedings with a religious invocation. And the Members of Congress open their sessions with a prayer. I just happen to believe that the school children of the United States are entitled to the same privileges as Supreme Court Justices and Congressmen.[5]

The Countercultural Left

At the other end of the ideological spectrum on social issues are the groups that set in motion the changes in the 1960s and 1970s which the New Right finds so distasteful: the remnants of the "New Left." The 1960s and early 1970s were characterized by a wave of new political movements, each of which raised fundamental challenges to historical modes of thinking and each of which generated political organizations that outlived the faddishness of times. The first of these was the civil rights movement, which ultimately not only generated new black civil rights organizations but also contributed to the climate in which Black Power, Hispanic, and other ethnic identity organizations emerged. On the heels of the civil rights movement came the peace movement, questing to end the Vietnam War and the arms race, and to redefine the U.S. role in the world. The coming of the 1970s saw the emergence of the ecology movement, which sought to protect the environment from the ravages of twentieth century technological development. Gathering momentum throughout this period but emerging with greatest force in the early 1970s was the women's movement, which, following the example of the civil rights movement, sought a political and ideological redefinition of the position of women in society. In the footsteps of the civil rights and women's movements came the organization of gay groups that further expanded the redefinition of social roles.

What these diverse groups shared was a dissatisfaction with traditional political institutions and traditional individual roles. Each went beyond raising any single social issue; rather, they sought to change the way the culture thought about the identity of particular groups and political institutions in general. A major work of the Black Power movement of the 1960s put the identity question this way:

> Black people must redefine themselves, and only *they* can do that. Throughout this country, vast segments of the black communities are beginning to recognize the need to assert their own definitions, to reclaim their history, their culture; to create their own sense of community and togetherness. There is growing resentment of the word "Negro," for example, because this term is the invention of our oppressor; it is *his* image of us that he describes. . . . When we begin to define our own image . . . the black community will have a positive image of itself that *it* has created.[6]

It was sentiments like these that pushed the term "Negro" out of general usage and made "black" the new usage. In the women's movement as well, there was great emphasis on women defining women's roles and identities, rather than accepting the roles and identities defined by patriarchal culture. In a similar manner, the peace movement sought redefinition of the U.S. role and identity in the world system, and the environmental movement sought redefinition of technology's place in the ecological system.

The American right is, with a few exceptions, almost universally committed to and evangelical about Christianity. Religion also plays a key role at the left end of the political spectrum, although on the left many groups are primarily secular rather than religious. The American left has produced leaders like Martin Luther King, Jesse Jackson, the Berrigan brothers, Dorothy Day, and others whose political activity was based in a deep Christian faith even as, like Christ, they opposed the orthodoxies of their time. But the counterculture left also has elements that are purely secular or profess non-Christian faiths.

Cultural Pluralism

The countercultural New Left groups gravitated toward the Democratic Party, and the Christian New Right groups aligned with the Republican Party. This is no accident; it reflects the different natures of the social blocs that historically have been at the core of each party. Yet these new ideological groups and the social issues they raised were deeply controversial and represented a threat to each party's ability to maintain its appeal to the political center, as the fate of the Goldwater and McGovern campaigns clearly showed. The centrist elements in each party sought to develop ideological formulations that would simultaneously allow them to mute the stridency of their ideological wings in order to appeal to the political center and yet signal to the ideological wings that their concerns were being heard. The centrist Democratic formulation can be called "cultural pluralism." The centrist Republican formulation can be labeled "cultural monism."

The Democratic Party has always been a collection of diverse groups. Will Rogers' famous line, "I'm not a member of any organized political party—I'm a Democrat," was uttered long before the countercultural movements of the 1960s emerged. The Democratic Party was the home of immigrant ethnic minorities long before the development of the civil rights movement or the Rainbow Coalition. But the developments of the 1960s put new strains on the Democrats' ability to hold together their diverse coalition, as their fate in recent presidential elections has shown.

The Democrats have tried to deal with these tensions through the ideology of cultural pluralism. They have tried to portray themselves as the party that is open to many groups, that balances many different points of view and brokers many competing interests. Perhaps the most significant example of this is the rules for delegate selection the Democratic Party developed for the 1972 convention. Democratic conventions in the 1960s had been torn by conflicts between all-white southern state delegations and blacks who demanded representation in these delegations, and by conflicts between the "old guard" party leaders who controlled their state delegations and the demands of the Eugene McCarthy and Robert Kennedy forces for a share of state delegations proportionate to their support among the public. As a result, new rules about delegate selection were devised which mandated that each state's delegation must reflect the level of support for particular candidates in that state and must have the same proportion of women, minorities, and youth as in the general population of the state. These rules reflected the recognition that distinct cultural groups had been systematically denied full representation in past conventions. This quota system has since been abandoned, but the attempt of the Democratic Party to recognize and appeal to distinct subcultural groups has not.

Cultural Monism

The problem for the Republicans of reconciling their polar and centrist tendencies is different and elicits a different strategy. The WASP social base of the Republican Party is more homogeneous. But in order to construct their presidential majorities and to have any hope of becoming a true majority party, the Republicans have to attract broader support. The new Christian right movement has been key in attracting evangelical Southerners to the Republican Party, people who, until the civil rights era, for historical reasons favored the Democratic Party. But any real Republican majority also needs considerable support from the more assimilated descendants of Irish, southern European, and eastern European immigrants. While certain themes of the Christian right resonate well with conservative Catholics and Jews, other themes of militant Protestantism can alienate these groups from the Republicans.

One key Republican strategy for finessing this problem is the development of ideological themes that emphasize a kind of nondenominational version of the "one true faith," a kind of civil religion of nationalism and national identity. Such appeals are particularly attractive to members of ethnic groups who wish to assimilate more completely into mainstream American culture, to lessen their sense of ethnic distinctness. This civil religion of an "American way" allows the Republicans to appeal simultaneously to Protestant evangelicals and to non-Protestant conservatives who can each read tenets of their doctrines into the nationalist creed. It also allows the Republicans to differentiate themselves from whatever social groups are perceived as outside the political mainstream or as challenging traditional values.

This strategy is not new to the 1980s. The "law and order" theme of the Nixon campaign in 1968 was aimed at unpopular social groups and was widely acknowledged as a code word for attacking minorities. Spiro Agnew was chosen as Nixon's running mate in large part to send the message he had sent as governor of Maryland: "The biggest race questions that are arising today come from the civil rights militants who are trying to create an unhealthy black racism in this country."[7]

Once in office Agnew turned his attack to the peace movement:

> We have among us a glib, activist element who would tell us our values are lies. . . . They mock the common man's pride in his work, his family, and his country. . . . America cannot afford to write off a whole generation for the decadent thinking of a few. America cannot afford to divide over their demagoguery, or to be deceived by their duplicity, or to let their license destroy liberty. We can, however, afford to separate them from our society—with no more regret than we should feel over discarding rotten apples from a barrel.[8]

There is certainly continuity between Agnew's attacks on unpopular social groups and the fusing of ethnic and ideological themes characteristic of the McCarthy period in the 1950s or the attacks on trade unions and socialists in the 1920s. One can even hear echoes of these themes in contemporary conservative attacks on "special interests."

Of course the Democrats also appeal to some sense of an American national identity. But because of the nature of their coalition, these appeals are cast in terms of cultural pluralism. The Democratic version of the American way is inclusive. It emphasizes that there are many "American ways," and celebrates diversity. The Republican version, on the other hand, has an element of exclusivity. It emphasizes a single national identity that is crucial in differentiating between those who meet its standards and those who deviate from its tenets.

CONCLUSION

The terms "conservative" and "liberal" are useful shorthand to indicate the ideological tendencies of presidents and their administrations. But the actual meaning of these terms for policy behavior is often vague. Further, presidents' rhetoric rarely is completely philosophically consistent, and administrations' actions often do not match their rhetoric. It is useful to break out the ideological spectrum into more categories and to distinguish between various types of issues. This chapter has developed more complex typologies that can help in understanding presidential ideologies in two areas of domestic policy—the political economy and social issues. Chapter 3 will take up foreign policy and pursue a more historical approach to characterizing the American ideological spectrum.

NOTES

1. Theodore Lowi, *The End of Liberalism* (New York: Norton, 1979).

2. Barry Goldwater, *The Conscience of a Conservative* (Shepherdsville, KY: Victor Publishing, 1960), pp. 16-17.

3. *Inaugural Addresses of the Presidents* (Washington, DC: U.S. Government Printing Office, 1974), p. 240.

4. Ibid., pp. 271-272.

5. Ronald Reagan, *Public Papers of the Presidents, 1983*, (Washington, DC: U.S. Government Printing Office, 1984), pp. 359-364.

6. Stokely Carmichael and Charles Hamilton, *Black Power* (New York: Random House, 1967), p. 37.

7. Jules Whitcover, *White Knight* (New York: Random House, 1972), p. 177.

8. Ibid., p. 309.

3

CHANGE, CONTINUITY, AND CONTRADICTION IN THE AMERICAN IDEOLOGICAL SPECTRUM

CHANGE IN IDEOLOGIES ABOUT RACE AND SOCIAL ISSUES

The typologies introduced in Chapter 2 provide a simple yet useful character-ization of the ideas that have shaped domestic policy-making in recent decades. But as presented so far, they are static and ahistorical, while the ideological process is dynamic over time. Because ideology changes over time, each typology of ideologies is valid only over a particular historical period. This chapter will reflect the dynamic quality of ideological formulations.

Ideologies about the political economy and economic policy have been somewhat more stable than those about social or foreign policy. The social democracy—social security—limited interest state—laissez-faire typology is useful for a period of over 50 years running from the latter half of the FDR administration into the 1990s. However, it would be stretching the typology too far to try to use it before the New Deal era. There are similarities in the debate about the activist state and the limited state in the pre-New Deal period. But there was much less experience with what an activist government would actually mean in such a wide variety of policy arenas. Therefore the debate about government activism had a much different character. It was not known to the extent it is known today what the real social and economic impact of incorpora-tion of groups into state structures would actually be. Rather than try to charac-terize the pre-New Deal debate in detail, this book will focus on post-New Deal ideological formulations.

Ideologies on social and racial issues have shown more change in recent decades, and thus the dynamic nature of ideology about these issues needs to be examined in more detail. The debate over cultural pluralism and cultural monism is as old as the republic. The issue of whether immigrants should be largely socialized into the prevailing "American way" or whether America is enriched by great cultural diversity dates back to the founding of the nation. The question of the status of those who come to the United States without the ability to speak English came up long before the term "bilingual education" was coined.

But there was a fundamental shift in the range of acceptable ideological debate about social and racial issues in the 1960s. The doctrine of the superiority of the white race was banished from polite political conversation and, more important, from effective political impact. This is the most dramatic case in the second half of the twentieth century of an ideological doctrine that had shaped public policy being totally routed from the political landscape. American ideologies about racial and cultural issues in the period reaching back to the beginning of the century up until the mid-1960s can be characterized along the following spectrum:

RIGHTS	CULTURAL	CULTURAL	WHITE
MOVEMENTS	PLURALISM	MONISM	SUPREMACY

The doctrine of the superiority of the white race had considerable political legitimacy throughout most of American history. It was strongest in the South, where most of the black population had been centered since slavery, and thus, the issue of race was most salient. However, belief in the inherent superiority of civilized, Christianized white peoples was certainly not exclusive to the South but was found in various respectable quarters throughout the nation. But it was in the South that the code of white supremacy was written into the laws of the states. The real political power of that doctrine can be seen in the content of southern law prior to national civil rights legislation. Blacks were segregated from whites in public schools, public transportation, and housing. They were denied all but the most menial jobs in white-owned businesses. They were denied the right to vote. The system of segregation was backed up not only by the force of law but also by the political terror of mob violence, which in its most stark form led to unpunished lynchings of black men.

At the other end of the political spectrum was the civil rights movement, which fought to have the basic rights established in the Constitution extended to people of color. After the Civil War, the Thirteenth, Fourteenth, and Fifteenth amendments to the Constitution seemed to guarantee national protection of the rights of the freed slaves. But national protection of these rights was abandoned when Reconstruction ended and Union troops left the South in the 1870s. The doctrine of states' rights asserted that the Constitution granted the states the autonomy to carry out racial repression. Black leaders' repeated appeals to the national government to enforce blacks' rights to participate in the political and economic life of the nation were largely ignored.

Most white politicians outside the South avoided confronting the issue of civil rights head-on. More progressive or liberal leaders would give some symbolic support to black leaders by meeting with them publicly or vaguely espousing the advancement of all people—in other words, by symbolic support of cultural pluralism. More conservative northern politicians would make clear their disdain for nonwhites by refusing to have any contact with groups who were traditionally not accepted by the dominant culture. However, by the middle of the twentieth century it became harder and harder to finesse the racial issue by symbolic politics.

The civil rights movement began to gain ground with the historic advances of the power of the national government under FDR and his successors. Civil rights advocates had some impact on the executive regulations issued by FDR and Truman that guided national government programs. Perhaps the most important political turning point came in 1954, when the Supreme Court abandoned its historic support of the doctrine of states' rights. The Supreme Court dealt a severe blow to the practices of white supremacy when it ordered all public schools desegregated. From that point on, the American nation was increasingly polarized on racial issues between the South, which wanted to maintain white superiority, and the rest of the nation, which increasingly supported enforcement of minorities' civil rights. Civil rights leaders such as Martin Luther King were increasingly successful in mobilizing black Americans to openly oppose the practices of white supremacy and thereby reveal to the rest of the country the brutality of its practices.

After a decade of increasing conflict and confrontation over minority rights, in 1964 and 1965 Congress passed civil rights bills that gave national protection to such basic rights as the right to vote, the right to use public services and commercial accommodations, and nondiscrimination in employment. The story of the civil rights legislation of the 1960s is told in more detail in Chapter 6. What is important to point out here is that these civil rights bills broke the back of white supremacy as a national political force. The open advocacy of white supremacy disappeared from national political dialogue.

Neither the defeat of white supremacy nor the success of the civil rights movement in entering the political mainstream ended ideological polarization on social and racial issues. New groups emerged on both the left and the right. Black Power, women's liberation, and other antiestablishment forces arose on the political left. Once they abandoned the discredited doctrine of white supremacy, conservative political forces concerned with maintaining the traditional American way reemerged with new vigor. But American public policy, as well as both the ideological left and the ideological right, was transformed by the victory of the civil rights movement over white supremacy.

There is one other significant anomaly in the ideological system before the 1960s that bears noting. Both the ideological left and the ideological right were located within the Democratic Party. In the current party system, the more ideological left is associated with the Democratic Party and the more ideological right is found in the Republican Party. For example, the Christian right has affiliated itself with the Republican Party and the left, countercultural elements have gravitated to the Democratic Party. But in the period from the 1930s into the 1960s, both the ideological left and the ideological right on social and racial issues made their homes in the Democratic Party. This unusual distribution of ideological forces had its basis in American history. It had been Republican presidents who had prosecuted the Civil War and then imposed the hated Reconstruction regime on the formerly dominant white elite. In response, the southern white racists had been the base of the Democratic Party in the post-Civil War era, the "solid South." For almost a century virtually every southern member of Congress was a Democrat. From the Civil War until the Great Depression the South provided most of the Democratic members of Congress and most of the votes for Democratic presidential candidates. Even after the Democratic Party became the majority party in the North in the 1930s, southern Democrats committed to the idea of white supremacy were a major, and highly unified, faction in the party.

However, the grand Democratic coalition constructed by Franklin Roosevelt in the wake of the Great Depression brought many new groups into the Democratic Party, including most northern and many southern blacks. Northern liberals, who now were the stronger faction in the Democratic Party, increasingly championed the cause of civil rights, although until the 1960s they were blocked from implementing major change by the power of southern Democrats in Congress. The triumph of liberal Democrats on civil rights in the 1960s eventually shattered the Democratic coalition that had dominated national politics for almost two generations. Many white Southerners who had for a century shunned the Republican Party because of its association with Reconstruction and minority rights now identified the Democratic Party with distasteful national intervention in southern affairs, and increasingly Republican candidates were able to compete effectively in what had once been the "solid" Democratic south.

CHANGING IDEOLOGIES ABOUT FOREIGN POLICY

Perhaps because world politics is more turbulent than the domestic political system, American ideologies about foreign policy have undergone more change in the twentieth century than ideologies about domestic policy. To understand the changing beliefs that have shaped U.S. foreign policy one needs to break the last 100 years into separate eras. First there is the period of emerging U.S. power, beginning prior to the Spanish-American War in 1898 and lasting through World War II. The second era is the cold war, which began in the late 1940s and which appears to have ended in recent years. A third era, which at present can only be characterized as the post-cold war period, is beginning in the 1990s. As in the case of domestic economic policy, this book will treat the early part of the twentieth century very lightly. This chapter will focus largely on the cold war era. Later chapters will explore changing East-West relations and offer some projections about ideology in any post-cold war era.

It is worthwhile to note briefly the ideologies that dominated foreign policy in the earlier periods of American history and those which emerged with the rise of U.S. power. The dominant foreign policy ideology in the nineteenth century was isolationism. George Washington, in his Farewell Address, laid down principles that were faithfully repeated for more than a century, particularly the fear of "entangling alliances" that would involve the United States in the bloody wars of European politics. The geographic isolation from European and Asian conflicts provided by the Atlantic and Pacific oceans allowed the policy of isolationism to thrive for more than 100 years. The principles of isolationism were often honored in the breach, particularly in the case of Latin America, where the Monroe Doctrine asserted a special U.S. role in hemispheric relations. But westward expansion across the American continent and domestic economic development, not foreign policy, took up most of U.S. governmental energy throughout the first century of the republic.

By the end of the nineteenth century, however, the frontier was rapidly becoming a thing of the past, American industry had become competitive with that of the most advanced European powers, and U.S. interests had come to span the Atlantic and the Pacific oceans. Increasingly the doctrine of isolationism came to be challenged in both theory and practice by a new philosophy of internationalism, of intervention in world affairs. In the first half of the twentieth century U.S. foreign policy debate centered on the conflict between the fading philosophy of isolationism and the growing power of the ideas of internationalism and interventionism in global politics. The new willingness to take an activist international role became clear in the Spanish-American War. Cuban rebellion against their Spanish imperial rulers was utilized as a justification for conflict with Spain. In victory the United States finally realized its long-term goal of ousting Spanish power from the Caribbean Sea and establishing an American protectorate in Cuba. The United States also routed the Spanish fleet in the Far East, seizing its first significant colony, the Philippines. The U.S. had now joined the ranks of imperial powers.

But the most important expression of the new American internationalism was participation in the two world wars. These fearsome wars, which engulfed and eventually destroyed all the great European empires that had constructed and dominated the modern world system, represented new heights in the destructive European conflicts that isolationism had warned against. Yet even as he proclaimed that the United States was different from the old imperial powers, Woodrow Wilson led the nation into World War I. Wilson's attempts to construct a new world order in the aftermath of the devastation were, however, thwarted in part by the resurgent political power of isolationist sentiment. Having tasted the horror of modern warfare, Americans were not sure they wanted to become permanently embroiled in foreign conflicts. Ironically, the Senate rejected U.S. participation in the League of Nations that Wilson had fought so hard to create.

It was not until the presidency of Franklin Roosevelt, during World War II, that interventionist internationalism finally prevailed over isolationist ideology. As FDR, much like Wilson had before him, prepared the United States to enter this war the Japanese launched their attack on Pearl Harbor. That attack obviated any need for FDR to justify U.S. participation in the war. It was now seen only as a question of self-defense. The United States emerged from World War II as by far the most powerful nation on earth, the only great power whose territory was virtually untouched by the devastation of the war. The very success of the U.S. efforts in both world wars had legitimated the philosophy of internationalist interventionism. From FDR on, the United States has been firmly committed to an activist role around the world. Its global strategy put it in conflict with Soviet communism, which also was moving into the vacuum created by the destruction in Europe and Asia. Thus the cold war was born.

The internationalist ideology that gained sway during this period contained elements of both idealism and realism. In their public statements all presidents used idealistic rhetoric to justify U.S. intervention in international conflicts. Even as the United States plunged more deeply into international power struggles, its presidents asserted that the exceptional history of the American nation gave it a special moral role in elevating the standards of world politics. If the United States was going to be a great power, it would be a different and better kind of great power. Woodrow Wilson was the embodiment of this messianic fusion of power and idealism. Even as he took the United States into World War I on the side of one group of old imperial powers, he called for a new world order to emerge from the death throes of the old. According to Wilson, the United States was fighting not for power but for democracy, self-determination, and the security of all nations of the world.

Woodrow Wilson on America's Special Role in the World

What we demand . . . is that the world be . . . safe for every peace-loving nation which, like our own, wishes to live its own life [and] determine its own institutions.

[The American troops] brought with them a great ardor for a supreme cause. . . . They saw a city not built with hands. They saw a citadel . . . where dwelt the oracles of God himself. . . . There were never crusaders that went to the Holy Land in the old ages . . . that were more truly devoted to a holy cause.

The men who . . . frame[d] this government . . . set up a standard to which they intended that the nations of the world should rally. They said to the people of the world, "Come to us, this is the home of liberty; this is the place where mankind can learn how to govern their own affairs . . . and the world did come to us. . . . They have looked to us for leadership.[1]

While all presidents spoke in idealistic terms in their efforts to win public support for an interventionist role for the United States, they also bent their idealism to power politics. The realist school of thought saw all nations pursuing not high ideals but real political power. Realists justified this pursuit of power as the right and natural goal of nation-states. Teddy Roosevelt perhaps expressed the pursuit of power at the root of the new internationalism most clearly. Speaking about shady U.S. maneuvers to gain the territory on which the Panama Canal was built, Teddy cut through the idealism of the Monroe Doctrine and simply stated, "I took the Canal."

Even the moral fervor of Woodrow Wilson was tempered by realistic assessment of power relations. Wilson's idealistic Fourteen Points argued in favor of self-determination for all subjugated peoples. But while the empires of the defeated Turkey and Austria-Hungary were carved up by the victors in the name of self-determination, the possessions of England and France not only were untouched but were enlarged through new grants of colonial powers over most of the Middle East. And of course, Wilson did not apply the principle of self-determination to the U.S. colony of the Philippines or to the military dependencies of Cuba and Nicaragua.

FOREIGN POLICY DURING THE COLD WAR

While the philosophy of isolationism was vanquished by World War II, the cold war brought new forms of debate over the appropriate role for the United States in the world. Later chapters will analyze the emergence and development of ideologies in the cold war era. This chapter will simply introduce a fourfold typology, shown below, that clarifies the ideas which animated the foreign policies of presidents during the cold war.

PEACE MOVEMENT	HEGEMONIC FLEXIBILITY	NATIONAL SECURITY STATE	HOLY WAR

The cold war brought a broad agreement about the general goals of U.S. foreign policy, what was called the bipartisan consensus. But debate over the place of ideals and morality in foreign policy was not over. The more centrist foreign policy ideologies stressed realism in the pursuit of national power. But both the ideological left and the right challenged the morality of the dominant centrist ideologies, although on different grounds.

The National Security State

The national security ideology was the dominant force in U.S. foreign policy from the end of World War II through the 1960s. It still plays a prominent role in shaping foreign policy today. The national security state's conception of the U.S. role in the world was shaped primarily by anticommunism. Communist expansion was seen as the principal threat to world peace in the latter twentieth century.

U.S. power was believed to be the only force that could check worldwide Soviet military and ideological power. The basic currency of international power was defined as military force. The Soviet military was seen as the heart of communist power, and the U.S. military was the prime means of opposing the communist threat.

In the national security state, all other elements of foreign policy were subordinated to the struggle against communism and the maintenance of a favorable military balance. The national security state extended U.S. military power through a series of alliances stretching from western Europe to the Pacific Rim. Cemented by trade and cultural relations, these alliances were seen as critical in the world military balance, and thus considerable energy was put into maintaining them.

Anticommunism and military force were also central in the way the national security state approached the Third World. The doctrine of counterinsurgency justified support for anticommunist regimes and movements. By backing anticommunist governments and supporting rebels against socialist governments the United States could sometimes achieve its objectives without directly risking American lives or prestige. So over the years the United States armed and trained forces of the governments of the Shah of Iran; Ferdinand Marcos in the Philippines; Central American military governments such as those El Salvador, Guatemala, and Honduras; and for a time the government in South Vietnam. The United States also supported rebels trying to overthrow socialist regimes in Nicaragua, Cuba, Guatemala, Chile, Iran, Afghanistan, Angola, Cambodia, and elsewhere.

The distinction between totalitarian (read pro-Soviet) and authoritarian (read pro-U.S. or neutral) regimes was used by the national security ideology to justify support for pro-U.S. dictatorships as well as aid to rebels fighting against regimes too friendly with Moscow. When U.S. interests or pro-U.S. regimes were threatened, the national security state called for political stability. But if a socialist regime showed any sign of weakness, the counterinsurgency was prescribed to destabilize it.

The national security ideology dominated U.S. foreign policymaking from the end of World War II through the 1960s. It has shaped the behavior of every president since Truman, Democrat and Republican alike. One of the clearest statements of the national security ideology can be found in the 1980 Republican Party platform.

The premier challenge facing the United States, its allies, and the entire globe is to check the Soviet Union's global ambitions. This challenge must be met, for the present danger is greater than ever before. . . . The Soviet Union is accelerating its drive for military superiority and is intensifying its military pressure and ideological combat against the industrial democracies and the vulnerable developing nations.

The scope and magnitude of the growth of Soviet military power threatens American interests at every level, from the nuclear threat to our survival, to our ability to protect the lives and property of Americans abroad.[2]

The platform concluded that the United States needed to embark on a military buildup and to be more willing to use its military power to contain Soviet expansion. This was the essence of the national security ideology.

The Holy War Ideology

The more idealistic holy war ideology shared with the national security state a central concern with the power of communism. But the differences in degree were so great as to make a real difference in kind. The holy war ideology viewed the atheistic Soviet Union as "the evil empire," as "the focus of all evil in the modern world." From this perspective, since communism was totally and incorrigibly evil, the only response of the forces of righteousness was to struggle at all costs until righteousness prevailed. For the righteous, there could be no compromise with the devil, only eternal enmity.

In contrast, while the rhetoric of the national security state often utilized this demonic image of the Soviet Union to mobilize Americans to particular conflicts with socialist forces, at its core it was a more realist philosophy. The national security state tended to see the Soviet Union as the primary opponent of the United States in a great power rivalry. The differences between the idealism of the holy war ideology and the realism of the national security ideology led to significant policy differences. While the national security state used sophisticated strategies to amass a broad range of allies in its anticommunist goals, the holy war state demanded adherence to its ideological doctrines and tended to view any force that did not agree with those doctrines as an inherent enemy. The national security state was cautious and reluctant to deal directly with the Soviets on issues of joint concern like nuclear weapons, but even such a tough-minded anticommunist realist as Richard Nixon negotiated an opening to China and an arms treaty with the Russians. However, the holy war state was unwilling to countenance any bargaining with the devil.

Barry Goldwater was one prominent conservative spokesman who called for holy war against the Soviet Union. In the book he released as he prepared to run for president, *Why Not Victory?*, Goldwater articulated themes he used repeatedly as the Republican presidential nominee in 1964.

> This is a conflict where one side or the other must win. . . . On this question the decision is out of our hands. The rules for the conflict have been laid down by the Soviet Union. . . . We have continued to delude ourselves with something called peaceful coexistence while communism has kept right on gobbling up one country after another.[3]

Before he became president and in the early years of his administration, Ronald Reagan at times seemed to call for holy war against communism. In his presidential campaigns in 1968, 1976, and 1980, Reagan had scorned all the major agreements negotiated between the United States and the Soviet Union as sellouts to communism. In Reagan's first term as president, arms control negotiations with the Soviets were broken off as the United States launched the largest peacetime military buildup in its history. With the emergence of the Gorbachev reforms in the Soviet Union, Reagan reversed his position toward the Soviets in his second term. But in his first term, a holy war mentality prevailed.

Hegemonic Flexibility

A more centrist opposition to the national security state came from those who advocated that the United States adopt the posture of a flexible hegemon. A hegemon is a dominant power in a global system, a nation strong enough to influence the shape of the world system itself. Great Britain was such a power in the period from the Napoleonic wars up until World War I. At the end of World War II, the United States was in such a position. As the only power whose homeland was untouched by the war, the United States was able to shape the character of the postwar world. It was the leading economic, military, and political power, and it used its influence to construct an alliance of capitalist powers in Europe and Japan while building a series of global economic institutions that survive today, even as U.S. power is in decline.

Like the national security ideology, the ideology of hegemonic flexibility was based on maintaining American power and leadership in world affairs. Like both the national security and holy war ideologies, the strategy of the flexible hegemon was premised on checking the power of communism, relying heavily on maintaining U.S. military capabilities. But the flexible hegemonic position rested on more than military force or even anticommunism. This ideology was more confident of the ability of the United States to influence world events through means other than military power—diplomatic, economic, trade, and technological leadership all also played a major role in the foreign policy of an flexible hegemon.

Hegemonic flexibility mixed elements of idealism with realism. It argued that moral values were part of America's strength as a world power. U.S. foreign policy needed to express America's special mission, which was crucial to animating the alliances it developed and to justifying its power in the eyes of the world. In this strategy, bargaining and negotiation played as important a role as naked force. Integration of the U.S. economy with its trading partners in western Europe and the Pacific Rim was seen as just as important as maintenance of the military preparedness of the alliances. Conflicts with Third World regimes were thought to be as susceptible to political negotiation as to counterinsurgency. Even conflict with the Soviet Union could be managed through arms control agreements, bargaining over the use of forces, and ultimately through widened trade and cultural relations. It was this differing emphasis on the various tools of foreign policy that distinguished the flexible hegemon from the national security state.

Hegemonic Flexibility in the Inaugural Address of John Kennedy

Global Role: Let every nation know, whether it wishes us well or ill, that we shall pay any price, bear any burden, meet any hardship, support any friend, oppose any foe to assure the survival and success of liberty.

The Western Alliance: To those old allies whose cultural and spiritual origins we share, we pledge the loyalty of faithful friends. United, there is little we cannot do in a host of cooperative ventures.

Aid to Anticommunists in the Third World: To our sister republics south of our border, we offer . . . a new alliance for progress—to assist free men and free governments in casting off the chains of poverty. But this peaceful revolution cannot become the prey of hostile powers. Let all our neighbors know that we shall join with them to oppose aggression or subversion anywhere in the Americas.

Peaceful Coexistence with Communism: To . . . our adversary, we . . . request that both sides begin anew the quest for peace, before the dark powers of destruction unleashed by science engulf all humanity in planned or accidental self-destruction. . . . We dare not tempt them with weakness. For only when our arms are sufficient beyond doubt can we be certain beyond doubt that they will never be employed. But neither can two great and powerful groups of nations take comfort in our present course. . . . Let us never negotiate out of fear. But let us never fear to negotiate.[4]

Opponents on the right often accused the advocates of hegemonic flexibility of replacing faith in military power with faith in diplomacy, of being overly idealistic and unrealistic about the role of power in world politics. It is true that the ideology of hegemonic flexibility invoked certain ideals, such as human rights and international law, more often than the national security ideology. But the real aim of this philosophy was to maintain the U.S. position as a hegemonic power. Hegemonic flexibility supplemented realistic pursuit of national power with idealistic justifications for that power. An appropriate image for this strategy would be the national symbol of the eagle carrying weapons in one claw and an olive branch in the other. Some of the concepts of hegemonic flexibility emerged in the administration of John Kennedy, although this philosophy did not really flourish until the administrations of Nixon, Ford, and Carter in the 1970s.

The Peace Movement

Even at the height of its dominance of U.S. foreign policy-making, the cold war was not without its fundamental critics. Throughout the cold war there were those in the U.S. political system who argued that the cold war was not necessary or desirable. This ideological tendency can perhaps best be described as the peace movement.

The peace movement rejected the basic premises of the cold war. It argued that there was no reason for the United States and the Soviet Union to be locked into positions of interminable hostility, and resisted defining every conflict in the world in terms of East-West struggle. America's assumption of a global military role was contested, as was the growing reliance of U.S. military planners on nuclear weapons. Instead, the peace movement called for fundamental transformation of the cold war world system, asserting that there were grounds for cooperation between the United States and the Soviet Union. The peace movement sought an end to the military confrontation between NATO and the Soviet Union in Europe and the eventual demilitarization of central Europe. It argued for arms control agreements that went beyond simply reshaping the direction of the arms race and that so sharply reduced nuclear arsenals as to end the threat of nuclear holocaust for Americans, Soviets, and the peoples of the world. The peace movement also sought to end the extension of U.S.-Soviet conflict into the Third World and to stop the superpowers from arming Third World allies and fanning the flames of local conflicts. Conflicts in the Third World were viewed as driven primarily by local issues rather than by Soviet manipulation. The peace movement believed that the world would be a safer place if military forces, and particularly nuclear weapons, could be reduced rather than continually built up. It argued world hunger, economic development, and global ecology deserved more attention than competition between the superpowers.

While the peace movement shared some surface similarities with the strategy of the flexible hegemon, it was much more idealistic. While the hegemonic position mixed realistic concern about national power with idealism about the ends of power, the peace movement was more acutely aware of the contradictions between the professed ideals of U.S. foreign policy and the pursuit of power. The peace movement differed fundamentally from any ideology of hegemony in its ultimate view about U.S. power. A flexible hegemon may apply many tools to achieve its ends, including appeals to moral principles, but its fundamental end is to retain its hegemonic position. In contrast, many in the peace movement saw a retrenchment, and eventually a rollback, of U.S. power and military commitments as not only inevitable, but also, in many ways, desirable. They sought a world in which a U.S. role as global policeman would become obsolete.

All presidents at one time or another gave voice to the sentiments expressed by the peace movement. Even that old cold warrior Richard Nixon, under the pressure of the withdrawal from Vietnam, and highlighting the signing of the SALT agreement and the opening to China, reflected some of the philosophy of the peace movement in his second inaugural address in 1973.

> The peace we seek in the world is not the flimsy peace which is merely an interlude between wars, but a peace which can endure for generations to come. . . . Let us build a structure of peace in the world in which the weak are as safe as the strong—in which each respects the right of the other to live by a different system—in which those who would influence others will do so by the strength of their ideas, and not by the force of arms.[5]

However, in the period from the late 1940s through the late 1980s, no president gave the premises of the peace movement priority over the premises of the cold war. From Truman through Ronald Reagan the United States remained locked in conflict with the Soviet Union. While the doctrine of peaceful coexistence that emerged in the 1960s moderated the competition, the United States and the Soviet Union remained enemies. While arms control agreements affected weapons systems at the margins, every year of the cold war left the world with more armaments and greater destructive power than before. Pro-U.S. and pro-Soviet proxy forces clashed in every region of the globe.

Characterizing Ideologies on Issues of International Trade

The foregoing typology is best suited for the more traditional foreign policy issues of international security. It helps in understanding how different administrations have dealt with topics like the Soviet Union, deployment of military forces, arms control, NATO, and emerging political forces in the Third World. It is less helpful in understanding how presidents deal with the newly pressing issue of the 1980s and 1990s—the trade deficit and the U.S. position in the world economy.

Trade has always been an important issue of public policy. In the nineteenth century the high tariffs the less economically developed United States placed on European manufactures to protect domestic industry were one of the most consistently contentious political issues. Rural consumers fought bitterly, but largely in vain, to break down these barriers and thus lower prices. But by the end of World War II the situation had changed entirely. Now the United States was the dominant manufacturing power in the world and sought open world markets for its cheap industrial goods. Throughout most of the postwar period the United States ran a significant trade surplus. The principal objective of trade policy was seen as opening international markets so superior U.S. corporations could operate. In the 1980s, however, foreign penetration of the U.S. market far outstripped U.S. exports. In recent years the United States has run trade deficits of over $100 billion. Suddenly many U.S. policy-makers have sounded like Third World leaders complaining about foreign domination of their markets.

It is notable that in the face of this international challenge, American politicians have dealt with the trade issue much as if it were an issue of domestic economic policy. On the right, the philosophical approach has been free trade. Free traders argue that international markets should be allowed to operate without government interference such as tariffs or other trade barriers. If the government has any role in this area, it should be to point out to other nations the benefits of further opening their markets to international trade. This is essentially a laissez-faire approach to international trade.

On the other hand, there are those who argue that U.S. workers and businesses should be protected from the vagaries of international markets. They argue that unregulated markets do not necessarily serve the national interest, asserting that the playing field is not level, that other nations use trade barriers, or subsidies, or low-wage labor to take unfair advantage of the American worker. Therefore, as in domestic policy, it is the responsibility of the government to protect the interests of those who are harmed by unregulated markets. In domestic policy, I have called this the social security philosophy. On the left, the argument goes beyond simply regulating markets. Jesse Jackson, for example, has emphasized how U.S. corporations have reaped large profits from investing abroad, where labor is cheap. He refers to this as "exporting jobs" and "purging American workers." The social democratic philosophy argues that the interests of the multinational corporation and the American worker are in conflict. According to social democrats, only by giving workers a voice in how profits are reinvested and by using government to restrict the investment of American capital in low-wage countries will the interest of ordinary Americans really be protected.

Public policy in the 1980s steered a course between pure laissez-faire and the social security philosophy. Ronald Reagan gave strong rhetorical support to the free market philosophy. But Reagan also took some protectionist actions, most notably against Japanese computer chips when they threatened high-tech, military-related industries and against Japanese autos. So the outcome of trade policy at this point can best be described as fitting the pattern of the limited interest state. Some of the most strategic and politically well-organized interests get protection. Yet government aid is not universal but is limited in the number and scope of interests it assists.

Foreign Policy Ideology in a Post-Cold War Era

The typologies of ideology presented in this book are not meant to be timeless categories of thought but characterizations of the ideas that shaped policy-making in particular historical periods. In recent years the world has begun to enter a new era in which the cold war, which has dominated world politics in the second half of the twentieth century, appears to be over.

If a truly new era of international relations is really dawning, it would be a risky exercise to try to predict exactly how American ideology will regard a system that is not yet fully formed. However, it is clear that there are two world historical trends that will have to be taken into account by all ideologies about U.S. foreign policy in the coming years. These are the disintegration of the Soviet Union and the growing importance to the United States of issues of international trade compared with the more traditional military and political issues. Despite the obvious difficulties of prediction, it is worth speculating how the American ideological spectrum might adjust to these changes in the world system. Chapter 13 does this. Here I will just point out that the categories which describe foreign policy debate in the cold war era are losing their grip on the public imagination and face revision or transformation in the coming years.

IDEOLOGICAL AFFINITIES ACROSS ISSUE AREAS

It is certainly possible for any individual to take a "left" position on one set of issues and a "right" position on another set of issues. The tendency of survey respondents to do just that, or to have very little ideological structure of any kind in their political thinking, has confounded empirical research into personal political ideology for a long time. While the attitudes of political elites and activists show more ideological structure than those of ordinary citizens, it is still possible for them also to be "left" on some issues and "right" on others. But despite such possibilities, there are also strong tendencies for political parties to attract groups from one ideological pole on most different issue sets and for administrations to pursue either left-center or right-center policies on most issues. A key factor in this is an implicit shared vision of political order that underlies left, right, and centrist tendencies in American politics. Figure 3.1 summarizes these dynamics.

Centrist Tendencies and the Existing Order

What is common to centrist tendencies in American politics is their belief in, preference for, and commitment to the existing order. The political center is characterized by acceptance of current political institutions and a cautious, even cynical attitude toward political change. Centrist forces not only take as a given constant the basic capitalist structure of the political economy, they also tend to see the interest group system as a relatively static set of voting blocs. The task of centrist politics is to practice distributive politics—to cater to large interest groups and voting blocs and to broker their demands through the interest group state.

Questions of political identity are unproblematic in centrist politics. Interest groups that have real political resources are assumed to represent the people they claim to represent. In the same way, the U.S. role in the world is taken as a given. The United States is, and should be, the legitimate leader of the "free" world; the only question is what strategies best serve this hegemonic identity.

Centrist politics tries to avoid social and economic issues that cleave large social blocs into opposing camps. Centrist politicians find it more congenial to deal in issues that can be resolved through brokered compromise and distribution of government benefits to well-organized interests, without upsetting the established political order. Centrist political tendencies can be further broken down into those which look at the existing order as expansive and those which see the existing order as restrictive. "Left-center" political forces see the existing political order as naturally responsive to a plurality of cultural groups and legitimately providing state benefits for a wide range of interest groups. "Right-center" political forces tend to be more restrictive in their view as to which cultural groups are a legitimate part of the existing order and which interest groups have claim to state benefits.

The Left and a New Political Order

Left political forces, however, have considerable grievances with the existing order. What ties together as political and ideological allies such obviously diverse groups as organized racial minorities, women, homosexuals, environmentalists, militant unionists, and peace activists is their shared desire for and interest in a new political order.

Organized minorities, women, and homosexuals all seek a new political order that will allow them new dignity in their nontraditional personal identities and that will erase existing obstacles to their personal development because they do not meet some abstract ideal. Environmentalists and militant unionists seek a new economic order that will protect the ecology or their jobs in a way the current one cannot, though they often conflict on what that new economic order would be. Peace activists seek a new global identity for the United States that would

Figure 3.1
The Contemporary American Ideological Spectrum

Policy Ideologies

ECONOMIC POLICY	Social Democratic	Social Security	Limited Interest	Laissez-Faire
SOCIAL POLICY	Counter Culture	Cultural Pluralism	Cultural Monism	Christian Right
FOREIGN POLICY	Peace Movement	Hegemonic Flexibility	National Security	Holy War

Attitudes Toward the Political Order

	A NEW ORDER	THE EXISTING ORDER	RESTORED ORDER
IDENTITY	New Identities	Static Group Identities	Restore old Identities
U.S. IN WORLD	New Global Role	Hegemonic Roles and Strategies	Restore U.S. Dominance
POLITICAL ECONOMY	Newly Activist State	Interest Group State/ Brokered Political Economy	Restore Pure Market System

protect the peace in a way the current one cannot. While there is certainly tension between many of these goals, or in any political party or movement that tries to appeal to all of these forces at the same time, the underlying unity that makes the label "left" appropriate is dissatisfaction with the current state of affairs and the desire for a new political order.

The Right and a Restored Political Order

The one thing that the political left and the political right have in common is a dissatisfaction with the current political order and a strong desire to change it. While from the point of view of conventional political labels it may seem paradoxical, as one moves to the right end of the political spectrum, one moves away from a desire to conserve the existing political order and toward a position based on restoring a real or imagined past political order. The political alliances of right groups, like those of left groups, are rooted in a shared dissatisfaction with the current political order and a shared vision of how it must be changed.

The ideological theme that holds together the political right is the vision of a restored political order in which some superior real or imagined past is recaptured. At the level of social issues and personal identity, the vision is of a return to the nuclear family, a common religious community, and received traditional values as the foundations of social life. On the economic level the vision is of the removal of complex bureaucracies, the return to the individual work ethic, and a revival of individual social mobility. On the international level, the vision is of a restoration of American domination of world politics in which the United States regains the role of the "new Israel," the world leader chosen by God.

CONTRADICTIONS OF AMERICAN POLICY IDEOLOGIES

Conservatism and the Limited State

While there are clear affinities across issue areas on both the left and right ends of the political spectrum, there are also ideological inconsistencies and contradictions. Since the politics of the 1980s was characterized by the ascendancy of conservative political philosophy, it is worth noting one example of such inconsistencies in conservative thought between the value of individual freedom and the use of activist government.

American conservatism is philosophically committed to maximizing individual freedom. The limited state is at the heart of conservatives' ideal political system. One of Ronald Reagan's favorite slogans crystallizes this attitude: "Government is not the solution, government is the problem." Certainly conservative Republicans act in many ways that can be thought to be consistent with this philosophy of limited government. For example, Reagan implemented tax cuts, cuts in social programs, deregulation of business, and other measures that could be justified by this principle of limited government. But the economic policies of conservative Republicans are not always consistent with the principles of true laissez-faire philosophy. So, for example, the Reagan administration also increased the military budget, farm programs, trade protection, and other forms of economic assistance to interest groups.

But the contradictions of conservatism run even deeper than the unwillingness of Republican presidents to implement pure free-market economic policies. At the philosophical level conservatism does not apply the principle of maximizing individual freedom and minimizing government interference in private lives in all spheres of public policy.

Instead, in the area of social policy it is conservatives who favor the activist use of government power to coerce individuals, and liberals who oppose such use of government. In social policy conservative Republicans have more often favored the use of government power to assert their cultural values over the claim of individual freedom of action. Critics of these contradictions have claimed that conservatives want to get the government out of the board room and into the bedroom. So conservative Republicans want to outlaw abortion while liberal Democrats favor individual choice. At the level of state government, conservatives have backed laws making homosexual activity and even certain heterosexual sexual practices illegal while liberals have argued for individual freedom. In the name of fighting crime conservative Republicans have supported stronger government powers for police to enter people's homes, use electronic eavesdropping devices, and generally engage in surveillance of citizens believed to have committed crimes or to be involved in subversive activities. A similar inconsistency can be seen in conservatives' support for U.S. military and political intervention in a wide range of foreign crises around the globe. While conservatives have little faith in the ability of government to effect positive change in domestic economic affairs, they often seem to have almost unlimited faith in the power of the military to effect positive results in a wide variety of international situations.

Ideological Debates That Obscure Real Policy Issues

In its discussion of the relationship between presidential ideologies and public policy, Chapter 1 emphasized the dual nature of ideology. Ideology at the same time both illuminates many of the motives for public policy and obscures many of the real forces shaping policy behind misleading official pronouncements. The typologies introduced in this chapter and Chapter 2 have illustrated what presidents and candidates have said motivated their policy prescriptions. But it is also worth reviewing how debate over contemporary presidential ideologies obscures the true nature of policy.

When the fourfold classification of domestic policy typologies was introduced, Theodore Lowi's analysis of the misleading nature of much of the domestic policy debate was alluded to.[6] Lowi points out that ideological conflict is typically between those who advocate an activist state whose purpose is to help the less fortunate and those who advocate a limited state. He correctly points out that most government programs help not the poor, but rather powerful, well-established political interests. It is also evident that true laissez-faire policies which restrict government to a few minimal functions have not been pursued since before the days of Franklin Roosevelt. Even in the pre-New Deal period, government engaged in many activities that could not be justified under the doctrine of laissez-faire. But in the post-New Deal period, it is truly anachronistic to talk of a government that performs only minimal functions in society.

The debate over whether government should take an activist role to help the powerless or be strictly limited to a few functions can be heard in virtually every political campaign and certainly has been central to most presidential campaigns. Yet simply said, it is a false debate. How can this shadow contest weigh so heavily in American political rhetoric? A large part of the answer lies in the fact that this kind of ideological debate obscures the true nature of most domestic public policies. It is the dirty little secret of American public policy that most government programs serve the interests of the wealthy and powerful, not ordinary citizens or the poor. But it would not be politic for public policy to be debated in these terms. It would not further the interest of incumbent presidents or members of Congress to openly proclaim that their purpose was to serve a limited number of powerful interests. They would prefer not to have policy debates that focus clearly on the true driving force of domestic policy, which is calculation of which interests are powerful enough to effectively demand government benefits. It is safer to debate public policy in the shadow world of egalitarian activism vs. minimal interventionism.

A similar kind of false debate can be seen in the conflict between realists and idealists in foreign policy. Realists believe U.S. foreign policy is, and should be, driven by concerns of national power and rational calculation of national interest nd little else. Idealists argue that foreign policy can, and should be, shaped by the moral vision of the American people. There are various strains of idealism in the ideologies of the peace movement, hegemonic flexibility, and the holy war ideologies. But reflection indicates that most realists are not very realistic and most moralists arc not very moral.

C. Wright Mills summed up the flaws in the realist school of U.S. foreign policy when he coined the term "crackpot realism."[7] Mills pointed out that "realist" military strategies have turned the world into two armed camps and populated the world with many thousands of nuclear weapons. He asked what realistic aims of national interest were served by policies that left Americans the target of thousands of nuclear missiles which could destroy not only U.S. power, but the nation itself. He questioned whether national interests were realistically served by maintaining a military presence in every corner of the globe and using U.S. power to contest virtually every insurgent movement against the established order—wherever the conflict and whatever the issues. These policies struck Mills more as an idealistic crusade against communism than as a realistic pursuit of U.S. power.

Opponents of the realist school often criticize its exclusive concern with national power and national interest. Idealists argue that moral values should also play an important role in foreign policy-making. But the professed moralism of the dominant strain of American idealism, that associated with the strategy of hegemonic flexibility, is as suspect as the hardheadedness of the so-alled realists. U.S. foreign policy-makers have often held double standards of morality, hypocritically criticizing adversaries for the same kind of behavior that they justify as moral when they engage in it. The father of American internationalism,

Woodrow Wilson, set the tone. While he self-righteously called for liberation of the subject peoples of the defeated empires of Austria-Hungary and Turkey, he participated in the carving up of many of Turkey's territories into new colonies for his allies, the British and the French. Further, Wilson never applied the standard of self-determination to the U.S. colony of the Philippines or the U.S. protectorates of Cuba and Nicaragua. The same hypocrisy characterized the cold war competition with communism. Brutal military dictatorships that were socialist or showed socialist inclinations were chastised for violations of fundamental human rights. But brutal military dictatorships that were U.S. allies against communism were characterized as part of the free world. In the earlier years of the cold war, the United States denounced Soviet domination of eastern Europe as an offense against the self-determination of peoples even as it was providing massive military assistance to the French in their efforts to retain their colonial possessions in Indochina, Algeria, and elsewhere.

Even as the idea of a new post-cold war world order emerges, the same double standards can be seen in the application of morality to U.S. foreign policy. When Islamic fundamentalists challenge U.S. power, as in Iran or Lebanon, they are characterized as crazed fanatics, devoid of reason. But when the same kinds of forces battle the leftist regime in Afghanistan, they are brave freedom fighters. When the Chinese communists suppress student movements with naked force, they are roundly criticized, but when the key U.S. ally South Korea suppresses student movements with naked force, not a peep is heard. When the Iraqis, Turks, and Iranians brutally suppress Kurdish independence movements, Washington is silent. But then Iraq becomes a military foe and the Kurdish problem explodes onto the front pages, although with little mention of the how the key U.S. ally Turkey treats either the refugees or its native Kurds.

CONCLUSION

The ideologies that animate presidential action show both continuity and change over time. In particular historical periods policy debate shows considerable consistency. But as the world changes, so do presidential ideologies. Ideologies that shaped presidential policies in one era may lose their power as circumstances change. The ideologies of racial supremacy and of isolationism have largely disappeared from American policy dialogue, giving way to new formulations.

There are also consistencies and inconsistencies in policy philosophies across issue areas. There are similar attitudes that characterize left, right, and centrist ideological positions on different dimensions of public policy. Centrists tend to be satisfied with the established order, leftists tend to want to create new policies, and rightists tend to want to restore some idealized past. Yet there are also inconsistencies across policy issues in popular philosophies. For example, conservatives generally are skeptical of the effectiveness of government action in issues of political economy and call for limited government when it comes to such issues. Yet conservatives show great faith in the ability of government to achieve positive results through activist, interventionist foreign and military policies.

Presidential ideologies have a dual nature. They often illuminate the purposes of presidential action, but they also can obscure the true meaning of public policies. Prevailing ideological debate does not necessarily fully reveal the real motives of policy. Instead ideologies must be critically analyzed if the true nature of policy is to be fully understood.

NOTES

1. Janet Podell and Steven Anzovin, eds., *Speeches of the American Presidents* (New York: H. W. Wilson, 1988), pp. 394-398 and 405-412.

2. Donald B. Johnson and Kirk H. Porter, eds., *National Party Platforms of 1980* (Urbana: University of Illinois Press, 1982), pp. 205-212.

3. Barry Goldwater, *Why Not Victory?* (New York: McGraw-Hill, 1962), pp. 39, 153-154.

4. John Kennedy, *Public Papers of the Presidents, 1961* (Washington, DC: U.S. Government Printing Office, 1962), pp. 19-28.

5. *Inaugural Addresses of the Presidents*, (Washington, DC: U.S. Government Printing Office, 1989), pp. 280-281.

6. Theodore Lowi, *The End of Liberalism* (New York: Norton, 1979).

7. C. Wright Mills, *The Causes of World War III* (New York: Simon and Schuster, 1958).

PART II

IDEOLOGY IN PRESIDENTIAL POLITICS

4

THE IDEOLOGICAL CROSSPRESSURES ON PRESIDENTIAL ADMINISTRATIONS AND CANDIDATES

STEERING ADMINISTRATIONS THROUGH IDEOLOGICAL CROSSCURRENTS

Ideology in the Bush Administration

When George Bush took office in 1989, there was much speculation about the policy direction his administration would take. On the one hand it was expected that there would be considerable ideological continuity between Bush and his predecessor, Ronald Reagan. After all, Bush had served in Reagan's administration for eight years without ever showing any serious policy or philosophical disagreements with Reagan. Toeing the conservative line had proven a winning strategy not only for Reagan but also for Bush in the 1988 election. When Bush began naming his cabinet, it included many familiar faces from the Reagan years. But some suspected there might be some changes in emphasis in the new administration. Freed from the stifling responsibility of a vicepresident always to support his president, Bush would now be his own man. Before he had accepted the vicepresidential role, he had had some serious disagreements with Reagan in the 1980 primary election campaign. While Reagan's ideological consistency had cemented a powerful political coalition, some of the policy failures of the Reagan years were beginning to undermine political support for the Republican Party among key opinion leaders and constituencies. Bush did not have the personal appeal of the former movie star, so his fate would hinge more on practical policy results.

Each approach held risks for the Bush presidency. To follow too closely in

Reagan's conservative footsteps would risk alienating the political center, leaving Bush isolated on the political right, without Reagan's media skills and personal charm. But moving too far toward the political center would undermine Bush's support among the polar ideological activists who are the backbone of the Republican Party. Without their support the Bush presidency could be left to drift aimlessly, at the mercy of the political winds of the moment.

In his first term Bush showed mixed ideological tendencies, at times taking a more centrist stance than his predecessor but at other times taking conservative positions. Bush did diverge somewhat from Reagan's relatively consistent stance that government was the problem, not the solution. He took relatively tougher action on the environment, supporting the Clean Air Act of 1990. He often talked of his desire to be an "education president" and proposed the expansion of the Head Start program to help impoverished children succeed in their early school years.

Yet on other issues, Bush took a hard conservative line. Although he reneged somewhat on his pledge of no new taxes, his antitax stance kept income taxes from rising significantly. Instead, Bush tried to cope with the massive budget deficits he had inherited from the Reagan administration by vetoing certain domestic spending legislation. He also took a conservative stance on social issues. He appointed conservatives to the two Supreme Court vacancies he faced. He supported the *Webster* Supreme Court decision that raised the possibility of new restrictions on the availability of abortions. He backed legislation that would make flag burning a crime.

On foreign policy Bush also sent mixed signals. In the early days of his administration he was slow to respond to the sweeping arms control proposals made by Soviet leader Mikhail Gorbachev. But in the wake of the collapse of the Soviet bloc, Bush made sweeping unilateral cuts in U.S. nuclear arms that went beyond the cuts negotiated in the long-awaited START treaty. Yet at the same time he was bringing the cold war to a close, Bush showed his toughness by using U.S. military forces to retake Kuwait from the invading forces of Iraq's Saddam Hussein. He also used the military to invade Panama, take control of its government, and capture its president, Manuel Noriega, for trial in the U.S. on drug charges.

As the Bush administration prepared to face the voters in 1992, there were other shifts in public policy. Foreign policy, which had taken center stage in the first three years of the Bush presidency, was downplayed. The recession pushed all other issues off the table and forced the incumbent to focus on economic policy. In his 1992 State of the Union message Bush tried to invoke the triumph of the Desert Storm campaign against Iraq, but media attention was on his domestic program. There were more proposals for tax cuts—for the rich, the middle class, and the poor; for families with children; for the real estate industry; for research and development; for businesses investing in plant and equipment or in the inner city poverty zones; and for businesses and individuals selling capital assets.

Bush's proposals also embraced expansion of activist government programs. More money was promised for Head Start for preschool children, for fighting crime and drugs, and for support of high technology. Most significant, both politically and ideologically, reacting to the various health care reform plans of his Democratic challengers, Bush proposed a major expansion of government health care benefits. Of course, amid all these proposals to cut taxes and expand programs was another promise to bring the budget deficit under control.

How can these different policy stances of the Bush administration be characterized? More generally, how can the political balancing act of presidents between the centrist and the polar ideological political forces be understood?

Characterizing Presidential Policies on the Ideological Spectrum

Chapter 3 developed a context in which the ideological dynamics of administrations can begin to be explored. Breaking out the ideological spectrum beyond conventional concepts of liberalism and conservatism helps to characterize the differences between presidential policies and philosophies. This chapter will explain the ideological crosspressures that presidential administrations face and show how administrations cope with these conflicting demands. Every president is crosspressured by forces that pull it toward the party's ideological wing and by forces that pull it toward the political center.

For example, in economic policy, Republican presidents are crosspressured between their party's true believers, who want to return to freer markets, regardless of the short-term economic or political costs, and their need for broad support in a political system where organized groups expect government benefits and the public largely accepts the doctrine of the activist state. Caught between these conflicting demands for a truly limited state and the need for support from a political system that accepts the activist state, Republican administrations often end up developing the practices of the limited interest state. Those interest groups which form the base of the party have their programs protected or even expanded. But it is a minimal winning coalition strategy.

Democratic administrations are crosspressured on economic policy in a different manner. On their ideological left are groups demanding not simply narrowly targeted benefits for their particular members, but rather that government take a leadership role in fundamentally transforming society, much as it did with race relations in the 1960s. On the centrist side, Democratic administrations face the fundamental skepticism about the ability of the state to effect any kind of positive change, which is the most powerful residue of the laissez-faire philosophy. The characteristic response of Democratic presidents to these crosspressures has been to pursue a more maximal interest group coalition strategy. Democratic presidents may also invoke the rhetoric of social democracy, which helps justify expansion of the role of the government in helping the disadvantaged or empowering or benefiting the ordinary citizen.

Figure 4.1
Political Party and Presidential Ideologies on Economic Policy

SOCIAL   SOCIAL   LIMITED   LAISSEZ-
DEMOCRACY   SECURITY   INTEREST   FAIRE

                          [Range of Policies of Republican Presidents]

        [Range of Policies of Democratic Presidents]

Figure 4.1 represents the differences in the responses of administrations to ideological crosspressures on economic policy schematically. Republicans, crosspressured between conservative activists and centrist political forces, will oscillate between somewhat pure laissez-faire positions and somewhat expansive interest group politics, with the central tendency being a limited interest group politics. Democratic administrations will oscillate between an expansive use of the state with some social democratic elements and the maintenance of the status quo of interest group politics.

This pattern has been consistent since the early days of the New Deal in the 1930s. The central tendency of Democratic presidents, including FDR in his second and third terms, Truman, Kennedy, and Carter has been to seek somewhat broader activism of the state to protect a wider array of interest groups. When Democratic presidents have large majorities in Congress and liberalism is riding high as a philosophy, they may seek more sweeping expansions of the state and offer programs with social democratic elements. This was the case in the early FDR and LBJ administrations.

Republican presidents show a different range of policy actions. They generally try to hold the line on government spending and limit the range of government activities. But they rarely pursue a consistent laissez-faire position. Instead, they have a tendency to shift a fixed spending "pie" toward programs that favor the interest groups lodged within the Republican Party. The practices of the limited interest state best describe the policies of Eisenhower, Nixon, Ford, the later Reagan, and Bush presidencies. Ronald Reagan is the one Republican president who at times pursued laissez-faire policies, particularly in his first term, but even his commitment to laissez-faire was more rhetorical and symbolic than substantive. Military spending, farm programs, and trade protection are just a few of the more important areas where the Reagan administration often violated its free market principles in actual policy practice.

The same pattern can be seen in social policy, as shown in Figure 4.2. Throughout the twentieth century, but particularly in the 1970s and 1980s, the Republican party has been the home of the Christian right. Yet it has also sought to woo non-Protestant social groups, particularly conservative Catholics and

Figure 4.2
Political Party and Presidential Ideologies on Social Policy

| COUNTER | CULTURAL | CULTURAL | CHRISTIAN |
| CULTURAL | PLURALISM | MONISM | RIGHT |

[Range of Policies of Republican Presidents]

[Range of Policies of Democratic Presidents]

Jews. Hence it has emphasized traditional values and national pride. Republican presidents have given at least rhetorical support to key items on the agenda of fundamentalists, such as banning abortion and reviving school prayer. But Republican presidents have generally relied more on secular themes of American nationalism and traditions than on fundamentalist doctrine in order to justify these policy positions. Bills outlawing flag burning are a perfect example of the Republican use of nationalism as a civic religion.

The Democratic Party has historically been open to a wide range of ethnic groups and thus has been the party of cultural diversity. Particularly since it has been purged of its segregationist right, it has increasingly been the home of groups historically excluded from the centers of power of American life, from blacks to feminists to environmentalists. Yet at the same time the Democratic Party has suffered from being identified too closely with unpopular groups, so it has also sounded the themes of national identity and solidarity. However, the Democratic version of the American way is a more pluralistic one.

The contrast between cultural monism and cultural pluralism can perhaps be seen most clearly by comparing the ethnic composition of Democratic administrations and judicial appointments with those of Republicans. Democratic administrations and judicial appointments generally reflect a broad mix of ethnic groups and a significant proportion of women. On the other hand, Republican appointments are distributed disproportionately to white people, particularly white Protestant men. Men from the ethnic groups that Republicans are targeting as potential supporters, such as conservative Jews and Hispanics, are somewhat more prominent in Republican appointments than groups that Republicans have written off, such as blacks.

Characterizing the policy behavior of administrations of different parties on foreign policy is more difficult than on domestic policy. Until the recent changes in the world system, the rhetoric of Republican leaders generally fit the pattern of the national security ideology of military confrontation with the Soviet Union. Since the fall of Lyndon Johnson the rhetoric of Democratic leaders has generally fit the more liberal philosophy of a more flexible approach to the Soviet Union. But the actual policy behavior of administrations cannot be so easily characterized. Even before the dramatic events of recent years, Republican presidents largely followed a strategy of talking a tough cold war line toward the Soviet Union but eventually pursuing a more flexible strategy of negotiations. Ronald Reagan's revival of the cold war in his first term is an exception, but in his second term even Reagan shifted to a policy of conciliation and negotiation with the Soviets. Nor have recent Democratic leaders always followed a consistent policy of accommodation with the Soviet Union. In its final year the Carter administration took a tough stance toward the Soviet Union, suspending ratification of the SALT II treaty, boycotting the Olympic Games, embargoing food sales, and threatening to use military force in the Near East crises.

The Republican strategy of talking conservative but moving to the left in actual policy has proven to be a winning one. Nixon gained credit for the first SALT treaty, Reagan won plaudits for the Intermediate Nuclear Forces treaty, and Bush has been praised for ending the cold war. The hard-line rhetoric has held the support of conservative true believers even as successful negotiations have quieted liberal critics. This Republican strategy has put the Democrats in a dilemma. When Democratic presidents pursued negotiations with the Soviets, Republican leaders reverted to their cold war stance and portrayed Democrats as weak and naive. During the Carter presidency, whenever the United States faced setbacks or was unable to influence events overseas, Republican critics would blame these troubles on Carter's lack of toughness and resolve. In the area of arms control, while Democratic senators have overwhelmingly supported treaties negotiated by Republican presidents, Republican senators blocked the ratification of SALT II and other treaties negotiated by the Carter administration. The result is that Republican presidents can claim credit for being skillful negotiators and the Republican Party can blame Democratic administrations for lacking effectiveness in foreign policy.

This contradiction between rhetoric and the actual policy behavior of Republican administrations has obscured a real paradox. In the supposedly "conservative" era of the 1970s and 1980s U.S. foreign policy generally moved to the ideological left, with the notable exception of the later Carter and early Reagan years. U.S. foreign policy in the early 1990s has more in common with the policy stances taken by the McGovern campaign than the Goldwater campaign. Democratic advocates of a more conciliatory policy toward Russia have actually had more influence on policy when they have been out of power than when they held the White House.

TACTICS FOR STEERING THROUGH IDEOLOGICAL CROSSCURRENTS

While the general ideological tenor of an administration can usually be predicted by the party of the president, the exact actions presidents will take on specific issues cannot. Over the course of a term, presidents respond differently to ideological crosspressures on different issues and at different times. There are various tactics administrations can use to steer through treacherous ideological crosscurrents. Five of the most important are (1) symbolic politics, (2) moving in different ideological directions on different issues, (3) shifting ideological emphasis over time, (4) the use of presidential messengers to send mixed ideological signals, and (5) rewarding both wings of the president's party in personnel selection.

Symbolic Politics

One response of administrations that are forced to the political center by the system yet are seeking to please the ideological pole of their party is to employ symbolic politics. That is, they engage in rhetoric which reassures their ideological wing that they are pursuing the doctrinal agenda while they are engaging in quite different policy behavior. Certainly much of the disjuncture between presidential rhetoric and policy reality can be attributed to this phenomenon.

All presidents engage in symbolic politics at one time or another. The Reagan administration continued to propose a constitutional amendment to require a balanced federal budget at the same time it was running $200 billion deficits. The Carter administration proclaimed its devotion to human rights at the same time it was wining and dining the brutal Shah of Iran in an attempt to keep his pro-Western regime in power. The Nixon administration talked of limited government at the same time it was using the White House staff and the FBI to illegally subvert its domestic political opposition.

Moving in Different Directions on Different Issues

Another tactic presidents use to steer through ideological crosscurrents is to move to the center on one issue at the same time as they are pleasing their ideological wing on another issue. This process can be seen clearly even in the most ideologically consistent presidency of recent times, that of Ronald Reagan. For example, in his first year, even as Reagan moved to dramatically alter the economic and budgetary policies of the nation, he downplayed the conservative social agenda on abortion, school prayer, and family issues that had been so crucial to his electoral success among evangelical Christians. This same tendency can also be seen in the later years of his administration. At the same time Reagan was moving from his historical hostility toward the Soviets to negotiate a new arms control agreement, he sought to shore up his support among conservatives with his nomination of the strong philosophical conservative Robert Bork to fill a vacancy on the Supreme Court.

Richard Nixon was a master at sending mixed ideological signals. In the early years of his administration, in domestic policy he attacked big government and appealed to southern conservatives with his first Supreme Court nominees. But at the same time he proposed legislative initiatives to expand the role of the national government in protecting the environment and giving financial support to state and local government. In 1971 Nixon even imposed wage and price controls so inflationary pressures would not undermine his reelection campaign.

In his later years Nixon covered his tracks by moving in one direction on foreign policy at the same time he moved in the other direction on domestic policy. As he abandoned his conservative anticommunism to pursue detente with the Soviet Union and China, he protected his base on the right by becoming ever more militant on budgetary and fiscal issues, taking a harder line against big government and big-spending Democrats.

Shifting Ideological Emphasis over Time

A similar tactic is taking different postures at different times. Administrations often make both strong polar ideological appeals and centrist appeals over the course of their term. Many presidents take a stronger liberal or conservative position in their early years and then move toward the political center over the course of their administration. The Reagan, Carter, Johnson, and FDR presidencies all fit this pattern.

Even before he became president, candidate Reagan showed he could shift his ideological messages when the time was right. In the 1980 Republican primaries he waged a very conservative campaign that appealed to activists on the party's ideological pole. But once he had won the nomination, Reagan mended fences within the party and blurred the sharp ideological image he had projected at the Republican convention, particularly through his selection of a vicepresidential candidate. First he tried to get former president Gerald Ford, who was identified with the moderate wing of the party, to become his running mate. Unable to achieve this, Reagan turned to George Bush, who had been his main opponent in the primaries and who had called his economic plans "voodoo economics." But the most dramatic ideological movement by Reagan was the shift in his stance toward the Soviet Union between his first and second terms. In his first term Reagan embarked on a massive military buildup and revived cold war attitudes toward the Soviets. But in his second term he had four summits with Soviet leader Gorbachev and negotiated the first nuclear arms reduction treaty.

A similar kind of ideological shift can be seen in the middle of the Carter administration. Early in his term Carter tried to continue the Nixon-Ford-Kissinger policy of detente and arms control with the Soviet Union. In his cabinet appointments Carter tried to strike a balance between the different wings of his party, naming liberals to some positions and moderates to others. But as his reelection campaign neared, Carter tried to move toward the political center. He purged several of the most prominent liberals from his cabinet and toughened his stance toward the Soviet Union. Following the Soviet invasion of Afghanistan in December 1979, Carter suspended his support for the SALT II treaty he himself had negotiated.

Sending Mixed Ideological Signals via Presidential Messengers

Another way that presidents and parties send mixed ideological signals is through party leaders who share some of the stature of the president. Certain members of the administration and the party share some of the charismatic aura of the presidency. They may be perceived to have the president's ear, or they may seem to have been delegated the authority and power to make administration decisions, or they may be former or potential presidential candidates themselves. Those who share in presidential authority can be called presidential messengers. Presidential messengers come from a number of sources. Vicepresidents are the clearest example. Key members of the White House staff or members of the inner cabinet may share the aura of presidential authority. Past presidents or losing presidential candidates of the major parties also have some of the stature of sitting presidents. Other potential presidential messengers are members of the Senate or governors who have made a close run for the party's nomination or are thought to be leading future candidates.

Presidents and presidential candidates use such messengers to send important ideological signals. One clear example is vicepresidential selection. Ideology is not the only factor that goes into this choice. Qualifications to become president and geographical balance are among the other important factors. But in 1988 Michael Dukakis chose Lloyd Bentsen in part to try to moderate his image as a northern liberal, just as John Kennedy had chosen Lyndon Johnson in 1960. Ronald Reagan chose his main opponent for the 1980 nomination, George Bush, to moderate his strong conservative image. Moderate presidential candidates do the same in reverse. George Bush chose Dan Quayle in part to solidify his position with conservatives who remembered him as the moderate challenger to Reagan in 1980. Jimmy Carter chose liberal Walter Mondale to send the message that he was not a traditional southern Democrat.

Parties also produce presidential messengers who serve as counterpoint to the dominant trend within presidential administrations or campaigns. Former presidential candidates and then Republican Senate Leaders Howard Baker and Robert Dole generally were more moderate than the Reagan administration, helping to broaden the appeal of the party. In the later stages of the 1988 campaign, ideological polarizers Jesse Jackson and Pat Robertson continued to cultivate their respective parties' true believers even as the nominees scrambled to occupy the political center.

Presidential messengers assist administrations in sending mixed ideological signals and thus limit the political damage of painful policy decisions. When controversial decisions are made, they are sent out on missions of damage control. A presidential messenger from the ideological wing of the party will reassure the party faithful that the president is really on their side. At the same time a centrist presidential messenger will be assuring the political establishment that the controversial policy really represents the triumph of moderation.

An example of this can be seen in the Clean Air Act of 1990. The Bush administration wanted the credit for taking tough action on the environment. Yet it also wanted to placate its business supporters, who were worried about the costs clean air legislation would place on them. So in public Bush proclaimed his commitment to the environment. He relied on Environmental Protection Agency (EPA) director William Reilly, who had credibility with environmentalists, to trumpet the strong new Bush activism to these groups. But at the same time powerful White House Chief of Staff John Sununu was working to weaken key provisions of the legislation and to soften the bill's impact on business. While Bush was personally taking a popular stand and EPA head Reilly was carrying the message to the faithful, Chief of Staff Sununu was reassuring business leaders that the president really had their interests at heart.

Sending Mixed Ideological Signals Through Personnel Decisions

Presidents also send mixed ideological signals through use of their appointment powers. All presidents try to reward each of the factions and both ideological wings of their party when choosing the people who will serve in their administration. Presidents with more polarizing ideological views will choose a higher proportion of appointees with similar views, and presidents with more centrist inclinations will select more like-minded moderates. But all presidents will people their administration with a mix of both polar ideologues and moderates.

For example, Ronald Reagan was more consistently ideological in his personnel decisions than most presidents, but even he sent mixed signals through his use of appointment powers. In naming new federal judges he followed a strict ideological test. All of his judicial appointees had very conservative judicial philosophies. Reagan also chose many people with strongly conservative views for his cabinet and White House staff. His choice of James Watt to head the Interior Department foretold the administration's lax stance on environmental issues. Watt's career before being selected for Interior was as a corporate lawyer who championed business interests in court cases involving environmental issues. Reagan's first foreign policy team reflected the hard line the administration would take toward the Soviet Union in its early years. Reagan chose the militant cold warrior General Alexander Haig as his first secretary of state. He also chose Kenneth Adelman, who had written several articles attacking the very concept of arms control, to be director of the Arms Control and Disarmament Agency.

But even the conservative Reagan administration contained some important moderates. Perhaps the most prominent of these was George Bush's associate,

James Baker, who was chosen for the crucial position of chief of Reagan's personal White House staff. This appointment was meant to reassure Congress and the public that Reagan could negotiate and compromise when necessary. Reagan also gave considerable authority to White House staffers Ed Meese and Michael Deaver, who together with Baker formed a triumvirate of White House power. Meese was a strong polar ideologue who had been with Reagan since his days as governor of California, and Deaver was closely associated with traditional Republican Party constituency politics. Thus a kind of balance was struck between the pragmatists and the polar ideologues in the powerful White House staff. Reagan's second choice as secretary of state was also a leading centrist, George Schultz. Haig had proven to be a loose cannon whose tough talk toward the Soviet Union and other socialist nations did more to frighten European allies and alienate Third World nations than to intimidate the Soviets. So after not much more than a year at State, Haig was relieved of his command and a more diplomatic man was chosen to head State.

George Bush's first cabinet and White House staff also contained a careful mix of strong conservatives and moderates, although moderates were somewhat more prominent than in the Reagan years. None of the four most prestigious cabinet posts—State, Defense, Treasury, or Attorney General—went to a strong polar ideologue. Moderate James Baker, who had moved from White House chief of staff to Treasury in the second Reagan term, was Bush's secretary of state. Former Pennsylvania governor and political centrist Richard Thornburgh was chosen for attorney general. Richard Cheney, chief of the White House staff under moderate Republican Gerald Ford, became secretary of defense. Prominent businessman Nicolas Brady was selected to head the Treasury Department. While all of these men were solid Republicans, they also were all political pragmatists.

Yet Bush did not forget the ideological wing of his party in the appointment process. Just as Reagan had sought to balance his conservative image by selecting a moderate as head of the White House staff, so Bush balanced his more moderate image by choosing a strong ideological conservative, New Hampshire Governor John Sununu, to lead his personal staff. Reflecting the conservative social agenda, Bush named outspoken conservative William Bennett to be the country's first "czar" of antidrug operations. He also selected one of his most conservative primary opponents, Jack Kemp, to head the Department of Housing and Urban Development. Bush chose conservative Congressman Manuel Luhan as secretary of the interior. Like James Watt before him, Luhan had spent much of his career battling environmentalists rather than fighting for the ecosystem. But Bush balanced Luhan by naming a man having strong credibility with environmental groups, William Reilly, to head the EPA.

THE IDEOLOGICAL DYNAMICS OF PRESIDENTIAL CAMPAIGNS

Dealing with Ideological Crosscurrents Sequentially

Presidential candidates use tactics similar to those used by sitting presidents to deal with the conflicting forces that push them toward the ideological poles and that pull them toward the political center. At some points in the campaign candidates will try to build their support with the ideological wing of their party. At other times they will try to appear more moderate and centrist. For example, most presidential candidates use a different strategy in the primary season than they will use if they reach the general election. The length of presidential campaigns allows candidates to make multiple appeals over the long haul.

Many observers have noted that in the final months of the general election campaign, candidates steer away from controversial issues and do everything to appeal to the mass of voters who do not have strong ideological beliefs.[1] If most of the voters are in the political center, no presidential candidate can win a general election if he is perceived as outside the political mainstream.

The Nomination Phase and the Ideological Poles of the Parties

But before a candidate can reach the general election, he must first win his party's nomination. However, the typical voter in the presidential primaries is different from the typical general election voter. Richard Watson has referred to the primary electorate as the "selectorate."[2] This term has a dual meaning. Not only does the selectorate "select" the nominee, it also consists of a "select" few who are highly politicized. Barely half the electorate votes in a general presidential election, and only a small minority of those participate in the primaries and caucuses. This minority "selectorate" is much more ideologically consistent than the ordinary citizen. The Republican selectorate is made up mostly of very conservative voters, and the Democratic selectorate consists mostly of very liberal voters.

The confirmation of this process can be seen in the surveys of the political beliefs of those who become delegates to the Republican and Democratic conventions. Republican convention delegates are consistently more conservative than the general population, and Democratic delegates are more liberal.[3]

Many political pundits have lamented that presidential candidates must win the support of the ideological wings of their parties before they can gain their party's nomination. And certainly the nomination of polar ideological candidates has hurt parties in particular elections. The Goldwater and McGovern candidacies come immediately to mind, although Ronald Reagan's political success proves that having a strong ideology is not always a fatal liability.

But the fact that candidates must appeal to the ideological wings of their parties serves crucial functions for the long-term strength of the parties. Perhaps the most obvious function of the polar ideological phase of presidential campaigns is to activate new blocs of voters who previously had not participated in the political process. In 1988 Pat Robertson brought multitudes of previously unpoliticized evangelical Christians into the Republican Party. In 1984 and 1988 Jesse Jackson inspired millions of blacks who had given up on the political process to enroll in the Democratic Party. It is exactly the ideological fire of the messages of such presidential candidates that attracts new blood into the parties.

At a deeper level, such polar ideological candidacies serve other functions for the parties. A political party needs a reason to exist beyond the simple quest for office of a few of its leaders. Political parties are successful over time because large numbers of voters come to identify with their themes. Polar ideological candidacies help establish a party's political identity.   For decades, millions of voters identified the Democratic Party as the party that protected their interests because they identified with the policies and beliefs of the administration of Franklin Roosevelt and his successors. Democratic presidential candidates throughout the years were successful in reminding voters that the Democratic Party was the party of Social Security, economic recovery, and government that helped solve people's problems. Appeals to this belief system cemented a political coalition and a social bloc that pulled together millions of voters.

Polar ideological candidacies also perform a system-level function. For voters in a democracy to have a real, meaningful choice, the parties must offer them real, meaningful choices between conflicting political beliefs and public policies. A political system that offers such choices is called a responsible party system. But the strong centrist pressures of an American general election tend to blur such differences as candidates scramble for the political center. Elections often turn on things like candidates' personalities or verbal gaffes. It is their ideological wings that pressure the parties to behave like responsible parties--to articulate a set of beliefs that voters can accept or reject.

Moving Toward the Center for the General Election Campaign

Thus the ideological wings of political parties are not simply destructive for the fortunes of the party or the nation, as some pundits believe. The most successful presidential candidates of the 1970s and 1980s began their campaigns with a strong ideological appeal to the party faithful. Not only Ronald Reagan but also George Bush and Richard Nixon won with this strategy. It is still possible to win a party's nomination and then the general election by beginning as a centrist candidate. In 1976 both Republican Gerald Ford and Democrat Jimmy Carter ran in the nomination process as centrists. But it is significant that Ford was the only Republican in the last six elections to lose and that Carter was unable to muster enough long-term political support to win reelection.

However, the conventional wisdom that a party's ideological wing can be destructive to its chances of winning a general election is often true. Once they have solidified their base within their party, presidential candidates must then move to the political center for the general election campaign. Candidates Goldwater, McGovern, and Mondale were not able to do this, and they lost in landslides. Ronald Reagan, on the other hand, was able to make this transition. Since Reagan ran the most consistently ideologically polarizing primary campaigns, and thus was the candidate who had the farthest to go achieve acceptance by the political center, it is worth examining how he did it.

Reagan was aided in his move to the center by the fact that in 1980 he was running against a vulnerable opponent. Goldwater and McGovern had had to run against popular incumbents who were riding high after political triumphs. Goldwater faced LBJ, the Southerner who had shepherded historic civil rights legislation through Congress and who was the chosen successor of the recently martyred John Kennedy. McGovern faced Nixon in the year the first strategic arms limitation treaty had been signed, the diplomatic door to China had been opened, and peace was near in Vietnam. Reagan's opponent, on the other hand, was burdened by double-digit inflation and the humiliation of the Iranian hostage crisis. Voters were already looking for an alternative to the Carter administration. Yet Reagan certainly helped his cause by his own behavior. Unlike Goldwater, who had very similar beliefs, on a personal level Reagan did not come across as a strident, angry ideologue. Instead, his warm and friendly demeanor, his self-deprecating humor, and his obvious ease before the camera presented a visual image of reasonableness. It was not so much what he said as how he said it. Despite all the attempts of the Carter campaign to portray him as outside the political mainstream, Reagan's personal manner overcame voters' doubts. The television debates were crucial in this process. Most voters just did not believe that the avuncular gentleman they saw on the TV screen could be the dangerous man Carter claimed he was.

However, Reagan also softened his philosophical stance in the general election. Gone were the proposals of the 1976 primary campaign to cut government spending by 25 percent. The tough line toward the Soviet Union was blurred by professions of the desire for peaceful relations. The buckshot blasts at the policies of the past decades took on less importance than carefully aimed shots at the particular and immediate failures of the Carter administration. It took more for Reagan to win the 1980 election than his personal charm. He had to soften his ideological message to appear more politically flexible than his philosophical soul mate Barry Goldwater had seemed in 1964.

Just as sitting presidents must sometimes take strong ideological stands and at other times take a more centrist approach, so too presidential candidates must appeal both to more ideologically attuned party activists and to the broader political center. The presidential selection process presents a series of incentives which make it predictable that most winning presidential campaigns will begin closer to the ideological pole of their party and then move toward the political center over time.

Ideology in the Nomination Campaigns of 1988

It is also predictable that different candidates will adopt different ideological strategies to win the approval of the selectorate, as can be seen in both the 1988 and 1992 nomination races. The different stances of the candidates along the ideological spectrum are classified in Figure 4.3.

In 1988, on the Democratic side Jesse Jackson and George McGovern sought to appeal to the party's more ideologically inclined activists with very liberal messages. Jackson had considerable success with a campaign targeted at those who had historically been excluded from political and economic power, seeking to create a common ground between minorities and the white working class. At the other end of the Democratic spectrum was Tennessee Senator Albert Gore. He was the candidate who put the most distance between himself and the policy positions that had been characteristic of the national Democratic Party in the 1970s and 1980s. While he avoided any close association with the still unpopular Jimmy Carter, Gore, like Carter, presented himself as the most moderate Democratic contender, and thus the one most able to win independent voters in the fall election.

While Jackson was the most consistently left-wing candidate, and Gore the most moderate, most of the candidates, including the eventual winner, Michael Dukakis, sought to find the ideological center of the Democratic Party. Two western Democrats, former Colorado Senator Gary Hart and former Arizona Governor Bruce Babbitt, ran as relative centrists on economic issues but relative liberals on social and foreign policy issues. Illinois Senator Paul Simon tried to capture the political center within the Democratic Party by reviving some of the themes that had united the party before the conflicts of the late 1960s. Simon's repeated use of the memory of Hubert Humphrey symbolized his campaign to revive the old Democratic coalition.

One of the candidates whose campaign seeking the center of the Democratic Party proved more durable was Missouri Congressman Richard Gephardt. His campaign emphasized the newly critical issue of foreign trade. Millions of American auto, steel, and textile workers had lost their jobs because of foreign imports. Gephardt recognized that while trade was a new issue, it tended to unite broad segments of the historical Democratic coalition—unionized workers concerned about their jobs and wages, farmers dependent on foreign markets and world prices for their crops, Southerners concerned about the fate of agriculture and the textile industry, and Midwesterners worried about the decline of heavy industry and the farm crisis.

The candidate who was ultimately successful in capturing the Democratic center was Massachusetts Governor Michael Dukakis. Like John Kennedy, also from Massachusetts, Dukakis tried to downplay the importance of political ideology in favor of a belief in technocratic management of government and the economy. Dukakis espoused the historic Democratic position of activist government. But he also highlighted his good relationship with the Boston

Figure 4.3
Recent Presidential Candidates on the Ideological Spectrum

Democratic Left	Democratic Center	Center (Moderates)	Republican Center	Republican Right
		1992		
Jerry Brown	Bob Kerry	Bill Clinton	George Bush	Pat Buchanan
Tom Harkin		Paul Tsongas		
		1988		
Jesse Jackson	Michael Dukakis	Albert Gore	George Bush	Pat Robertson
	Richard Gephardt		Robert Dole	Jack Kemp

business community and touted the "Massachusetts miracle," the rapid economic growth that state had experienced during his governorship. This Dukakis attributed to a partnership his administration had created between activist government and the private sector. In contrast with the chronic fiscal crisis in Washington, Dukakis portrayed himself as prudent manager, pointing to the annual balanced budgets that he had submitted as governor.

The situation in the 1988 Republican primaries was somewhat different. Since the Goldwater convention in 1964 the Republican Party had shown less ideological diversity than the Democratic Party. In the Reagan era virtually all Republican officeholders professed some form of conservative philosophy. The contest on the Republican side was over who could rightly claim to be Reagan's true successor as the leader of political conservatives.

The Republican candidates basically pursued two strategies. Several less well-known candidates emphasized their passionate commitment to the conservative Reagan philosophy. Congressman Jack Kemp, Reverend Pat Robertson, and General Alexander Haig emphasized ideological conservatism and endorsed the conservative agenda on all major issues. But there were clear differences in the issues they used to frame this appeal. Kemp focused on economic policy, pointing to his authorship of the popular tax cut legislation of the first Reagan term. He portrayed himself as the candidate most committed to supply side economics, which, he argued, was the basis for the prosperity of the 1980s.

Robertson, on the other hand, emphasized social issues. Opposition to abortion, support of school prayer, and the commitment of the nation to Christian values were at the heart of the his campaign. Robertson's strategy was to try to mobilize in even greater numbers the millions of fundamentalist Christians who had been drawn to the Republican Party in the 1980s by its conservative stance on social issues. Haig focused on his area of expertise, foreign policy. He lamented the drift of Reagan foreign policy toward the political center in the second term and pointed out cases where the tough talk of the Reagan administration had not been matched by tough action.

Washington insiders Vicepresident George Bush and Senate Minority Leader Robert Dole had different strategies, emphasizing their pragmatic skills at implementing the Reagan agenda. Each tried to portray himself as the man with the greatest political skill in turning the conservative agenda into public policy. As the men considered the leading contenders, and as candidates fighting for the same niche, each saw the other as his main opponent. Dole tried to capitalize on the inherent weakness of the office of vicepresident to portray Bush as an ineffective "wimp" who had done less to further the Reagan agenda than he had.

As Reagan's vicepresident, Bush presented himself as the logical successor to the Reagan legacy. Front-runner Bush was stung in the first test, in Iowa, by Dole's challenge to his political skill and Robertson's challenge to his conservative credentials. But Bush's loyal service as second in command in the most politically successful Republican administration in a generation eventually paid off, not only in the nomination process but also in the general election.

Ideology in the Nomination Campaigns of 1992

Despite his victory in 1988, George Bush was never able to completely reassure many Republican conservatives that he was really one of them. After three years of coping with real-world problems and negotiating with congressional Democrats, Washington bureaucrats, and foreign leaders, Bush was further compromised in the eyes of many of the conservative faithful. As the recession which began in 1991 dragged on, conservative political columnist Patrick Buchanan decided to challenge Bush for the Republican nomination in 1992. Although he had never held public office, in the New Hampshire primary in February, Buchanan stung President Bush by drawing 37 percent of the vote and keeping the president's total to 53 percent. Nearly half of the Republican voters had rejected a sitting Republican president. Buchanan was able to draw votes from both ideological conservatives and those suffering from the recession by presenting himself as a means to send a message to Washington.

Buchanan continued to garner about a third of the vote in most of the early Republican contests, throwing quite a scare into the Bush campaign. At a minimum, the Buchanan vote demonstrated the softness of support for Bush. More seriously, if Buchanan had been able to ride the media attention his unexpected strong showing in New Hampshire generated to win just one early primary, he could have emerged as a real threat to Bush's renomination. But Buchanan topped out at about a third of the vote and eventually lost media and voter interest because he was no longer perceived as a mortal threat to the president.

Still, the fact that a political columnist who had never held public office could score so well against a sitting president shows that incumbents running for reelection are in no way immune from ideological crosscurrents. In three of the last four elections where there has been an incumbent, he has faced a challenge from the ideological wing of his party. George Bush was not the first sitting president to be stung by competition from a party leader who thought he had abandoned the faith. In 1980 Jimmy Carter faced a challenge from the left from Ted Kennedy, and in 1976 Gerald Ford nearly lost his party's nomination to the more conservative Ronald Reagan. Carter and Ford later went on to defeat in the general election. The stakes involved in the ideological messages sent by an incumbent president clearly are quite high.

Since the changes in the nomination process in the 1960s and early 1970s, the only president running for reelection to avoid such a test has been Ronald Reagan, whose conservative credentials could not be doubted by the party faithful. The general tendency of a president to move to the political center over the course of his administration, in order to position himself for reelection, clearly is limited by the tendency of such maneuvers to provoke a serious challenge from disillusioned party activists.

On the other hand, the power of the left ideological pole of the Democratic Party appeared largely blunted in 1992. The early leaders were Arkansas Governor Bill Clinton and former Massachusetts Senator Paul Tsongas, both of whom ran as moderate, centrist Democrats not tied to the liberal dogmas of the past. Clinton was the head of a national group of moderate Democratic Party leaders who had been trying for years to soften their party's association with liberal causes. Tsongas ran as a "pro-business" Democrat who skewered both big-spending liberal Democrats and tax-cutting Republicans with the line, "I am not running for Santa Claus, I am running for president of the United States." There was no one in the race as far to the left as Jesse Jackson had been in 1988, but Iowa Senator Tom Harkin and former California Governor Jerry Brown adopted strategies of appealing to liberal activists in the Democratic selectorate that had been successful in recent years. Harkin targeted labor and the old-line liberals who had supported Walter Mondale. Brown targeted the middle class, countercultural new liberals and independents who had supported George McGovern and Gary Hart. Harkin was forced to drop out early. Brown's unorthodox fundraising tactics allowed him to outlast most of his competitors, but he was unable to win the big state contests that would have demonstrated that he was a potential nominee.

Clearly, after twelve consecutive years of conservative Republican presidents even the liberal Democratic selectorate was looking for an electable Democrat not tied to the failures of the Democratic past. Changes in the presidential selection process made it easier for Democratic moderates and tougher for liberals. Before the 1988 campaign, ideologically moderate southern Democrats had tried to use the primary process to move their party toward the political center. Party leaders in most of the southern states agreed to set their primary elections on the same day, "Super Tuesday," which would come early on the nomination calender. The hope was to nominate a southern moderate and in any case to make it impossible for anyone who could not appeal to the moderate southern voters to win the nomination.

Super Tuesday backfired on the southern Democrats in 1988. Because of the large number of black voters in the South, the candidate most advantaged by Super Tuesday in 1988 was the most liberal one, Jesse Jackson, although Southerner Albert Gore also benefited. Super Tuesday also probably spared the Republicans a long and bitter nomination fight by allowing Southerner George Bush to take a commanding lead early in the process. But in 1992 Super Tuesday did contribute to thrusting moderate Democrats to the front of the pack.

NOTES

1. Anthony Downs, *An Economic Theory of Democracy* (New York: Harper, 1965).

2. Richard Watson, *The Presidential Contest* (New York: John Wiley, 1984).

3. George C. Edwards III and Stephen J. Wayne, *Presidential Leadership* (New York: St. Martin's Press, 1985).

5

PRESIDENTIAL IDEOLOGIES AND THE PARTY SYSTEM

A TYPOLOGY OF PRESIDENTIAL ELECTIONS

Not all presidential elections are created equal. Not all presidential elections have the same historical significance. Some elections put into motion a political coalition and a set of public policies that shape the nation for decades to come. Other elections have little long-term impact on the political system or public policy. It is useful to have a classification of the kinds of presidential elections based upon their impact on public policy and the party system.

Political scientists have coined the term "critical election" to refer to a presidential election that realigns the political system by setting in motion historical changes in party politics, public policy, public institutions, and political ideology which endure into succeeding decades.[1] Another important type of election is one that "dealigns" the existing party system by significantly weakening the hold of a dominant party over the political system.

There are also elections where a presidential candidate has long electoral coattails that pull many members of his party to victory in congressional races and produce an "ideological majority." These elections do not permanently alter the party system, but they do create congressional coalitions that make major shifts in public policy which endure beyond the temporary electoral majority. Other presidential elections can be classified as succession elections or simple reelections. (See Table 5.1.)

Table 5.1
A Typology of Recent Presidential Elections

Critical Election	Dealigning Election	Ideological Majorities	Succession Elections	Simple Reelections
1932	1968	1980	1988	1984
		1964	1976	1972
			1960	1956
			1952	

CRITICAL ELECTIONS, REALIGNMENT, AND DEALIGNMENT

The Critical Election of 1932

The critical election of twentieth century American politics is the election of 1932, which not only put FDR in the White House but also inaugurated an era of Democratic Party dominance of the national political system and historic changes in public policy and philosophy. The Republican Party had been the dominant political force since the election of Abraham Lincoln in 1860. From 1860 until 1932 the Republicans controlled the presidency for 56 of 72 years and held majorities in Congress in 48 of those years. But in 1929 the stock market crashed and the Great Depression began. A massive shift in political fortunes soon ensued as the Republican Party was blamed for the turmoil. In 1928 the Republicans had won their third straight presidential election and roughly 60 percent of the seats in Congress. In 1932 the Democrats won the presidency and gained control of both houses of Congress. By 1936 they had won roughly 75 percent of the seats in Congress and in the presidential election carried every state except Maine and Vermont.

More important, after 1932 the Democrats replaced the Republicans as the dominant force in American politics. The Democrats were able to institutionalize their gains. They held on to the presidency for 20 consecutive years. Their control of the House of Representatives endures today, interrupted for only 4 of the last 62 years. From 1932 to 1980 the Democrats controlled the Senate for 44 of the 48 years. The New Deal coalition that FDR hammered out withstood the test of time. The New Deal social bloc included northern white liberals, conservative white Southerners, northern ethnic minorities from southern and eastern Europe and Ireland, and northern blacks. The New Deal economic coalition included workers, farmers, the organized elderly, and, increasingly during the 1940s, elements of big business. FDR pulled together big city ethnic machines, southern courthouse politicians, and progressive reformers.

These changes in party politics brought with them some of the most significant changes in public policy and political ideology in the twentieth century. The New Deal coalition dealt a decisive blow to the prior public philosophy of laissez-faire economics and institutionalized an activist role for government in economic and social affairs. It committed the United States irrevocably to international leadership, decisively defeating the philosophy of isolationism.

From Democratic Dominance to a More Competitive Party System

Critical elections are historically significant because they set the basic structure of the American party system for generations to come by realigning the party system. They change which party dominates the political landscape. They construct a new coalition around a new issue or set of issues that changes the basic cleavage or polarization of the political system.

But over time a party system tends to lose strength. The political basis for a coalition erodes as the importance of old issues and old battle lines fades and new issues arise that divide members of the coalition from one another. The "out" party develops new issues and new ways of appealing to elements of the dominant party's coalition. New issues and new social cleavages will work against the prevailing political alignment, offering opportunities for the "out" party to become more competitive.

Eventually a new political crisis may emerge that will totally realign the political system. But this is usually preceded by a period of dealignment, a period when neither party is clearly the dominant political force. This dealignment process can be seen in the relative decline of the Democratic Party and the relative rise of the Republican Party since the critical election of 1932. These changes in the party system can be characterized by three periods: (1) 1932-52: Democratic Dominance, (2) 1952-68: Democratic Predominance, and (3) 1968-92: Divided Government.

The pinnacle of Democratic electoral success of the early FDR years could not be maintained, and with some significant exceptions, the electoral position of the Democrats has been eroding ever since. The electoral comeback of the Republicans, however, has never been characterized by such a rapid and dramatic shift as occurred in the early 1930s.

The Republicans began to recover from their stunning post-Depression losses in the congressional elections of 1938. By 1946 they were able to regain control of Congress for one term. However, the Truman upset victory of 1948 both delayed any Republican capture of the White House and returned control of Congress to the Democrats.

In 1952, led by the popular General Dwight Eisenhower, the Republicans gained control of the presidency and both houses of Congress for the first time since 1928. During the Eisenhower period a new pattern began to emerge:

divided government. In 1952 the Republicans not only won the presidency, they won control of Congress, picking up 22 seats in the House and a crucial Senate seat. However, in the period from 1954 to 1964 the Democrats were able to reassert their primacy. They regained control of Congress in 1954. In 1956, even as Eisenhower won a landslide reelection, the Democrats held control of Congress. In 1958 congressional elections the Democrats picked up 16 Senate and 51 House seats.

The pattern of divided government was based on voters splitting their tickets, voting Democratic for congressional and local candidates even as they voted for the Republican presidential candidate. As a hero of World War II, Eisenhower had a personal popularity that transcended party. But the party system was also changing. The party loyalties established during the 1930s were beginning to weaken. Memories of the Depression and of the FDR era were fading. New voters were entering the system who had never known FDR or experienced the Depression. Many families were now more prosperous and thus less receptive to appeals to class politics. New issues were arising that tended to divide the Democratic Party, particularly civil rights.

However, in the late 1950s and early 1960s the New Deal party system showed new life. In 1960 the Democrats recaptured the presidency. In the Johnson landslide of 1964 the Democrats gained their largest congressional majorities since the early FDR years and enacted another set of sweeping changes in the roles of activist government. But the Johnson administration was the culmination of the era of Democratic predominance.

THE ELECTION OF 1968 AS A DEALIGNING ELECTION

A Republican Presidential Majority

The Johnson landslide proved to be the last hurrah for Democratic dominance of the presidency. The Republicans won the presidential election of 1968, and now have won five of the last six presidential elections, most by landslides. The coalition that elected Nixon has dominated subsequent presidential elections, creating a Republican presidential majority. The Democrats have won more than 46 percent of the presidential vote only once in the last 24 years. In 1976 Jimmy Carter barely squeaked past Gerald Ford, who had been appointed president by the disgraced Richard Nixon. The new pattern is divided government in which the Republicans generally control the presidency and the Democrats generally control Congress.

The Republican presidential majority is based on a new coalitional pattern. The formerly "solid South" the Democrats used to rely upon has gone Republican in five of the last six elections. While southerner Carter carried the South on regional pride in 1976, he lost it to Reagan in 1980. Conservative southern Democrats have increasingly placed philosophy above party in presidential

choice. Memories of Republican Reconstruction have been replaced with association of the Democratic Party with civil rights and the welfare state.
Urban ethnic groups have also loosened their ties to the Democratic Party. The more these groups have assimilated into the American mainstream, the less they have identified with the Democrats' championing of the cause of cultural minorities and the underprivileged. Young people, less influenced by traditional political ties and more influenced by the media presidency, have also moved toward the Republicans.

Ideology in the New Deal Party System

The Republicans have been able to construct their presidential majority by capitalizing on new issues and introducing new polarizations into the political system. The effect of these new issues and new polarizations can be seen by comparing the party system of the 1940s and 1950s with that of the 1970s and 1980s. The New Deal party system was centered on a polarization, or cleavage, based on economic class. The Democratic Party had the support of working people, lower-to-moderate income voters. The Republican Party had the support of upper-income voters. Most of the very disparate elements of the Democratic Party—union members, white Southerners, urban ethnics, small farmers, and blacks—were united by "bread and butter" issues, by the Democratic philosophy of using the activist state to aid working people. Economic issues also worked to the advantage of the Democrats because they were perceived as the party of good times, whereas since the Great Depression the Republicans had been associated with hard times.

In the 1940s and 1950s the party system was also characterized by very ideologically diffuse and inconsistent parties. In the early 1960s James MacGregor Burns characterized the New Deal party system as actually being a 4 party system, with both the Democrats and the Republicans having liberal presidential wings and conservative congressional wings.[2] The only two presidents from the mid-1940s through 1960 had been Truman and Eisenhower, each identified with the liberal-to-moderate wing of his party.

In contrast, a coalition of conservative Republicans and conservative southern Democrats controlled Congress. The conservative "Dixiecrats" faced no Republican opposition in the historically one-party South and thus had long careers. This gave them immense advantage in Congress, where powerful committee chairs were allocated on the basis of seniority. When the powerful Dixiecrats joined with conservative Republicans, they could control the content of legislation.

The Ideological Polarization of the Parties Since 1964

A new set of issues and political forces arose in the 1960s that changed this system. The civil rights movement and the Vietnam War introduced new issues that tended to polarize the political system along new lines. At first the civil rights movement worked to the advantage of the liberal Democrats. But since 1966 these new polarizations have been crucial to the Republicans' ability to construct a presidential majority.

Pressures to end practices of racial oppression, and particularly the official segregation of the races in the South, built throughout the late 1950s and early 1960s. As blacks increasingly raised nonviolent opposition to segregation, the brutalities of the system were revealed on the TV screens of the rest of the country. White support for a redress of these grievances grew. After a number of halfhearted measures, in 1964 northern and western members of Congress united to pass a sweeping civil rights bill that banned discrimination in employment and public accommodations.

It is largely forgotten today that a higher percentage of congressional Republicans than Democrats supported the 1964 civil rights bill. But at the presidential level, conservative Barry Goldwater won the 1964 Republican nomination in part by emphasizing his opposition to the civil rights bill. Goldwater offered "a choice, not an echo." He was able to defeat the liberal wing of the Republican Party, which had dominated Republican presidential politics since 1940, through a strategy of uniting South and West in resentment against the Eastern, liberal establishment. However, in the general election Johnson defeated Goldwater in a landslide. This massive Republican defeat led to an unusually large liberal ideological majority in Congress from 1964 to 1966.

But the Republicans were not through with their "southern strategy." The politics of the South had been transformed forever. In this period, the association of the Democratic Party with civil rights opened up the once solid South to Republican penetration on racial and ideological grounds. At the same time, the enfranchisement of southern blacks set in motion the demise of the segregationist Dixiecrats. The Republicans' southern strategy added conservative Southerners to the party's western and midwestern conservatives. They formed the new center of gravity in the Republican Party, relegating the "eastern establishment" Republicans to the sidelines.

Social Issues

By 1968 racial tensions had heightened in the North as well. The nonviolence of the civil rights movement had been overshadowed by race riots in most northern cities. As racial conflict and the impact of civil rights legislation spread north, many northern whites came to oppose any further action on minority issues.

The party system was also affected by the escalation of the Vietnam War and the growing domestic opposition to the war. In 1965 LBJ introduced hundreds of thousands of U.S. troops into the war. But even this force was not able to turn the tide. As the war dragged on, protests against it spread much like the civil rights demonstrations that the war protesters consciously emulated. Clashes between student demonstrators and the police were added to pictures of cities in the flames of racial riots on the evening news.

These new polarizations worked to the advantage of the Republicans in 1968. Nixon emphasized what came to be called the "social issues." One of the key slogans of the Nixon campaign was "law and order." This slogan appealed to genuine concerns of city dwellers about the rising crime rate. But it was also a coded message that a Nixon administration would not be sympathetic to the positions of minorities and of student protesters. Whereas economic issues had united the traditional Democratic coalition, social issues divided them. As the importance of social issues grew, many white Southerners and urban ethnics were dislodged from the Democratic Party. This process was made easier by the fact that compared with the 1930s and 1940s, many southern whites and urban ethnics were more prosperous. The good times of the 1950s and 1960s had allowed of them to improve their economic circumstances. The historic Democratic association with the underprivileged had lost some of its appeal to middle-income voters even before such appeals came to be associated in many voters' minds with minority issues.

The election of Nixon in 1968 intensified the polarization of the parties. After 1968 the center of gravity of the Democratic Party was moved leftward. The segregationist Dixiecrats, the most conservative element in American politics, were becoming extinct. Freed from the political necessity of supporting Johnson's Vietnam policies, the Democratic Party became the home of those opposing the war and calling for a rethinking of the U.S. role in the world. In 1972 the antiwar, anticorporate establishment, countercultural McGovern campaign captured the Democratic nomination and white conservative flight from the Democrats accelerated.

Since 1972 both parties have worked hard to gain the support of white Southerners and northern ethnics. But the quest for the support of the white conservative voter has affected the ideological consistency of the parties differently. The Republicans want to emphasize political philosophy, using ideological appeals to reach voters on the basis of chosen issues. The Democrats fare better when they emphasize historical cultural ties and downplay their philosophical differences.

Ideological Polarization in the Presidential Selection Process

A major factor in the ideological polarization of the parties was change in the way presidential candidates were selected. Since before the Civil War, parties had selected their candidates at national conventions dominated by powerfully entrenched leaders, often called party bosses. Since the turn of the century, opponents of the boss system had advocated primaries where all members of the party could vote on convention delegates as a way of democratizing the process. Over the years many states had adopted primaries. But until the 1960s the bosses still dominated the presidential selection system.

In 1964, however, the Goldwater insurgency capitalized on the intense support of its adherents to defeat the formerly dominant eastern establishment of the Republican Party. By making strong ideologically conservative appeals, Goldwater was able to win a large number of delegates in the primaries. He was even more successful in motivating his supporters to attend and fight vigorously in the party caucuses that selected delegates in nonprimary states. However, it was ideological conflict in the Democratic Party that dealt the boss system a death blow. Following the Goldwater example in the Republican Party, in 1968 the anti-Vietnam War candidates Eugene McCarthy and Robert Kennedy sought the Democratic nomination by running in every Democratic primary and contesting every party caucus. Vicepresident Hubert Humphrey chose the more traditional strategy of relying on party bosses to control delegations for him. Humphrey did not put his name on a single primary ballot, and thus did not win any popular votes. McCarthy and Kennedy won roughly 6 million votes between them before Kennedy was assassinated on the night of the last primary. Yet at the Chicago convention the party nominated Humphrey as its standard-bearer. Not surprisingly, Humphrey lost in the general election.

While the antiwar forces lost the battle, they won the war. The manifestly undemocratic nature of such a system was clear. In an attempt to unify the party, the 1968 convention set up a commission to reform the future selection process. The McGovern Commission required the opening up of the party caucuses that the bosses had used to select delegates. They required that every delegation reflect the popular strength of the candidates in the state as well as the racial and gender mix in the state. They made operating caucuses so logistically difficult that many former caucus states switched to primaries. Since the McGovern reforms went into effect in 1972, no candidate of either party has been able to win his party's nomination without running in every primary and defeating his opponents in gathering popular votes.

But reliance on primaries and open caucuses to select presidential candidates is not perfectly democratic. The voters who tend to vote in primaries or attend caucuses do not reflect the ordinary voter. This minority "selectorate" tends to be much more ideologically consistent than ordinary voters. Those who vote in Democratic primaries are much more liberal than the general electorate, and those who vote in Republican primaries are much more conservative. The new presidential selection process has been a major factor in the ideological polarization of the parties.

CHANGES IN THE REGIONAL BASES OF THE PARTIES

The magnitude of the political changes of the 1960s can be seen in how the political bases of each party's strength in presidential elections has changed. It must be remembered that presidents are not elected on the basis of the popular vote, but indirectly through the Electoral College. Each state is allotted as many electoral votes as it has senators and members of the House of Representatives. Each state has at least three electoral votes because each state has two senators and at least one member of the House. The larger the population of the state, the more additional electoral votes it has. States cast their electoral votes in a bloc. If a presidential candidate wins a majority of the votes in the state, he wins all that state's electoral votes. It currently takes 270 total electoral votes to win the presidency. The Republicans have won five of the last six presidential races and Figure 5.1 shows how. Because most elections after 1968 have been so one-sided, the Democratic victories in 1964 and 1960 have been included to highlight areas of relative Democratic strength. If only the elections since 1968 were included, the results would be similar.

The 17 states shown in white went Republican (or third party) in seven of these eight elections, representing a solid core of 135 electoral votes under the 1984-1988 distribution. The 23 shaded states, representing 246 electoral votes, have been probable Republican states, going Democratic in only two or three of these eight elections. The Republicans only need to hold their base and win 55 percent of their probable states to put together an Electoral College majority. Broken down slightly differently, the Republicans only need to carry the states that have voted Republican in 75 percent of the elections since 1960 to gather an Electoral College majority.

In contrast, the Democratic Party electoral vote base is smaller and less secure. Its core consists of the 5 states and the District of Columbia, with 40 electoral votes, that have voted Democratic in at least six of the last eight elections. Five key states with a total of 112 electoral votes have gone Democratic in four or five of the last eight elections, including the big prizes of New York, Pennsylvania, and Texas. It has been more than 40 years since the Democrats have won an election without carrying each of these 3 key states. Even if the Democrats win all of the states where they have historically done well, they have about half of the electoral votes they need to win.

There is a clear regional base to each party's Electoral College strength. This pattern can be seen by breaking the country into four regions: Northeast, South, Midwest, and West and examining the closer elections in this period: 1988, 1976, 1968, and 1960. This breakdown shows the difficulties the Democrats have faced in recent presidential elections. The Republicans start with a big advantage, a secure base in the West. The Republicans have won 90+ percent of the West's electoral votes in every election since 1952, except in 1988 when they won 85 percent. The smaller, less secure Democratic base is in the Northeast. Close elections are largely fought and won in the central time zone.

Figure 5.1
Electoral College Results, 1960-1988

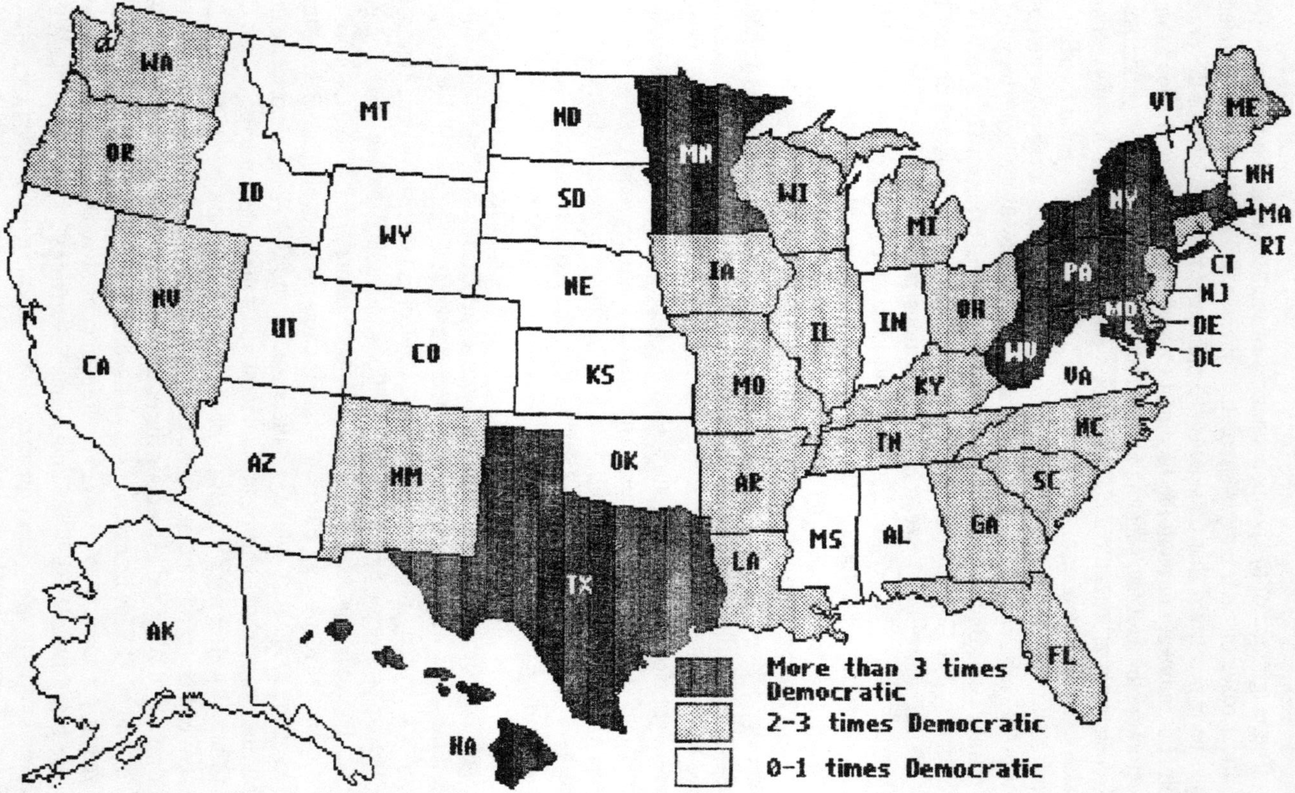

Source: *Presidential Elections Since 1796* (Washington, DC: Congressional Quarterly, 1991).

The Democrats cannot win without holding their base in the Northeast and scoring well in the South and the Midwest, as can be seen in Table 5.2. The importance of the South in the historical Democratic coalition is apparent. In 1960 and 1976 the Democrats won most of the South and won the national election. In the other years they did not win the South and they lost the election. The Midwest is also crucial in the winning Democratic coalition. In 1960 and 1976 the Democrats won roughly half of the Midwest, votes they needed to win.

Table 5.2
The Importance of the South and Midwest in Recent Close Elections

The Northeast   127 Electoral Votes in 1992
                    153 Electoral Votes in 1960

Winning Democrats	Electoral Votes	Losing Democrats	Electoral Votes
Carter	108	Dukakis	62
Kennedy	141	Humphrey	123

The South   147 Electoral Votes in 1992
                128 Electoral Votes in 1960

Winning Democrats	Electoral Votes	Losing Democrats	Electoral Votes
Carter	118	Dukakis	0
Kennedy	81	Humphrey	25

The Midwest   120 Electoral Votes in 1992
                  141 Electoral Votes in 1960

Winning Democrats	Electoral Votes	Losing Democrats	Electoral Votes
Carter	67	Dukakis	29
Kennedy	71	Humphrey	31

The West   144 Electoral Votes in 1992
               115 Electoral Votes in 1960

Winning Democrats	Electoral Votes	Losing Democrats	Electoral Votes
Carter	4	Dukakis	21
Kennedy	10	Humphrey	13

The Shift in Electoral College Results and the Sunbelt Strategy

There is marked contrast between the regional support of the parties before and after the elections of the 1960s. The Sunbelt strategy of the Republicans has dramatically shifted the regional base of each party. Figure 5.2 illustrates this shift.

Since the formation of the Democratic Party and particularly after the Civil War its base was in the "solid South." Because of the Republican Party's association with the post-Civil War Reconstruction, several deep southern states had never given the Republicans their electoral votes from the formation of the party up until the Nixon landslide in 1972. From 1932 until the Eisenhower period, the West was also largely Democratic. The Republican base was in the Midwest, and they were competitive in the industrial states of the Northeast and Great Lakes.

The Republicans' Sunbelt strategy has allowed them to penetrate first the West and then the historic Democratic stronghold of the South. Since 1960 the Republican presidential nominee has come from California five times, twice from Texas, and once from Arizona. Only in 1976 did the Republicans nominate a non-Westerner, and they lost that election. This strategy has turned a once largely Democratic region into the Republican stronghold at the presidential level.

The other dimension of the Sunbelt strategy is the penetration of the historically Democratic South. Once this was accomplished, the Republicans had reversed the presidential situation they faced in the 1930s and 1940s. Now they had a secure Electoral College base and the Democrats did not. Now the Democrats had to win most of the competitive states to assemble an Electoral College majority.

The Republicans' Sunbelt strategy puts demographics on their side. Population growth in the United States has been greater in the West and the South than in the North. Since the days of the 13 colonies the American population has been moving westward. The energy crisis of the 1970s also began a flow of people to the southern states, where energy costs are lower and/or heating needs are not as great.

This means that western and southern states are picking up strength in the Electoral College while northern states are losing their formerly strategic position. In the 1870s New York and Pennsylvania together had 17 percent of all the votes in the Electoral College, a third of the votes needed to win. California, Texas, and Florida together had a total of only 18 votes, half as many as New York.

Today California has 10 percent of all the electoral votes. Texas is nearly tied with New York as the second largest prize, and Florida has passed Pennsylvania for fourth place. Clearly, the Republicans' base in these states gives them a huge advantage in presidential elections.

Figure 5.2
Electoral College Results, 1932-1956

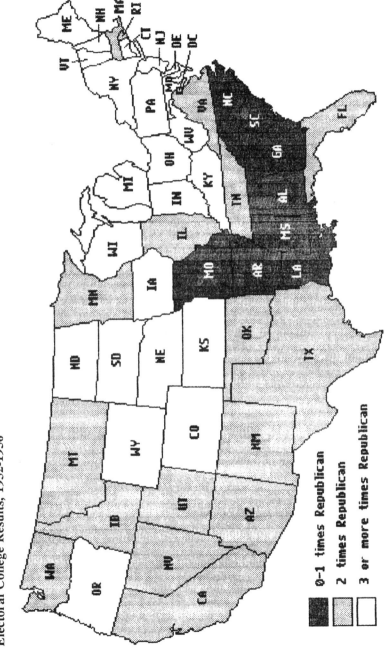

0-1 times Republican

2 times Republican

3 or more times Republican

Source: Presidential Elections Since 1796 (Washington, DC: Congressional Quarterly, 1991).

The 1988 Election Results and Democratic Party Strategy

Figure 5.3 show that the results of the 1988 election largely fit the pattern established since the Republican presidential majority first emerged in 1968. The Republicans enjoyed a secure base in the West and South, did well in the Midwest, and were competitive in the Democratic base in the Northeast. But a closer analysis of the results shows that the Republicans are beginning to pay a price for their Sunbelt strategy, with its strong conservative ideological appeals to win the South. If one looks at the states in which the Democrats got 48-49 percent of the vote and the states where they got 45-47 percent of the vote, one can see a potential winning Democratic presidential coalition that does not rely on the South. If the Democrats had run two points better nationwide, they not only would have won their entire northeastern base, they also would have added the biggest prize of all, California, to their Pacific northwest victories in Washington and Oregon. They would also have won most of the Midwest. The Democrats got at least 45 percent of the vote in the most of the Northeast and Midwest, and in a number of western states. This pattern suggests a potential new Democratic strategy of uniting the northeastern and midwestern "Rustbelt" with the larger western states that could provide an Electoral College victory without a single southern state.

This Rustbelt plus penetration of the West strategy would have significant benefits, but also real risks, for the Democratic Party. It would allow their candidate to take a more consistent ideological position. Freed of fear of losing the South, the Democratic nominee could accept the liberal-conservative ideological polarization and run on a consistent philosophy rather than being compelled to blur the issues. Such a strategy would help particularly in the more populous, urban states. Democrats could more starkly highlight conservative Republican positions that are not very popular in urban areas: the status of women, environmental protection, and cuts in popular social programs. Recent Democratic candidates have raised all these issues in their campaigns. But they have not dared to articulate a consistent philosophy to justify them for fear of losing conservative southern voters.

However, such a strategy could cost the Democrats their congressional majority. Even as the South has abandoned Democratic presidential candidates, it has continued to be the most Democratic region in congressional elections. If a Democratic presidential ticket simply wrote off the South, Republicans could make sharp inroads at the congressional level.

The irony is that this new Democratic presidential coalition would look much like the pre-FDR Republican regional base that united North and West against the old Democratic South. The reversal of the regional bases of the parties begun by the Republican Sunbelt strategy in presidential campaigns would then be complete, with the Republicans based in the South and the Democrats in the North and West.

Figure 5.3
Close States in the 1988 Election

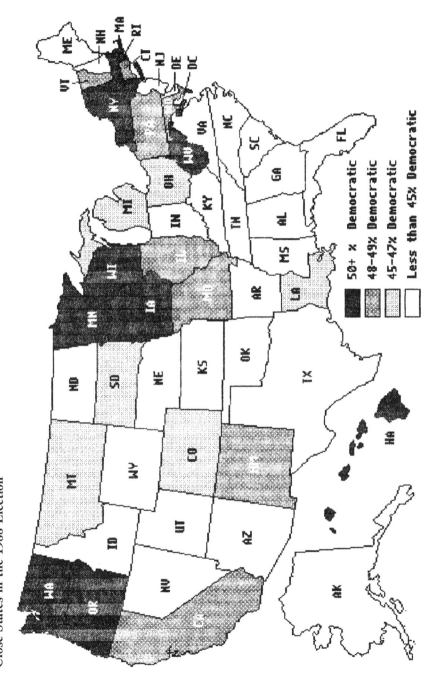

50+ % Democratic
48-49% Democratic
45-47% Democratic
Less than 45% Democratic

Source: Presidential Elections Since 1796 (Washington, DC: Congressional Quarterly, 1991).

DIVIDED GOVERNMENT

Just looking at the presidential level exaggerates the power of the Republican Party. While the pattern of presidential elections has changed dramatically since the 1960s, the pattern of congressional elections has not. The Democrats have won control of the House of Representatives for 38 consecutive years, and by 1992 they will have controlled the Senate for 50 of the last 60 years. Parliamentary systems must produce party government because the executive is elected by the legislature. Therefore one party or coalition of parties will control both the legislature and the executive branch of government. But since in the American system the president and Congress are elected separately, government power can be divided between the parties. Table 5.3 shows the periods of divided government, when one party controlled the presidency and the other party controlled at least one house of Congress.

Several factors have contributed to the emergence of divided government. It would not occur if voters were not splitting their tickets, voting for one party at the presidential level and another at the congressional level. Ticket splitting expresses weakening party loyalties among voters. Survey research shows that fewer voters identify strongly with either major party. Party is no longer as important to most voters as the character of the candidate. Most citizens today vote for the man or woman, not the party.

Divided government also reflects the different nature of the electoral coalitions of the parties. The social base of the Republican Party is relatively homogeneous, made up primarily of white Protestants, those in upper income brackets, and ideological conservatives. The Democratic Party coalition is a much more

Table 5.3
Eras of Divided Government and Party Government

	Number of Years of Divided Government	Number of Years of Party Government
1801-1843	4	38 (34 Democratic)
1843-1861	12	6
1861-1875	0	14 (all Republican)
1875-1897	16	6
1897-1969	14	58 (32 Democratic) (26 Republican)
1969-1993	20	4

heterogeneous group, including blacks, various southern and eastern European ethnics, white Southerners, feminists, union members, and ideological liberals. It has been very difficult for the Democrats to hold together all these elements at the national level. The Republicans, with their more homogenous base, need only chip away a few of the Democratic constituencies to assemble a national majority.

The picture is somewhat different at state, congressional district, and local levels. Not all the elements of the Democratic coalition will be important in any one congressional district. Few Democratic congressional candidates face such a heterogenous set of constituencies as their national standard-bearer. In a particular congressional district the problem of holding together all the elements of the local Democratic coalition against Republican raids is less complicated.

Once the pattern of divided government began to be set, several factors tended to maintain it. Perhaps most important was the increasing ability of individual members of Congress to insulate themselves from the impact of national electoral trends. In the era of weakened party loyalties, incumbents have developed a series of electoral advantages that mean they tend to win reelection over time. If a member of Congress "brings home the bacon," that is, assists individual constituents with their problems with the federal bureaucracy and wins federal money for local projects, he or she can build political support in the district that goes beyond issues of party. The longer a member serves, the more seniority he or she accumulates, and thus the more "pork" he or she can win.

Incumbents also have the advantages of name recognition and fund-raising capacity. An incumbent can use the powers of office to keep his or her name before the voters throughout the term. A challenger gets no corresponding attention in the media.

The advantages of incumbency cumulate. The success rate of congressional incumbents is known to interest groups and political pundits. Interest groups generally prefer to back winners, for a loser can do little for their constituency. Therefore, the power of incumbency becomes a self-fulfilling prophecy. Campaign contributors favor incumbents because incumbents are the favorites.

As the system of divided government has become entrenched, the parties have seemed to specialize as executive and legislatively oriented organizations. The Republicans have largely been unwilling to risk their new presidential majority by trying to turn presidential elections into referenda on which party should control Congress. Instead, they have generally focused on the personalities of presidential candidates and forms of campaigning that split the Democratic coalition without producing clear mandates for their party. In the same way, Democrats have seemed primarily concerned with maintaining their congressional majority. They have avoided any consistent ideological message that might mobilize voters around their presidential candidates in order to maximize their ability to appeal to every element of their legislative coalition.

As the system of divided government has persisted, individual voters have developed rationales for their split-ticket voting. Some voters talk of splitting their ticket as a kind of check and balance—putting one party in the White House and the other party in Congress to keep an eye on them. Voters seem to like the appeal of conservative Republican presidential candidates who promise to keep overall government taxing and spending low, but at the same time favoring congressional candidates who promise to protect the programs that are of special importance to them, who will fight to maintain the programs that are popular in their section of the country.

PRESIDENTIAL ELECTIONS THAT PRODUCE IDEOLOGICAL MAJORITIES

In certain presidential victories the president has coattails. In a "long coattail" election not only does the president win, but his party will peak in its level of strength in Congress, a large number of his party's congressional candidates will ride in, "hanging on his coattails." If the winning president has run a highly ideological campaign that emphasized certain issues, he can proclaim a mandate to change public policy. Whether the voters intended a broad mandate or not, they have given the president a chance to effect major policy change. If he is politically successful in using his strength in the first two years of his term, he may construct an ideological majority in Congress that has a major impact on public policy.

The relationship between presidential power and the strength of the president's party in Congress is tricky. In the American constitutional system, presidents really have limited power unless they can move Congress to follow them. The American party system allows individual members of Congress great latitude in their decisions whether to support presidents in their policies. So simply having a party majority in Congress is no guarantee of success for a president's policies.   There are moderate elements in both parties, and conservative Southerners in the generally liberal Democratic Party. Both the Democrats and the Republicans were more ideologically diverse in the 1940s and 1950s than in the more polarized party system of the 1970s and 1980s.

However, even today interpreting the impact of the size of a party's congressional delegation on the policy power of presidents is difficult. The Democratic Party has generally controlled Congress since the 1930s. But because the Democratic delegation has contained moderates and conservatives as well as liberals, liberals have rarely had control of Congress during this period. On the other hand, when southern Democrats combine with Republicans, the resulting conservative coalition can be more powerful than the number of Republican seats might indicate.

Since the FDR era there are four cases when a party has peaked in its strength in Congress at the same time it controlled the presidency, and in two cases particularly strong presidents have emerged who have used temporary ideological majorities in Congress to set in motion policy and philosophical

Figure 5.4
Party Strength in Congress, 1930-1990

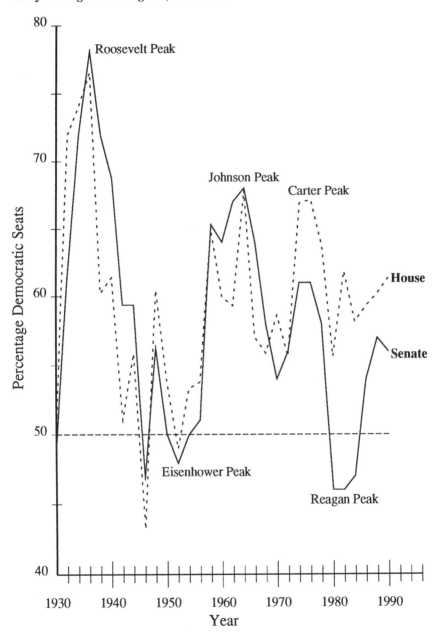

Source: World Almanac and Book of Facts (New York: Pharoh Books, 1992)

movement uncharacteristic of the rest of the period. The Democratic Party has peaked in strength twice since FDR: in 1964-1966 and in 1976-1978. The 1964 electoral triumph brought the rush of legislation labeled the Great Society.

The Republican Party has also peaked in strength in Congress while holding the presidency twice in this period. In 1952-1954 they last gained complete control of Congress and the presidency. In 1980-1982 the Republicans elected Reagan, won control of the Senate, and reached one of their highest peaks since the Eisenhower years in the House of Representatives. This set the Reagan "revolution" in motion. What stands out is that the presidents who had strong ideological agendas—LBJ and Ronald Reagan—were able to turn their electoral majorities into working congressional majorities that altered public policy. Dwight Eisenhower and Jimmy Carter had similar congressional majorities. But Eisenhower and Carter were anti-ideological, centrists who eschewed close ties to the party's historical agenda, and thus left considerably less impact on public policy.

REELECTIONS AND SUCCESSION ELECTIONS

Simple Reelections

Critical elections of the 1932 variety are historically rare. Elections that produce ideological majorities like those of 1964 and 1980, or major shifts in party balance like that of 1968, are also relatively rare. The bulk of elections, which do not fit these types, can be classified based on the length of time the incumbent party has held power. It seems there is a definite time pressure on the ability of a party to hold the White House. Parties seeking their second term in office usually win. Since 1956 there have been five elections where the incumbent party was seeking a second term—1984, 1980, 1972, 1964, and 1956. The incumbent party won four of those five elections. The elections of 1984, 1972, and 1956 all fit the pattern of what I have called "simple reelections." In each case an incumbent Republican was returned to office, but there was very little change in the strength of the parties in Congress. In each case a pattern of divided government and relatively little domestic policy innovation characterized the next four years.

Succession Elections

However, parties seeking to hold the presidency for a third consecutive term usually lose. These elections can be called "succession elections," since usually a new candidate is seeking to succeed a member of his own party. Since 1956 there have been four succession elections—1988, 1976, 1968, and 1960. George Bush is the only one to win a succession election, thus confirming the durability of the Republicans' presidential majority.

Table 5.4
"Six-Year Itch" Losses in Party Strength in Congress

	House Seats	Senate Seats
1958 Republicans (Eisenhower)	-47	-12
1966 Democrats (Johnson)	-48	-4
1974 Republicans (Nixon/Ford)	-48	-5
1986 Republicans (Reagan)	-6	-7
(1982 + 1986 Republican House Losses)	-31	

Regular pendulum-like swings in party strength can also be seen in a party's congressional delegation. The national congressional elections that are held at the midpoint of each presidential term in which the entire House of Representative and one-third of the Senate are elected can have a significant impact on a president and his party even though he is not standing directly before the voters. For example, after a party has been in power for six years, voters tend to turn toward the other party in congressional races. Table 5.4 shows the impact of what has been called the "six year itch." It usually foreshadows a defeat for the party's next presidential candidate.

In the past, the six year itch cost the incumbent party most dearly in the House of Representatives. The Republicans in 1986 were able to minimize their losses in the House, in part because they had already lost many House seats in the 1982 election. However, in the Reagan victory of 1980 the Republicans had won control of the Senate for the first time since the 1950s. But in 1986 all the freshmen senators who had been swept into office on Reagan's coattails were vulnerable, and the Democrats were able to regain their majority. It seems that the longer a party controls the presidency, the more it comes to be blamed for negative political conditions and events. The six year itch is a particularly dangerous warning signal to a party in power. It is significant that the Republican presidential majority has become so durable that in 1988 they were able to win their first succession election since 1928.

MIDTERM ELECTIONS AND THE PULL TO THE CENTER

Honeymoons, Mandates, and Midterms

The phenomenon of the six year itch shows that presidential elections are not the only elections which exert influence on the ideological direction of an administration. Because the incumbent president's party generally loses seats in Congress, midterm elections generally move administrations toward the political center. When a new president is elected, he is usually granted a period of good feeling and political support that will probably be uncharacteristic of the later part of his term. Citizens, political players, pundits, and even to some degree the opposition party wish to see any new president succeed in coping with the difficult policy problems of the nation. There is often a case to be made that the new president has won a mandate from the people, particularly if his party has also gained seats in Congress. In any case, a new administration has had little time to offend key political forces or voting blocs. This period of good feeling is often called the president's honeymoon. New presidents who have had long coattails, who have come to power along with many new members of Congress of their party, have a particular chance to use the honeymoon period to put their stamp on public policy. After the massive shift in party strength in the election of 1932, FDR turned his honeymoon period into the famous "hundred days" of legislation that created the New Deal.

In 1981 Ronald Reagan used newly won Republican control of the Senate and unusual Republican strength in the House to create a conservative majority in Congress. During his honeymoon period Congress passed his new budget priorities of tax cuts, a military buildup, and cuts in social spending. Lyndon Johnson had a particularly long honeymoon period because his succession of the assassinated John Kennedy was followed by the 1964 election that built up his congressional majority. In 1965 the Great Society social legislation passed Congress.

Not all presidents enjoy such success during their honeymoon period. If they face a Congress under control of hostile political forces, or if they are unable to mobilize their strength in Congress, presidents may find that the honeymoon period offers them little chance to mold public policy but only a temporary respite from political attack.

Even if a president has a successful honeymoon period, this special opportunity eventually comes to an end. Midterm elections are often a key point in the shifting political fortunes of even successful administrations. The impact of midterm elections can be seen in several presidencies, including those of Reagan, Carter, Johnson, and FDR. The shifting ideological stances of recent presidential administrations is illustrated on Figure 5.5.

Midterm Elections in the Reagan Years

When the Reagan administration first came to power, it sought to strike while the iron was hot and reverse what it perceived as the liberal domination of public policy-making. Reagan's first budget represented the most dramatic shifting of taxing and spending policies since the passage of Great Society legislation by LBJ in 1965. The Reagan landslide of 1980 had a significant impact on party strength in Congress. The Republicans picked up 12 Senate seats to gain control of the chamber for the first time since 1954. The Democrats maintained control of the House, but the Republicans gained 35 seats. These gains enabled them to form a coalition with conservative southern Democrats to pass Reagan's economic and budgetary policies in 1981.

But in the 1982 elections the Republicans lost 24 House seats. The conservative ideological majority evaporated as the Democrats regained effective control of the House of Representatives. From that point on, Reagan was forced to compromise with the Democratic leadership in the House in order to pass legislation. The pull to the center had begun. On such key issues as taxes and Social Security reform, the Reagan administration ended up endorsing compromises that were inconsistent with its conservative ideology.

In the 1986 congressional elections the Republicans lost nine Senate seats, and control of the Senate returned to the Democrats. The centrist pressures on the administration gained even greater momentum. At this point Reagan made even more dramatic reversals in foreign policy, particularly in negotiating a new arms control agreement with the Soviets.

Midterm Elections and Democratic Presidents

A honeymoon followed by disillusionment can also be seen in the Johnson presidency. The Johnson landslide of 1964 gave Democrats two-thirds of all the seats in Congress. LBJ used this majority to pass a series of new domestic programs he called the Great Society. But in the midterm elections of 1966 the Republicans gained 47 House seats and 4 Senate seats. The honeymoon was over, and so was the innovative period of the Great Society.

The case of FDR is instructive because the shift in party strength was even greater. FDR had bigger majorities in Congress and a greater impact on policy than any president in the twentieth century. The Democrats actually gained seats in FDR's first midterm election, in 1934. It was not until he had been in office for six years that the Democrats lost ground in a congressional election. In 1938 the Democrats lost 70 House seats and 7 Senate seats and FDR's dominance of Congress was over.

Even though Jimmy Carter was one of the less ideologically consistent presidents, the midterm election of 1978 had a distinct impact on his administration. Throughout his term Carter tried to downplay ideology in order to keep his administration from being identified with the polar ideological wing of his party. Carter was widely criticized during his term for indecisiveness and flip-flopping on issues, taking one position at one time and an opposing one at a later time. Even so, the ideological stance of the Carter administration was affected significantly by a midterm election.

The perception of ideological inconsistency began early in his term when, as part of his first budget, Carter proposed a tax rebate to stimulate the economy,

Figure 5.5
The Ideological Shifts of Recent Presidential Administrations

Democratic Left	Democratic Center	Center	Republican Center	Republican Right
			Early Bush	
		Later Reagan (Foreign Policy)	Later Reagan (Economic Policy)	Later Reagan (Social Policy)
				Early Reagan
		Later Carter		
	Early Carter			
		Later Nixon (Domestic Policy)		Later Nixon (Foreign Policy)
			Early Nixon	
	Later Johnson (Domestic Policy)			
Early Johnson (Domestic Policy)				

then a few months later withdrew the proposal as inflationary. A similar flip-flop occurred in arms control policy when the administration first proposed a set of innovative proposals to move beyond the cautious SALT I framework of the Nixon-Ford years, then quickly abandoned it when the Soviets balked. But even within this context a clear shift in the ideological stance of the administration can be identified.

In its early years the Carter administration had an ambivalent relationship with the traditional Democratic leadership and the policies they represented. On the one hand, Carter sometimes seemed to go out of his way to step on the toes of old-line Democrats. Perhaps the most politically damaging of such actions was his attempt to cut back on the water projects that were the kind of traditional constituency-pleasing pork barrel on which Democratic members of Congress had historically built their political support.

Yet Carter's policy positions on a number of key issues did represent an attempt to find a middle way between the old New Deal Democrats and the new generation of post-Vietnam, neoliberal Democrats. Although Carter was averse to costly new social initiatives, some programs were expanded. The CETA public jobs program grew considerably under his tenure. Social Security finances were bolstered by a tax increase to keep pace with benefits. Maternal and child health and nutrition programs were expanded. In foreign policy Carter sought to continue and even accelerate detente with the Soviet Union.

However, after the Democratic Party suffered significant losses in the midterm elections of 1978, Carter consciously sought to widen the distance between his administration and the liberal wing of his party. Democratic majorities in Congress had swelled in 1974 and 1976 in the wake of the Republicans' Watergate scandals. But in 1978 the pendulum swung the other way, and the Democrats lost 16 House and 3 Senate seats. It was no accident that major personnel changes followed in 1979.

After retreating to Camp David, Carter sacked several of the leading liberals in the administration, the most prominent being Secretary of Health, Education, and Welfare Joseph Califano, who had been closely identified with Johnson's Great Society and with Senator Ted Kennedy. In the foreign policy field hardliners like National Security Adviser Zbigniew Brzezinski and former Nixon-Ford cabinet member James Schlessinger took more prominent roles as the more liberal Secretary of State Cyrus Vance had his role downgraded and was eventually forced out.

NOTES

1. The concept of critical elections was introduced by V. O. Key, Jr., "A Theory of Critical Elections," *Journal of Politics 17* (February 1955). Other seminal works are James L. Sundquist, *Dynamics of the Party System* (Washing-

ton, DC: Brookings Institution, 1983); Walter Dean Burnham, *Critical Elections and the Mainsprings of American Politics* (New York: Norton, 1970); and Jerome M. Clubb, William H. Flanigan, and Nancy H. Zingale, *Partisan Realignment* (Boulder, CO: Westview, 1990).

2. James MacGregor Burns, *Deadlock of Democracy* (Englewood Cliffs, NJ: Prentice-Hall, 1963).

3. Data about Electoral College results are taken from *Presidential Elections Since 1796* (Washington, DC: Congressional Quarterly, 1991).

PART III

PRESIDENTIAL IDEOLOGIES AND PUBLIC POLICY

6

THE TRIUMPH OF THE ACTIVIST STATE

THE CONFLICT BETWEEN LIMITED GOVERNMENT AND THE ACTIVIST STATE

The Emergence of the Activist State

The next several chapters examine changes in presidential administrations, political philosophy, public policy, and party politics. This chapter covers domestic policy from the beginning of the twentieth century through the presidency of Lyndon Johnson, giving particular attention to the New Deal of Franklin Roosevelt and the developments in domestic policy since then. The twentieth century brought the triumph of the philosophy of activist government over the previously dominant doctrine of the limited state. Along with the ideology of the activist state came the doctrine of the activist presidency. As the twentieth century progressed, the president was increasingly expected to devise programmatic responses to the problems that the nation faced.

In this period there were four bursts of expansion in the size and scope of government mixed with longer periods of general maintenance of the status quo. The principles of activist government and an activist presidency were first established in the era of Progressive reform that ran from 1900 to 1916. Theodore Roosevelt and Woodrow Wilson exerted strong presidential leadership to achieve the Progressive agenda of using government to control monopoly power and the worst excesses of unregulated corporate capitalism.

The Great Depression of the 1930s was the stimulus to the most significant expansion of presidential power and government involvement in the domestic economy. The administration of Franklin Roosevelt began the development of the American welfare state. In the 1940s, during World War II and the cold war that followed, FDR, and his successor Harry Truman, established the other major component of contemporary American government, the warfare state, or the military-industrial complex, as it has been called by its critics. The final burst of growth of U.S. government came in the 1960s under Lyndon Johnson, when the welfare state was expanded as a response to the racial conflict and heightened concern about social justice of that era.

But despite their historic significance, these periods were more the exception than the rule. The more characteristic pattern of public policy, particularly since the 1950s, has been slow, incremental growth of government, accompanied by some lesser paring of more politically vulnerable programs.

The Progressives and the Rise of the Activist State

The dominant public philosophy in the nineteenth century was limited government, although public policy was never been wholly consistent with this doctrine. The philosophy of limited government did not stop politicians from taking activist measures to aid the railroads and other key industries, nor to use police and even military force to strike against the rising trade union movement, to take just two examples. But even if the policies they pursued were often out of step with their rhetoric, presidential administrations throughout the nineteenth century, and particularly in the last third of the century, preached the doctrine of limited government.

Of course there were periodic challenges to the ideology of the limited state throughout the nineteenth century. For example, in the 1880s Congress had passed the Sherman Antitrust Act and the Interstate Commerce Act to limit the power of huge industrial corporations.

In 1896 the populist crusade of William Jennings Bryan against the dominance of industrial capital threw a real scare into the eastern political establishment. Bryan tried to unite southern and western farmers with northern workers and immigrants to contest the industrial interests, but in the end his challenge was beaten back. However, building on many of the themes of Bryan's populism, the Progressive movement had much more influence on public policy. The Progressives represented a different coalition, one between the urban middle class and western farmers, both of whom were critical of the excesses of unregulated capitalism. The Progressives fused the moral indignation of American Protestantism with nineteenth-century faith in science and progress to form the doctrine that economic and political systems could be reformed by men of goodwill.

As the twentieth century began, the Progressives' influence was first felt in the administration of Theodore Roosevelt, who became president when McKinley was assassinated in 1901. In contrast with his predecessors, Roosevelt believed in a highly visible, highly activist presidency and in active use of government to reform the excesses of corporate capitalism. Early in his term Roosevelt prosecuted one of the biggest trusts for violating laws against monopoly practices. He also took on the railroads, the symbol of corporate arrogance, in a series of legislative acts designed to regulate their rates. He supported the creation of the forerunner of the Food and Drug Administration, which checked the unhealthy practices of the meat-packing industry and regulated the quality of medicinal drugs. His administration made efforts to conserve natural resources by protecting them from uncontrolled exploitation by industry.

Following the precedent that informally limited presidents to two terms, Roosevelt stepped down in favor of William Howard Taft as his party's nominee in 1908. But after a few years of enforced retirement, he attempted to recapture the presidency in 1912 by running on the Progressive Party ticket. This split the Republican vote and led to the election of only the second Democratic president since the Civil War, Woodrow Wilson. Wilson, like Roosevelt, was in tune with the Progressive movement, and another wave of reform was begun in his first term.

Wilson attacked the monopolies on two fronts. The Clayton Antitrust Act put new limits on trusts. But monopoly practices had proven so difficult to define legally and new practices inevitably arose when old ones were banned. So the Federal Trade Commission was created to be an ongoing watchdog of corporate practices and to develop new regulations to meet the evolution of corporate monopolies. The Federal Reserve Board was created to regulate the banking industry and to control the money supply. New legislation expanded farmers' access to credit. Protective tariffs that had shielded U.S. business from international competition were slashed. A national system for compensating workers injured in industrial accidents was devised. New laws banning child labor were passed. However, Wilson's first term proved to be the final burst of Progressive reform at home. War broke out in Europe, and Wilson's second term was consumed by fighting the war and negotiating the postwar peace. In 1920 the Republicans swept back into power, promising a return to normalcy, which meant a return to the limited state.

Yet the Progressive era had been historically significant. It had established the twin precedents of using activist government to regulate economic and social forces and presidential activism in pursuit of these goals. However, the effect of the Progressive reforms on the power of industrial capital can be overstated. Many of the reforms actually worked in favor of corporate interests. To take just one example, the Federal Reserve Board did more to rationalize the control of big banks over the financial world than to democratize financial institutions. Still, the precedent of governmental activism set in the Progressive period had continuing impact on American government.

FDR AND THE ACTIVIST STATE

Action in the Economic Crisis

The prosperity of the Roaring Twenties proved more powerful than the reform impulse, and the presence of conservative Republicans Harding, Coolidge, and Hoover in the White House meant a revival of the doctrines of isolationism and the limited state. Coolidge perhaps captured the spirit of the times best when he said, "The business of America is business."

But in 1929 the stock market crashed and suddenly the Great Depression swept over the land. Prosperity was a memory as the United States faced the worst economic crisis the country has ever known. All over the country family fortunes and family farms were being lost, corporations were going bust, and working people were being thrown out on the streets. Nearly one of four workers was unemployed, and economic output was half of what it had been before the stock market crash. The previously dominant public philosophy of letting the market work was not working.

Being in power, the Republican Party absorbed the blame for the Depression. In the congressional election of 1930, literally hundreds of Republican legislators were swept from power as Democrats took control of the House of Representatives. In 1932 the Democrats nominated Franklin Delano Roosevelt, a relative of Theodore Roosevelt, as their presidential candidate. The election gave Roosevelt a resounding mandate for change. Not only did he win in a landslide, but the Democrats won by margins of almost three to one in the House of Representatives and almost two to one in the Senate. FDR recognized that the country expected active leadership from the White House to tackle the economic crisis.

FDR embarked on many programmatic innovations, which he called the New Deal, in order to try to lift the country out of the throes of the Depression. In its first hundred days in office, the Roosevelt administration passed emergency legislation reforming the banking and securities systems, establishing national recovery planning for industry and agriculture, beginning public works projects to put some of the unemployed to work, and providing relief for some of the unemployed and impoverished. Later in his first term, in what has been called the second New Deal, FDR won legislation establishing social insurance for the elderly and unemployed, and protecting the rights of workers to organize trade unions and bargain with employers.[1]

FDR never really had a comprehensive theory to justify the actions he took in expanding the functions of government so dramatically. He was a pragmatist at heart, taking up problems as they presented themselves and seeking what he thought were reasonable solutions. But over time the philosophy of the New Deal revealed itself in the choices the administration made in trying to revive the faltering economy.

Three key elements can be seen in the policies of the early FDR presidency: economic stabilization, economic planning, and social reform. Each of these policy goals reflected a deeper philosophical basis. Many economic stabilization measures, such as the restructuring of the banking system, were based on the ideology I have called the social security philosophy, the belief that major sectors of the economy should be protected from large losses of income. New Deal legislation for industrial recovery reflected a belief that joint government and corporate planning would lead to more rational economic development than would unregulated free markets. The recognition of the rights of trade unions and strengthening of their bargaining position with owners reflected a belief that government had the obligation to protect and foster the democratic rights of working people in the economy and society.

The most immediate crisis the Roosevelt administration faced was the crisis in the banking system. The Depression had led to a number of bank failures as withdrawals ran far ahead of new deposits. The panic fed on itself as depositors worried about the security of their savings rushed to remove their funds before their bank became the next to fail. Upon taking office, FDR issued an executive order closing the nation's banks. He then submitted emergency legislation to Congress to pump new credit into the system. The first hundred days also brought legislation to provide federal guarantees of bank deposits through a government insurance system, new federal regulation of the securities industry, federal assistance for the refinancing of home and farm mortgages, and abandonment of the gold standard.

One of the most important products of the tumultuous first hundred days of the Roosevelt presidency was the National Industrial Recovery Act (NIRA). NIRA envisioned a restoration of prosperity through the organization of industries into associations of producers. These "modern guilds" would mutually agree to maintain existing production and price levels. They were designed to stem the tide of layoffs and deflation, and to preserve aggregate production and demand levels. This was the president's plan to return economic activity to pre-1929 levels.

FDR also moved to stabilize the farm economy. In the 1930s one-third of the population was still working in agriculture. The most important farm bill was the Agricultural Adjustment Act (AAA), which sought to raise farm prices by curtailing production. This was to be accomplished by committees of local farmers who would apportion crop allotments among themselves. This was a kind of agricultural equivalent of the NIRA. The AAA also attempted to keep farm prices up by government guarantees. If farmers could not sell their products on the open market, the government would buy them for a predetermined price. In addition, the Farm Credit Act assisted farmers with mortgages and set up a system of regional rural banks to provide new credit to farmers.

The Depression had thrown millions of people out of work. While the Roosevelt administration sought to revive industrial and agricultural production, it also had to deal with the army of unemployed. The old system of private charity and relief by state governments was overwhelmed by the Depression. The Federal Emergency Relief Administration was created to expand the relief system by making grants to state and local agencies.

New Deal planners tried to combat unemployment and boost national economic production through public works projects that provided employment and increased purchasing power for workers and new facilities for communities. Federal public works programs went through a series of administrative evolutions due to shifting political and budgetary tides, but the purposes of public job creation remained the same. Public construction projects included roads and highways, airports, schools, parks, water and sewage systems, power plants, and shipbuilding for the navy.

The epitome of the New Deal public works philosophy was the Tennessee Valley Authority (TVA). The TVA was an ambitious public project for multipurpose regional development. Its responsibilities included hydroelectric power generation, fertilizer production, flood control, soil and forest conservation, land use planning, and raising living standards in one of the poorer rural regions of the country. The TVA was a visionary model for public planning for regional development. But it was only the largest of a series of measures aimed at rural revival that included the Civilian Conservation Corps, the Soil Erosion Service, and the Rural Electrification Administration.

While FDR's new activist programs were not successful in ending the Depression, they were politically popular. In the midterm election of 1934 the Democrats added to their massive majorities in Congress.

FDR on Activist Government

Second Inaugural Address: We recognized a . . . need to find through government the instrument of our united purpose to solve for the individual the ever-rising problems of a complex civilization. Repeated attempts at their solution without the aid of government had left us baffled and bewildered . . . we knew that we must find practical controls over blind economic forces and blindly selfish men.

The NIRA: It represents a supreme effort to stabilize for all time the many factors which make for the prosperity of the nation. . . . Its goal is the assurance of a reasonable profit to industry and living wages for labor. . . . [It] proposes to our industry a great spontaneous cooperation to put millions of men back in their regular jobs.

Social Security: The establishment of sound means toward a greater future economic security of the American people is dictated by a prudent consideration of the hazards involved in our national life. . . . We can eliminate many factors that cause economic depression, and we can provide the means of mitigating their results. This plan for economic security is at once a measure of prevention and a method of alleviation.[2]

In 1935 the New Deal entered a new phase, turning to issues that had been deferred because they were even more politically contentious than the questions that had been addressed. While in the first hundred days the Roosevelt administration had dealt with the industrial and farm crises, it had not faced the demands of organized labor and the organized elderly. Trade unions and associations of the unemployed had been growing rapidly as wages and employment remained at low levels. Many elderly had joined groups that pressed for government pensions for those too old to work.

In 1935 Congress and the Roosevelt administration responded with the passage of the Social Security Act which expanded federal relief aid, set up a national system of unemployment insurance, and, most important, began a national system of old age insurance. The Social Security program ensured the income of workers after they retired. The government would now tax an individual's income while he or she was in the work force, and keep the revenues in a separate fund. Benefits would be paid to retired workers, based on how much they had paid into the fund while they were working.

In 1935 Congress also passed the Wagner Act, which for the first time in U.S. history conclusively guaranteed the right of workers to organize into trade unions and bargain with employers over wages and working conditions. It set up the National Labor Relations Board to oversee the collective bargaining process between unions and management. The Wagner Act banned or regulated many of the most successful tactics companies had used to divide and conquer their workers. Most important, it mandated that if a majority of workers endorsed a union as their representative, it would be the sole bargaining agent for all the workers in the bargaining unit. This undercut past company practices of splitting their work force by treating nonunion workers better than union workers or workers in company unions better than members of more militant unions.

Steering Between Class Conflict and Economic Cooperation

The massive changes in policy and philosophy of the New Deal did not come without intense opposition and conflict. During the Depression crisis FDR was not averse to pointing to the class cleavages of American society and the economic forces behind the political conflicts over the New Deal.

Opponents of the New Deal assailed it as socialism, as undermining the very foundations of the American constitutional system and American capitalism. This certainly is not what the Roosevelt administration intended. In crafting their coalitions in Congress and administering the new programs, the New Dealers employed a rhetoric of joint effort of all elements of American society in the national effort to restore prosperity.

The NIRA sought the cooperation of business in the maintenance of industrial production. The AAA sought the cooperation of large and small farmers in the maintenance of crop prices and agricultural production. The reforms in the financial system kept the private banking and securities systems largely intact.

The intent was to save the system, not to revolutionize it. But conservative opponents of the New Deal were not persuaded. They saw the new aggregation of power at the federal level as inevitably leading to total government control of the economy and society.

The New Deal also faced attack from growing radical movements on the left. Millions of workers were joining trade unions or associations of the unemployed. Dispossessed farmers were another source of militant discontent. Many intellectuals, even a few within the administration, saw the planning mechanisms of the New Deal as a wedge for developing new institutions of public power that could challenge the dominance of private economic institutions. But most New Dealers saw their reforms as a middle course between revolution and reaction.

Roosevelt was not averse to confronting his opponents on the ideological front. In his first inaugural address he reflected the popular resentment at the prior generation of economic and political leadership, which had allowed the crisis to deepen and had resisted the use of government to redress the suffering it had caused.

In preparation for his first reelection campaign, FDR renewed the attack on the old elite and the old order. In his speech accepting the Democratic nomination for a second term, he labeled his opponents on the right "economic royalists." FDR also had harsh words for his opponents on the left, but he saw them as less of an immediate threat.

FDR on Class Conflict

The royalists of the economic order have conceded that political freedom was the business of Government, but they have maintained that economic slavery was nobody's business. They granted that Government could protect the citizen in his right to vote, but they denied that the Government could do anything to protect the citizen in his right to work and his right to live.

Today we stand committed to the proposition that freedom is no half-and-half affair. If the average citizen is guaranteed equal opportunity in the polling place, he must have equal opportunity in the market place.

These economic royalists complain that we seek to overthrow the institutions of America. What they really complain of is that we seek to take away their power.

Government in a modern civilization has certain inescapable obligations to its citizens, among which are protection of the family and the home, the establishment of a democracy of opportunity, and aid to those overtaken by disaster.

Governments can err, Presidents do make mistakes, but the immortal Dante tells us that divine justice weighs the sins of the cold-blooded and the sins of the warm-hearted in different scales.

Better the occasional faults of a Government that lives in a spirit of charity than the consistent omissions of a Government frozen in the ice of its own indifference.[3]

The theme of class conflict was not unknown to the Democratic Party. The populist William Jennings Bryan, who had led the Democratic ticket in three unsuccessful presidential campaigns at the turn of the century had tried to unite discontented farmers and workers against the dominance of industrial interests. Bryan had crystallized resistance to the power of banks and trusts when he castigated them for "crucifying mankind on a cross of gold." FDR's skewering of the "economic royalists" captured the same resentments of the economic system that had failed so many so tragically.

New Priorities in the Second Term

Roosevelt largely had his way in his first term, buoyed by the ratification of his policies in the midterm election of 1934 and his landslide reelection in 1936. But the New Deal and its expansion of government programs ran into more serious trouble in his second term. On the one hand, the New Deal lost momentum because it had not met its primary goal, ending the Depression. On the other hand, its political and social successes eased the crisis atmosphere that had made the country so responsive to urgent action and rapid change.

FDR also spent valuable political capital battling with the Supreme Court, which was still dominated by laissez-faire Republicans. Since the Civil War the Supreme Court had been the bastion of the theory of limited government, striking down all kinds of national and state regulation of the economy as unconstitutional extensions of government power. In 1935 the Supreme Court declared the NIRA invalid because it too broadly delegated Congress' constitutional powers to the executive branch. The Roosevelt administration had largely lost faith in NIRA as a mechanism for restoring prosperity and so was not unhappy with its demise. But it was determined not to let the Court put the entire New Deal in jeopardy.

In retaliation, Roosevelt took advantage of the fact that the number of justices who sit on the Supreme Court is determined by Congress, and proposed to increase their number. Since the president appoints justices with the confirmation of the Senate, this would allow Roosevelt to pack the Supreme Court with supporters of the New Deal and end the court challenges to his program. However, in many quarters this was seen as an unprecedented attack on the independence of the judicial branch, and the court packing scheme was opposed even by many of FDR's supporters.

The Supreme Court ultimately backed down before the court packing scheme came to a vote by ruling in favor of the administration in some key cases. But the court packing scheme it took to achieve this cost FDR dearly in political terms. The Republicans picked up 75 House seats and 7 Senate seats in the 1938 election, which decisively shifted the political balance away from new government activism.

As New Deal reformism bogged down, the attention of the administration turned abroad. The outbreak of war in Asia and then in Europe shifted the nation's primary concern from domestic to foreign policy. In order to achieve his foreign policy objectives, FDR recognized that he had to mend fences with his opponents in the business world. By 1939 the United States was beginning to mobilize for the possibility of war. This required coordination between political and military leaders and big business to develop the mechanisms for war production. Early attempts at coordination included the National Defense Advisory Commission, the Office of Production Management, and the use of the Reconstruction Finance Corporation to subsidize defense-related industries.

Several key elements of the new cooperation between business and the Roosevelt administration were worked out during this period. Contracts were to be let on a basis of incurred cost plus profit, thus effectively guaranteeing a profitable return. War industries were granted massive tax breaks, such as accelerated depreciation of their investments. FDR promised to block any excess profits taxes on windfalls from war production. Private risks incurred in war production would be underwritten by federal credit guarantees.

When the Japanese attacked Pearl Harbor, the problem of war production intensified. Early in 1942 the War Production Board was created to oversee all military-related production. The administration and the business community were now united in pursuing the war effort, although conflict over the tactics of war mobilization could not be entirely eliminated.

What Kind of Activist State?

The New Deal and the war production efforts of the Roosevelt administration represented a conclusive triumph of the activist state over the philosophy of the limited state. But it is important to see clearly what were the main components of this new activist state. The policies of the New Deal had three basic elements: economic stabilization, economic planning, and social reform. Behind these policies stood a more basic philosophy.

Behind many of the economic stabilization measures lay the principle of securing the income of many of the key sectors of the economy from large losses, or what in Chapter 2 was called the social security ideology. Behind the planning mechanisms of the New Deal lay the belief that corporations and government working together could rationalize economic production. The programs of the first hundred days were a mix of the social security philosophy and corporate planning.

The banking reforms, the NIRA, and the AAA all fused the goal of securing the income of the major sectors of the economy with the technique of joint corporate and government planning. Bankers, farmers, and industrial producers would organize self-regulating cartels and work together with government to ensure their income streams. The public works and relief programs served the same function by restoring income for unemployed workers. This combination of programs extended economic security programs broadly throughout society.

The Social Security Act of 1935 represents another elaboration of the philosophy of protecting the income stream of major sectors of society, in this case the elderly and the unemployed. These social insurance programs stabilized the income of workers over time, protecting them from the effects of temporary unemployment in economic downturns and providing a minimal pension once they were too old to work.

The other major philosophical component of the New Deal was social democracy, the redistribution of power and income. FDR often employed the ideal of social democracy in his rhetoric, although most of the programs of the New Deal sprang from less visionary origins. But certain New Deal programs did redistribute power or income. For example, the Social Security Act had the effect of redistributing income, not across class lines but across generational lines.

Perhaps the most clearly social democratic of the New Deal programs was the Wagner Act, which recognized the rights of trade unions in the workplace. It substantially altered the balance of power between capital and labor in the marketplace, ending the historic policy of using government power to suppress the trade union movement.

The TVA also had elements of social democracy in its makeup. In some ways the TVA was simply a huge public works employment program. But, unlike most other planning in the New Deal, the TVA program asserted the primacy of public power over private power. The TVA was a public corporation, and its planning mechanisms provided for input not only from local industrialists but also from small farmers and businesses, local residents, and others affected by the project. Its goals included not only making a profit but also leading and shaping the economic development of an entire region.

With regard to domestic policy, the FDR era can be broken into three periods. In each period there was a different relative emphasis on elements of the activist state. In the first two years, the emphasis was on economic stabilization and planning. The first hundred days sought primarily to secure the income of major sectors of society and establish mechanisms of corporate planning.

The "second" New Deal of 1935 combined elements of the social security philosophy with social democracy. The legislation of this period dealt more broadly with securing the income of working people and redefining the power relations between labor and capital. After the defeat of his court packing scheme and the swing to the right in the 1938 midterm election, FDR largely abandoned domestic reform in order to prepare for the war in Europe. In this period a new form of corporate planning took center stage, planning for war production.

The policy outcomes of the FDR years irrevocably changed the nature of U.S. government. Many of FDR's initiatives survive today as major government programs, either in their original form or modified over the years. Others were abandoned as the years passed and left no lasting mark on public policy.

Programs reflecting the social security ideology had the highest rate of survival and growth. The Social Security program established in the 1930s is now the single biggest government program, providing hundreds of billions of dollars in benefits to over 30 million recipients. The multibillion-dollar savings and loan rescue legislation passed in 1989 was an elaboration of the system of banking insurance established during the New Deal.

Programs based on the philosophy of corporate planning fared less well. Government planning for industrial policy and comprehensive national public works programs like TVA have long since been abandoned as public policies. Corporate planning has survived where it had been put in the service of social security goals. So today certain sectors of the economy still engage in sectoral planning. Agriculture still operates on the government subsidies, protection, and planning established in the FDR era. The close cooperation between military contractors and the Defense Department established during World War II continues today. But this kind of planning is quite different from the more general national industrial policy envisioned by the NIRA. Instead, the government-business planning mechanisms that have survived are those which put government power at the service of particular sectors of the economy, promoting and subsidizing one set of economic interests.

In terms of the typology introduced in Chapter 2, the New Deal promises of social democratic transformation and security for all segments of society were only partially fulfilled. Instead, a limited number of interests were secured. Financial institutions were shored up and their operations insured by the government. Large parts of the agricultural community were protected from the worst vagaries of the market. Organized labor had its rights to collective bargaining recognized and protected. Those who had been a regular part of the work force had their earnings partially protected from the effects of unemployment and a minimal pension ensured.

But the social democratic, redistributional rhetoric of the New Deal was largely unrealized. Unemployment and poverty persisted as social problems long after the economy recovered. The trade union movement was channeled into narrow concerns about wages in single industries. Minorities and women remained largely relegated to peripheral roles in the economy and society. The minimal welfare state of the New Deal did a better job of protecting the position of unionized workers and the income of higher-earning workers during recessions and at retirement than it did of advancing the interests of workers in more marginal positions. The activist state was effectively confined to a limited number of social roles.

THE CONSERVATIVE COALITION AND THE LIMITED
INTEREST STATE

From 1938 on, and particularly from 1946 into the 1960s, Congress was dominated not by the liberal New Deal Democrats, but by the "conservative coalition," the alliance between conservative southern Democrats, who controlled most of the key congressional committee chairs, and conservative Republicans. The watering down of the provisions of the full-employment bill in 1946, the passage of the Taft-Hartley Act in 1948 with its restrictions of the power of unions, and the McCarthy anticommunist witch-hunts in the 1950s reflected this conservative dominance of Congress.

The 1940s and 1950s was a period of greater attention to international affairs than to domestic reform. Most expansion of government programs during this period came in the military and intelligence agencies that were part of the new national security apparatus. From 1940 through the early 1960s, more than half of all government expenditure was on the military and security apparatus.

Roles of Government and Conflict over the Full-Employment Bill

The postwar political environment was inimical to expansion of domestic programs. The philosophy of the activist state had taken firm hold, and many of the new roles that the state had taken on in the 1930s survived the war and the postwar recovery. But in the postwar years the doctrine that the government should take on only a limited, if now expanded, set of roles rebounded ideologically.

The renewed power of the ideology of the limited state can be seen in the watering down of the Employment Act of 1946, which was designed to deal with an economy demobilizing from the massive war effort.[4] The war had ended the Depression, and it was now feared that the end of the war would bring the return of hard times. Sponsors of the original full-employment bill sought to counteract any contraction of the postwar economy through economic planning and large-scale public works and public employment projects if the private economy failed to maintain high employment and production levels.

Sponsors of the full-employment bill were acting from a New Deal-like mix of philosophical principles. Most important, they wanted to broadly secure the income streams of working Americans. Many backers of the bill also wanted comprehensive national economic planning to overcome the tendency of the market economy toward severe cyclical fluctuations and periodic depressions. Some of the bill's supporters also sought to establish the principle of democratic public steering of the economy over the primacy of private interests.

Many conservatives opposed the full-employment bill on pure free-market grounds. But the more politically tenable position was to try to limit the scope of the bill. The conservative alternative to the full-employment bill recognized the federal government's role in macroeconomic stabilization, in trying to keep employment and production up and inflation down in the postwar period. It accepted the creation of the Council of Economic Advisers to give the president expert opinion on how to use fiscal and monetary policy to achieve these goals. But the conservative alternative struck from the bill provisions for comprehensive economic planning, public works and public jobs, and any idea of supplementing the private sector with public power. It even purged the bill of any reference to the term "full employment."

It was this conservative alternative that formed the basis of the Employment Act that won passage through Congress in 1946. In perhaps the most important political test of the early postwar period, the principle of limiting the scope of activist government had prevailed over a more expansive vision of activist government.

Truman and Eisenhower on the Role of Government in the Economy

Truman on the Employment Act of 1946

The history of the last several decades has been one of speculative booms alternating with deep depression. . . . Democratic government has the responsibility to use all its resources to create and maintain conditions under which free competitive enterprise can operate effectively--conditions under which there is an abundance of employment opportunity for those who are willing to work. . . . It is not the government's duty to supplant the efforts of private enterprise to find markets, or of individuals to find jobs. The people do expect the Government, however, to create and maintain conditions in which the individual businessman and the individual job seeker have a chance to succeed by their own efforts.

Eisenhower on the Role of Government

In a modern industrial society, banishment of destitution and cushioning the shock of personal disaster on the individual are proper concerns of all levels of government, including the Federal Government.

The aspiration of most of our people can best be fulfilled through their own enterprise and initiative, without Government interference. The administration, therefore, follows two simple rules: First, the Federal Government should perform an essential task . . . only when it cannot otherwise be adequately performed; and second, in performing that task, our Government must not impair the self-respect, the freedom, and incentive of individuals.[5]

Eisenhower and the Republican Acceptance of the Activist State

The newly resurgent Republicans won control of Congress in 1946. Their hopes for return to power were frustrated by Truman's upset victory and the loss of control of Congress in 1948. But with the war hero Dwight Eisenhower leading the ticket, they won control of both Congress and the presidency in 1952. However, the Democrats regained control of Congress in 1954 and fattened their majorities in 1958.

The return of Republican control of the national government in the Eisenhower landslide of 1952 did not bring return of the laissez-faire philosophy to the scene. Eisenhower's victory in the Republican nomination struggle over Senator Robert Taft represented the continuing dominance of the liberal eastern wing of the party that had accommodated itself to activist government, if not to all of its programs. The Republicans, chastened after 20 years out of power, did not make a frontal attack on the activist state. Instead, they tried to distinguish their philosophy from that of the Democrats by prescribing a more limited role for the activist state.

Eisenhower's public philosophy is perhaps most clearly expressed in his State of the Union addresses. For example, in his first State of the Union message Eisenhower sounds much like FDR or Truman regarding the premise that the activist state should insure the income of individuals under certain conditions. In his second State of the Union message, Eisenhower provides some rules of thumb for when government action should be considered legitimate and when it should not.

The pattern of the limited interest state can be seen by examining government budgets from the presidencies of Hoover through Eisenhower. When Herbert Hoover took office in 1929, national government expenditures were a small fraction of total economic output. Under FDR and Truman, government expenditures rose dramatically, first for the New Deal, then much more explosively for World War II and the Korean war. Government expenditures climbed to over 40 percent of GNP during the second world war, shrank to 13 percent after the war, and then climbed to over 20 percent during the Korean war.

Under Eisenhower government expenditures stabilized, ranging from 15-20 percent of GNP. Big government was here to stay, but the growth of government was limited during the Truman and Eisenhower administrations. Most of the domestic programs that had survived the FDR period were retained, although a few were eliminated and many were pared back. The world war and the cold war made military production the central element of the limited interest state, consuming more than half of all government expenditures during the 1940s and 1950s.

LYNDON JOHNSON AND THE GREAT SOCIETY

John Kennedy and Domestic Deadlock

In the 1960 campaign John Kennedy promised to get the country moving again, to bring a new generation of leadership and a new dynamism to American politics after the surface tranquillity and the lack of innovation in domestic policy in the Eisenhower years. He succeeded in this, perhaps more than he ever wished. The 1960s were a period of rapid political change, particularly in the immediate aftermath of Kennedy's assassination.

On the one hand, Kennedy's election was the result of the mobilization of new political forces like the emerging civil rights movement and a renewed political vigor of the more traditional elements of the old New Deal coalition like organized labor. On the other hand, his victory, coupled with his rhetorical and stylistic calls for change, served as a spur to further mobilization of these groups, particularly the civil rights movement.

The Kennedy campaign reactivated the old New Deal coalition, which despite its political survival, had been dormant as a force for policy innovation since early in the second FDR term. Kennedy's call for a New Frontier echoed FDR's call for a New Deal. Programmatically, Kennedy backed federal aid to education and a new government medical insurance program to guarantee the elderly could get health care. Later, as the civil rights mobilizations intensified, a broad-based civil rights bill and the war on poverty were added to the agenda. However, the conservative coalition still dominated Congress and was able to block these programs throughout the Kennedy years.

In November 1963 the nation was shocked as Kennedy was struck down by an assassin's bullet. It seemed especially tragic that such a young and dynamic leader could be erased from the national scene, cut down before the great promise of his presidency could be realized.

The Civil Rights Act of 1964 and the Defeat of White Supremacy

Kennedy's martyrdom contributed to the realization of his program. So did the political skills of his successor, Lyndon Johnson, who had mastered the art of legislation in his years as Senate majority leader prior to being selected as vicepresident. Johnson moved quickly to use his grace period of succession to enact key elements of the Kennedy program.

Johnson the Southerner was in a particularly good position to sell the civil rights act to the country. As a senator from segregated Texas, he had opposed prior civil rights bills more on grounds of electoral prudence than on principle. But as president, Johnson had a national constituency. Because of his southern roots, he recognized both the seriousness of the crisis and the key role it would play in perceptions of him as a national, rather than a regional, leader. He applied the full force of his office and his considerable legislative skills to the task of passing civil rights legislation.

Since the slaves had been freed after the Civil War, southern whites had used their state governments to develop an elaborate system of white supremacy that relegated blacks to second-class citizenship. A series of measures like all-white primaries, the poll tax, and discriminatory voter registration practices had denied blacks in the South the elementary right to vote. Blacks were segregated from whites in both public and private facilities. Blacks attended separate schools, rode in separate sections of buses, stayed in separate hotels, and even ate at separate lunch counters. Blacks generally held the lowest-paying jobs and were excluded from positions of power in white-owned businesses.

The system of segregation was justified by the ideology of white supremacy. Many whites believed blacks were inferior to whites in intellectual capacity and moral development. It was widely believed among whites that it was right and natural that blacks should be subordinated to whites in the political and economic system. The doctrine of states' rights asserted that any national intervention to alter segregation would be an unconstitutional interference in the affairs of the states, a new tyranny of the national government.

The civil rights movement demonstrated to the rest of the country how brutal white supremacy actually was. As the TV news entered most American homes in the 1950s, it increasingly showed southern blacks petitioning for such elementary rights as voting and entrance to state schools being met with police dogs, billy clubs, fire hoses, and even bullets in the night. The Kennedy administration, which had tried to walk a fine line between racial justice and holding the support of racist southern Democrats, finally was forced to ask Congress to pass civil rights legislation. But it fell to the Southerner Johnson to shepherd the bill through Congress.

The Civil Rights Act of 1964 ended the system of white supremacy and official segregation in the South. It banned discrimination in public accommodations. Businesses would have to treat white and black customers alike. Discrimination by employers in the hiring and promotion of their workers was banned, and strong legal sanctions were put in place against states and businesses that continued discriminatory practices. The Justice Department was empowered to sue states or businesses that did not comply, and the penalties for continuing discriminatory practices were substantial. States could lose federal subsidies for programs that discriminated. Businesses could lose federal contracts.

The Civil Rights Act was followed by the Voting Rights Act of 1965. White supremacists had excluded blacks from participation in the southern political system down to the level of denying the right to vote. The Voting Rights Act provided national guarantees for blacks' and other minorities' ability to participate in the political process.

The philosophical shifts in racial policy in the mid-1960s can be characterized by comparing the dominant ideologies on racial issues prior to the passage of the Civil Rights Act and the 1964 election with the prevailing public philosophy on racial issues in their aftermath. Prior to the 1960s, white supremacy was the dominant ideology in the South. Open support for white supremacy was not common outside the South, but most nonsouthern whites felt a stronger cultural sympathy with white Southerners than with blacks. In the first half of the twentieth century, open advocacy of civil rights was heard only from the most liberal leaders. FDR, Truman, and Eisenhower had taken only halting steps in the direction of enforcing civil rights.

In the 1950s and early 1960s the civil rights movement laid bare the ugly truths of racial hatred and challenged the conscience of the nation. The racial polarization in the South forced the country to make some clear choices between civil rights and segregation, and the philosophy of white supremacy was completely routed. The Civil Rights Act of 1964 and the Voting Rights Act of 1965 decisively defeated the doctrine of white supremacy. Even when racial tensions rose again during the urban riots of the summers of 1966-1968, open advocacy of white supremacy was relegated to a place beyond legitimate ideological debate.

The Expansion of Government During the Great Society

Along with the passage of civil rights legislation, Johnson called for a war on poverty. In part the war on poverty was designed to meet the economic demands of the civil rights movement, which argued that it did little good to be able to sit at the same lunch counter with whites if one did not have the price of a meal. But the war on poverty also was an attempt to cast the newly activist federal government in a role that white working people could identify with, that of provider of public goods and services. It is in talking about the war on poverty in his first State of the Union message that Johnson's philosophy of government is most clearly revealed.

Lyndon Johnson on the War on Poverty

Unfortunately many Americans live on the outskirts of hope—some because of their poverty, and some because of their color, and all too many because of both. . . . This administration today here and now declares unconditional war on poverty in America . . . we shall not rest until that war is won.

Our chief weapons . . . will be better schools, and better health, and better homes, and better training, and better job opportunities to help more Americans. . . . Our aim is not only to relieve the symptoms of poverty but to cure it; and above all, to prevent it.

—We must enact youth employment legislation to put jobless, aimless, hopeless youngsters to work on useful projects.

—We must distribute more food to the needy.

—We must, by including special school aid funds as part of our education program, improve the quality of teaching and training and counseling in our hardest hit areas.

—We must build more libraries in every area, and more hospitals and nursing homes . . . and train more nurses to staff them.

—We must provide hospital insurance for our older citizens.

—We must . . . provide more housing for our poor and our elderly, and seek . . . a decent home for every American family.[6]

The war on poverty legislation passed in 1964 fell far short of LBJ's rhetorical flourishes. Other elements of the presidential program were completely stalled in Congress. The 1964 election was a key turning point. In large part in reaction to civil rights legislation, a new social mobilization was appearing on the right that led to the nomination of Barry Goldwater by the Republican party. Goldwater led the most aggressive ideological campaign against government activism since the 1930s.

In his 1960 book, *Conscience of a Conservative* Goldwater laid out his philosophy of "limiting the functions of government"

Throughout history, government has proved to be the chief instrument for thwarting man's liberty. Government represents power in the hands of some men to control and regulate the lives of other men. And power, as Lord Acton said, corrupts men.

The federal government has moved into every field in which it thinks its services are needed. . . . The result is a Leviathan, a vast national authority out of touch with the people, and out of their control.[7]

While Goldwater's campaign prefigured the successful Republican strategies applied by Nixon and Reagan, in 1964 it led to a decisive Democratic victory. Not only did Johnson win in a landslide, but the already strong congressional Democrats picked up 37 House seats. The two to one majorities in both houses of Congress were the largest the Democrats enjoyed since the 1930s. For the first time since the 1930s the liberal Democrats had the votes to overpower the conservative coalition in Congress.

The result was the most activist legislative session since FDR's first term. The first broad-based federal aid to education was voted, targeted to school districts with large poverty and minority populations. The Medicare and Medicaid programs were created, providing government health insurance programs for the elderly and the poor. The Voting Rights Act provided national guarantees of minorities' ability to participate in the political system. The war on poverty and its community action programs were dramatically expanded. Federal job training programs were expanded and targeted toward the chronically unemployed. Access to welfare was expanded. Federal aid to the inner cities was increased. Community action programs tried to mobilize the poor to fight for their rights.

The Fragmenting of the Democratic Coalition

The year 1965 was the high point of the Great Society. 1965 also brought the major commitment of U.S. ground forces in Vietnam. As in the later FDR administration, guns began to replace butter as the national priority. The Republicans gained 47 House seats in the 1966 congressional elections. The innovative period of the Great Society was over, although government spending for programs voted in the early Johnson years continued to rise into the 1970s.

In 1965 Johnson believed that he had to move quickly to utilize the historic opportunity presented by the convergence of the national desire for change in race relations and social policy and his landslide victory, because such a chance would not likely come again soon. History proved him right in that assessment.

As the Vietnam War escalated, unrest on the college campuses did likewise. At the same time the war on poverty bogged down and race rioting swept the urban ghettos. The coalitions LBJ had carefully crafted began to fragment. By 1968 he was facing a serious challenge within his own party from Minnesota Senator Eugene McCarthy and then from Robert Kennedy, the martyred president's brother. Rather than face a sustained battle for renomination, LBJ withdrew.

But the fault lines in the Democratic coalition were deeper than the feuds among the top leaders. The moderates of the 1950s who had counseled that confronting the civil rights issue would irrevocably split the historic Democratic coalition ultimately were proved correct. Richard Nixon, expressing popular frustrations with the quagmire in Vietnam and the growing racial and political polarization, swept into office in the election of 1968.

NOTES

1. Arthur Schlesinger, *The Age of Roosevelt* (Boston: Houghton Mifflin, 1957).

2. Franklin Roosevelt, *Nothing to Fear*, ed. B. D. Zevin (Boston: Houhgton Mifflin, 1946), pp. 87-92 and 107-115; and *The Roosevelt Reader*, ed. Basil Rauch (New York: Rinehart, 1957), pp. 144-145.

3. Rauch, *The Roosevelt Reader*, pp. 148-152.

4. Stephen Bailey, *Congress Makes a Law* (Westport, CT: Greenwood Press, 1980).

5. Harry Truman, *Public Papers of the Presidents, 1946* (Washington, DC: U.S. Government Printing Office, 1947), p. 125; and Dwight Eisenhower, *Public Papers of the Presidents, 1954 and 1955* (Washington, DC: U.S. Government Printing Office, 1955 and 1956), p. 19, and p. 18.

6. Lyndon Johnson, *Public Papers of the Presidents, 1964* (Washington, DC: U.S. Government Printing Office, 1965), pp. 112-118.

7. Barry Goldwater, *Conscience of a Conservative*, (Shepherdsville, KY: Victor Publishing, 1960).

7

THE TRIUMPH OF THE NATIONAL SECURITY STATE

THE COLD WAR AND THE NATIONAL SECURITY STATE

The United States and the Soviets in the Postwar World

In the early decades of the twentieth century, the primary ideological conflict over foreign policy was between those who wanted the United States to take an activist role in world affairs and those who wanted to isolate the United States from the travails and turmoil of the world across the oceans. The American victories in the world wars sealed the triumph of internationalism. After World War II an increasingly bitter rivalry emerged between the most powerful of the wartime allies, the United States and the Soviet Union. As this struggle intensified, much of the world was split into two hostile camps. The Soviet army had driven the Nazis from eastern Europe, and now this region fell under Soviet control. The United States, Britain, France, and other European countries coalesced into the western bloc.

Thus Europe was divided into two spheres of influence, controlled by the Soviet Union and the United States respectively. But large parts of the world were still up for grabs. Certain countries in central Europe fell in between the boundaries of the two blocs. Germany was split into four different zones of occupation, and eventually divided into East and West Germany. Pro-U.S. and pro-Soviet forces each had influence in Greece, Austria, Czechoslovakia, and Yugoslavia.

Much of Asia was also being contested. Japan had surrendered to the United States after the dropping of the atomic bombs, and fell under U.S. control. In

China the civil war between communist and nationalist forces that had preceded the Japanese occupation raged once again after the Japanese were driven out. In southeast Asia and India the old colonial powers, Britain, France, and the Netherlands, faced nationalist resistance movements, often led by socialists or communists, when they tried to reestablish their rule over their former colonies. Hostile nationalist movements also met Western attempts to maintain control over the Middle East and Africa.

As the world war drew to a close, the United States and Britain sought agreements with the Soviets over the shape of the postwar world. The war-weary Allies had hoped to extend their cooperation to find a basis for a more peaceful world. At conferences at Yalta and Potsdam they appeared to be making progress toward this goal. But it soon became increasingly evident that each side had very different ideas about how power should be distributed and what sort of social order should prevail in the postwar world. The differences between the American and Soviet ideologies and their attitudes toward international politics made mutual understanding difficult and added to the suspicions each had about the motivations of the other.

In the early postwar years there was uncertainty in the United States about Soviet intentions, about whether the Soviet Union truly wanted an understanding between the great powers or whether they were bent on the classical Marxist-Leninist goal of world conquest. Policymakers debated whether the Soviets would respond more to open, frank negotiations or threats of force. Eventually the view of the Soviets as a hostile expansionist power that could be influenced only by superior military force won out.

The Dawn of the Nuclear Age

In one sense the postwar conflict between the United States and the Soviet Union was a classic great power rivalry. But one thing made it very different from any previous great power rivalry—the existence of the atomic bomb. Now not only was the power of great nations at stake, but the very existence of their peoples and perhaps of the entire human race.

The United States was the first to develop atomic weapons. It also is the only nation ever to use nuclear weapons. In order to speed the unconditional surrender of the Japanese and to test the impact of the new weapon, the United States dropped atomic bombs on Hiroshima and Nagasaki, killing hundreds of thousands of civilians. The terror of the nuclear era had begun.

At the end of the war the United States enjoyed a nuclear monopoly. Many in the Truman administration and Congress wanted to use that monopoly to extract concessions from the Soviet Union. But others, aware that the Soviets would be able to develop their own bomb and fearful of the consequences of a nuclear arms race, counseled that the United States should seek agreements with the Soviets to renounce the manufacture of nuclear arms and for international control of nuclear technology.

The question of nuclear weapons was a critical test of U.S.-Soviet relations in the postwar world. The United States did take some halting steps to try to avoid a nuclear arms race. In 1946 President Truman appointed a commission to develop proposals for international control of atomic technology. But serious efforts to control the development of nuclear weapons ran against the theses of the emerging cold war. Negotiations over international control of nuclear energy broke down on the key issue of whether the existing U.S. program or the developing Soviet program would be controlled first.

There was intense opposition in both the Truman administration and Congress to the idea of sharing nuclear technology with the communist enemy. The hard-liners thought the nuclear monopoly would allow the United States to shape the postwar world in its favor. They did not believe that Soviet science was capable of producing the bomb in the foreseeable future. Many policymakers doubted the Soviets would keep any agreement. Perhaps most important, few policymakers really comprehended how nuclear weapons had changed world power politics.

As the cold war intensified, the Truman administration relied ever more heavily on nuclear weapons as part of its strategy for checking Soviet military power. U.S. military strategy was increasingly based on plans to retaliate against any advances of Soviet ground forces in Europe or Asia with atomic attacks against Soviet military and civilian targets. This became known as the doctrine of deterrence. The United States would deter war by meeting Soviet aggression with an atomic response.

However, the hope that the nuclear monopoly could be used to extract Soviet political concessions quickly proved to be an illusion. The Soviets knew the United States would not risk general war to achieve lesser foreign policy aims, and could simply call the bluff when the United States brandished its atomic weaponry. Once the U.S. monopoly on nuclear weapons ended in 1949 as the Soviets exploded their own weapon, threats to use the bomb to control Soviet behavior rang even more hollow.

Yet U.S. policymakers continued to see advantages in nuclear weapons. It was believed that even if the actual use of these weapons was too terrible to contemplate, threats to use them could still be used to deter the Soviets from taking action against U.S. vital interests. Nuclear weapons were also cheaper than conventional forces, in both economic and political terms. A few nuclear weapons could substitute for divisions of soldiers who would have to be either drafted or recruited, and who would require heavy costs to maintain.

The Truman Doctrine

The U.S.-Soviet stalemate over the control of nuclear weapons was only one symptom of the deterioration of relations. The United States and the Soviets could not agree on the composition of postwar regimes in Germany, eastern and southern Europe, the Middle East, China, southeast Asia, and elsewhere. As tensions rose, positions hardened and a consensus began to form in the United States that cooperation was no longer possible, that the only way to deal with the Soviets was through confrontation.

The most important statement of the forming American consensus was an address President Truman made to Congress in 1947. The immediate issue was U.S. assistance to pro-Western forces in Greece and Turkey facing communist opposition. But more important, the speech outlined what came to be known as the Truman Doctrine of containment of Soviet expansion. It was one of the first general statements of the emerging national security ideology.

The Truman Doctrine stated the essential principles of the national security ideology that guided U.S. foreign policy from the end of World War II into the 1970s. The United States was portrayed as facing a threat to its very existence. The physical security of Americans was under challenge from enemies abroad and their sympathizers at home. The geographical isolation from foreign powers and conflicts that the Atlantic and Pacific oceans had provided in the nineteenth century was forever gone. The hostile communist world was on the march, and only a newly activist U.S. foreign policy could protect its citizens and its way of life. The United States had to counter communist insurgents, to manipulate faraway events and peoples or face eventual national extinction.

The national security ideology proclaimed the moral superiority of the Western world. Western capitalist democracies were presented as the embodiment of all civic virtues. Soviet socialism was portrayed as brutal totalitarian dictatorship. Conflicts between the United States and the Soviet Union were contests between good and evil, darkness and light.

Moreover, the Soviets were pictured as the aggressors. Western military and political action was characterized as purely defensive, simply trying to "contain" Soviet expansionism. The Soviet Union was portrayed as acting aggressively; the United States was seen as merely reacting to Soviet moves. The expansionism of the Soviet Union made conflict inevitable. If the West was to survive Soviet aggression, it must be ready to fight. It must deter war through military strength.

The Truman Doctrine assigned particular importance to U.S. leadership of the West. No other power was deemed capable of meeting the Soviet challenge. Before the war, Greece and Turkey had been British spheres of influence, but Britain was now too weak to maintain control. The situation was similar in other parts of the world, such as French Indochina. The national security ideology asserted that only if the United States led the way, could the expansion of Soviet influence be checked.

The doctrine of containment was global in nature. Every country was critical on the global chessboard. The fall of any nation into the Soviet orbit was likely to be followed by others. In the 1960s this came to be known as the domino theory. If one domino falls, it will set off a reaction overturning a chain of other dominoes. The United States must counter Soviet-backed insurgencies around the world in order to keep such a chain reaction from beginning.

The Truman Doctrine

Totalitarianism or Democracy

Totalitarian regimes imposed upon free peoples, by direct or indirect aggression, undermine the foundations of international peace and hence the security of the United States. . . . Every nation must choose between alternative ways of life. The choice is too often not a free one.

One way of life is based upon the will of the majority and is distinguished by free institutions, representative government, free elections, guarantees of individual liberty, freedom of speech and religion, and freedom from political oppression. . . . The second way of life is based upon the will of a minority forcibly imposed upon the majority. It relies on terror, oppression, a controlled press and radio, fixed elections, and the suppression of personal freedoms. . . . I believe that it must be the policy of the United States to support free peoples who are resisting attempted subjugation by armed minorities or outside pressures.

Containment

If Greece should fall under the control of an armed minority, the effect upon its neighbor, Turkey, would be immediate and serious. Confusion and disorder might spread throughout the entire Middle East.
Moreover, the disappearance of Greece as an independent state would have profound effect upon those countries in Europe whose peoples are struggling against great difficulties to maintain their freedom and their independence. . . . If we falter in our leadership, we may endanger the peace of the world—and we shall surely endanger the welfare of this nation.[1]

The Truman Doctrine faced stiff political opposition. Weary from the human, economic, and spiritual costs of the world war, Americans had turned away from the Democratic Party they associated with the domestic deprivations of the war. In the midterm elections of 1946 the Republicans regained control of Congress for the first time since the days of Herbert Hoover. Truman's aid package for Greece and Turkey, and the Marshall Plan for even wider ranging economic aid to Europe that followed on its heels, had to pass a Congress controlled by a Republican Party with a large isolationist wing. However, by working with Senator Arthur Vandenberg of Michigan and other prominent internationalist Republicans, the Truman administration was able to win a majority of Republican votes. Aid to Greece and Turkey passed by 67-23 in the Senate and 287-108 in the House. In 1948 the Marshall Plan passed by larger margins.

The Formation of the National Security State

The national security ideology that was triumphant in the postwar era was codified in the National Security Act of 1947, which created a set of political institutions devised to fight the budding cold war with the Soviet Union. The National Security Act restructured the executive departments that made foreign policy and formulated a coordinated military and intelligence apparatus to implement the new role the United States was taking in the world. It was widely believed that the old system of fiercely independent services, competition between the War and State departments for policy leadership, and limited intelligence capacities was inadequate for the struggle against communism.

The National Security Act unified command of the military by putting the formerly autonomous Army, Navy, and Air Force departments under the direct control of the renamed Department of Defense and the newly established military chief of staff. The ability of the secretary of defense and the chairman of the Joint Chiefs to control the services was assisted by specific grants of authority and by increased staffing. The National Security Act also created the Central Intelligence Agency (CIA) to provide the executive with independent intelligence gathering and evaluating capability.

To coordinate the entire apparatus and provide overall direction to foreign policy, the legislation also established the National Security Council (NSC). The NSC consisted of the president and vice president, the secretaries of state and defense, the heads of the CIA and the Joint Chiefs, and the newly created national security assistant to the president, who headed the NSC staff. The NSC's mission was to get advice from each of the players in the foreign policy process, devise long-term policies and strategies that looked beyond the parochial view of any one agency, and coordinate the implementation of policy.

The Bipartisan Consensus on the National Security Ideology

The platforms of the major parties in the election of 1948 illustrate the elements of an emerging bipartisan consensus on the national security ideology. The Democratic and Republican platforms were the products of highly contentious conventions racked by intense political battles. But the cold war internationalists won the struggle in both major parties. The final statements of the Democratic and Republican conventions sound much as if they were written by the same author. Both were fully internationalist with no hint of residual isolationism.[2]

Republicans and Democrats alike began from the central cold war assumption: that the keystone of U.S. foreign policy should be containment of an aggressive Soviet Union. The two parties supported the extension of U.S. military power globally, favoring extensive aid to anticommunist forces around the world, although both also called for international control of nuclear arms. The newly formed United Nations and the Organization of American States were endorsed by both parties, as was the Rio Pact's mutual defense arrangement for the western hemisphere. The newly emergent state of Israel was also supported. Both parties called for extensive trade agreements with western European nations to integrate the capitalist economies of the West.

The contrast of a third party platform is instructive. The Progressive Party had been an important force in the early part of the century, winning many seats in Congress and even carrying states in presidential elections. In 1948 the Progressive presidential candidate was Henry Wallace, who had been FDR's second vicepresident and would have become president if FDR had died just one year earlier than he did. As a member of the Truman cabinet, Wallace had counseled postwar cooperation with the Soviet Union. His campaign for maintenance of good relations with the Soviets led Truman to fire him in 1946.

Wallace and the Progressives rejected the policies of the cold war and containment. They had a different vision of the kind of world order that could emerge from the ashes of war. The Progressives called for negotiations rather than confrontation with the Soviet Union, criticizing the rise of the national security apparatus and the deployment of U.S. military forces around the world. They sought an end to the military draft.

Despite being labeled a communist front by the major news media and the major parties, the Progressives did capture over one million popular votes in 1948. But that represented only 2 percent of the total vote. The bipartisan foreign policy consensus had triumphed and would not again receive a significant political challenge from the left until the late 1960s.

THE KOREAN WAR, THE NATIONAL SECURITY STATE, AND THE IMPERIAL PRESIDENCY

The Korean War

As the twentieth century reached its midpoint, the attention of U.S. foreign policymakers was centered on Europe. The postwar division of Germany, the composition of regimes in southern and eastern Europe, Western military cooperation, and the Soviet blockade of the Western outpost in West Berlin were at the center of policy deliberations. The year 1949 had brought the signing of the North Atlantic Treaty Organization (NATO) charter, which bound the United States, Britain, France, Italy, Canada, and most of western Europe into a permanent military alliance. West Germany, which had been created out of the U.S., British, and French postwar occupation zones, was at the core of the new organization, although it was not made a full member until a few years later.

But the ultimate test of the national security ideology did not come in Europe. It came in Korea. The Korean peninsula has the unhappy fate of being placed in a strategic vise, between China and Japan, at the convergence of Soviet and U.S.

power in the Pacific. After World War II this former Japanese colony was divided between the West and East blocs along the thirty-eighth parallel.

In June 1950 war between the two Korean regimes broke out, and North Korean forces invaded South Korea. President Truman committed United States forces to the conflict on the side of the South. While the Soviet Union boycotted the proceedings, the U.S. obtained a United Nations Security Council resolution backing South Korea.

President Truman justified his actions to the United Nations, the Congress, and the American people with the doctrines of the national security ideology. In a radio address to the nation in 1951, Truman laid out his reasons for fighting and for conducting the war as he had.

Truman blamed the war on aggression by communist North Korea. To him, the war was an act of a global conspiracy directed and masterminded by the Kremlin. U.S. national security was at stake—if communism were not contained in Korea, it would eventually spread around the world. Truman called for the noncommunist world to unite in an alliance against communist aggression, yet he also warned that the United States should conduct the war in a limited fashion. He feared that escalation would drag the United States into a land war in China, provoke greater direct participation by the Soviet military, and/or cause the Soviets to take action in other areas around the world where the West was more vulnerable, like Berlin.

Truman on the Korean War

Global Communist Aggression

The Communists in the Kremlin are engaged in a monstrous conspiracy to stamp out freedom all over the world. If they were to succeed, the United States would be numbered among their principal victims.
The attack on Korea was part of a greater plan for conquering all of Asia.
. . . The whole Communist imperialism is back of the attack on peace in the Far East. It was the Soviet Union that trained and equipped the North Koreans for aggression. The Chinese Communists [threw] 44 well-trained and well-equipped divisions . . . into battle when the North Korean Communists were beaten.

Limited War

The question we have had to face is whether the Communist plan of conquest can be stopped without general war. . . . The best chance of stopping it without general war is to meet the attack in Korea and defeat it there.[3]

After initial losses the U.S.-led U.N. forces overwhelmed the North Korean army and had soon occupied much of North Korea. But then the newly established Chinese communist regime entered the war on the side of North Korea, driving the U.N. forces deep into the southern end of the peninsula. There the U.N. forces regrouped and fought their way back into control of most of South Korea until the war stalemated. In 1953 a truce was signed that largely reestablished the prewar situation.

The National Security State and the Imperial Presidency

Policy-making in the Korean conflict showed just how much the national security state had changed the balance of power in the institutions that made foreign policy. The national security state required a strong presidency, able to act quickly in international crises.

The national security ideology saw a world defined by the international communist menace backed by Soviet military power. The threat was both global and unpredictable; at any time any part of the noncommunist world might be threatened by communist aggression. The only meaningful deterrent or counter to communist expansion was U.S. military power. In such a world the United States must be able to respond rapidly to repeated emergencies around the globe. And in order to be successful in sustaining such commitments, it must show a national unity of purpose.

Yet the American Constitution divides the power to make war and foreign policy, as it divides most other powers, between the Congress and the presidency. The president is designated commander in chief of the armed forces, but Congress is given the power to declare war. The president is given the power to negotiate with foreign powers, but the Senate must approve treaties by a two-thirds vote. The president has executive power over the military establishment, but no forces can exist without congressional authorization and appropriation of funds.

The framers of the Constitution had several reasons to divide war powers between the Congress and the president. The decision to go to war is the most important decision a country can make. The framers did not believe that decision should lie with just one man.

They knew from their own experience and European history that monarchies with strong executives were prone to go to war. Monarchs often benefited politically from leading winning military campaigns, from being perceived as brave heroes, and from bringing home the spoils of war. Wartime emergencies also gave monarchs an excuse for suppressing domestic dissidents, claiming it was necessary to maintain national unity. The framers of the Constitution were deliberately making it more difficult for the president to commit the country to war. More had to be involved than the benefit of the executive or imperial pride.

The framers also believed foreign policy would be refined through shared powers and the consultation that shared powers required. The executive is limited in its perspective, in its ability to see possible policy options and to anticipate the consequences of its actions. As in other areas of governance, the framers believed that if Congress were involved in policy formulation, serious errors in judgment could be recognized and avoided. Consultation also built a certain degree of delay into the process. This might be a disadvantage in some cases, but it would mean that unreflective action in the heat of conflict would be avoided; that in the midst of a crisis, cooler heads could prevail.

The division of war powers under the Constitution is clearly, as one scholar has phrased it, an "invitation to struggle," and throughout American history Congress and the president have done just that. The circumstances of the cold war and the ideology of the national security state tipped the balance much further in favor of the president than ever before in American history.

The Imperial Presidency and the Korean War

President Truman had to fight to pass aid to Greece and Turkey, the Marshall Plan, and the NATO treaty through Congress. But the national security ideology and the perceived emergency smoothed the way for congressional acquiescence to executive domination of the decision-making process in the Korean War.

The president's decision to send troops into the Korean conflict was made with only the barest consultation with Congress. So was the decision to try to conquer all of Korea after South Korea had been initially secured. At no point during the war did the Truman administration seek a congressional declaration of war.

The Truman administration argued that under emergency conditions, authority over the use of military forces lay with the president and not Congress. A *Department of State Bulletin* summarized the key elements of the theory of presidential prerogative:. "The President, as Commander in Chief of the Armed Forces of the United States, has full control over the use thereof." The State Department also asserted that there is a "traditional power of the President to use the armed forces of the United States without consulting Congress," and that this had often been done in "the broad interests of American foreign policy."[4]

Opposition to the development of the imperial presidency in Congress was irregular and ineffective. There was residual isolationist sentiment to keep the United States out of overseas conflicts. There were members who feared that simply acquiescing to unilateral executive decision-making was a bad precedent and a bad way of making policy. But few challenged the principle of containment of communism and few were ready to bear the political costs of opposing the president in a time of perceived national crisis. The most significant challenge to Truman's warmaking authority came not from those who questioned his unilateral commitment of U.S. forces but from those who advocated a wider war, such as the commander of U.S. forces in Korea, General Douglas MacArthur.

EISENHOWER AND THE NATIONAL SECURITY STATE

The Return of the Republicans

The Democratic Party of FDR and Truman had controlled the presidency throughout the tumultuous decade of the 1940s, in which the United States had shed its last isolationist illusions, fought in the world war, and taken an ever more activist role in shaping the postwar world. Throughout this period Republicans in Congress had largely ratified the broad policy direction of Democratic presidents, although they had also often questioned the effectiveness of Democratic administrations.

In 1952 the Republicans recaptured the White House for the first time in 20 years by heading their ticket with the popular hero of D-Day, Dwight Eisenhower. In 1952 they also won control of Congress, but the Democrats regained Congress in 1954 and held it throughout the rest of Eisenhower's term. Now the bipartisan foreign policy consensus faced a new challenge—that of a Republican president working with Democrats in Congress.

The Eisenhower administration also faced a difficult political task within its own party—holding together its liberal, eastern, internationalist wing and its more conservative midwestern and western wing. Twenty years out of power had led to bitter conflict over who was at fault for the party's decline. Yet it had also provided a powerful incentive for Republicans to pull together to make their new president a success.

Eisenhower had won the Republican nomination as the champion of the liberal, internationalist wing whose candidate had won in every Republican convention since 1940. But the conservative wing was strong in Congress, and Eisenhower needed its support to be successful. In order to understand the pressures Eisenhower faced within his party on issues of foreign policy, one must understand the changing world outlook of the Republican right.

Changes on the Republican Right: From Isolationism to Anticommunist Crusade

The Republican Party had gone through many changes in its period of exile from power, but perhaps the most dramatic was in the isolationist foreign policy positions of its conservative wing. In the period between the end of the second world war and the conclusion of the Korean War, the Republican right had undergone a remarkable conversion from isolationism to anticommunism.

During the world war and the Korean War it had been politically unpopular to question the purpose of fighting. After the world war it was politically difficult to question the policies that had made the United States the predominant power in the world. In the age of globe-spanning transportation and communication networks, it was hard to argue that the two oceans could buffer the United States against world events.

Rising new stars on the Republican right were better attuned to the politics of the day. General Douglas MacArthur was the hero of the victory over the Japanese and the commander of U.S. forces in Korea until he was removed by Truman for openly advocating a wider war. But MacArthur remained a hero to many, and his bold call for all-out war against communism expressed the frustrations many Americans felt with the inability of the United States to decisively defeat communism in Korea.

The wartime emergency also elevated Senator Joseph McCarthy of Wisconsin to national prominence. McCarthy built his career on exposing alleged communist subversives and sympathizers who held positions of power in the U.S. government. McCarthy shared with isolationists a visceral distaste for things foreign, things not American.

It was not a long ideological distance from America-first isolationism to anticommunist internationalism. America's European allies were, after all, white, Christian people. But communism as a philosophy was openly atheistic. The communist powers were Russia and China, whose populations could be used to evoke images of Asiatic hordes sweeping across the world stage. In an age when isolationism was no longer politically tenable, holy war against international communism became the doctrine of the Republican right.

The Eisenhower administration dealt cautiously with the Republican right. It never openly opposed McCarthy until his wilder charges had turned public opinion against his witch-hunts. It incorporated much of the rhetoric of holy war against communism in its foreign policy statements. Secretary of State John Foster Dulles was particularly noted for the messianic zeal with which he opposed world communism. The Eisenhower era was a period of expanding global commitments to contain communism, of an ever broader definition of what containment of the Soviets required. But Eisenhower's policy actions also showed caution in committing U.S. forces to shooting wars like Korea and Indochina.

Concluding the Korean War

The dominant foreign policy issue in the campaign of 1952 had been the stalemate in Korea. Frustration with the Korean situation had played a large part in the rejection of the Democratic Party and the return of the Republicans to power. Many voters hoped that the man who had led the successful D-Day invasion would have the expertise to solve the mess in Korea. On the eve of the election Eisenhower promised to go to Korea, highlighting his attention to this issue without making any commitments about what kind of policy he would pursue.

The new Eisenhower administration had the advantage of not having deep investments in the policies that had led to the stalemate. It could act to end the war without being held politically responsible for the fact that three years of war would end with essentially the restoration of the status quo ante.

Upon taking office, the Eisenhower administration considered escalating the war by attacking military targets in communist China and even using nuclear weapons. But there was little real domestic support for the greater casualties of a wider war, and the nuclear threat rang hollow, given the Soviet capability to retaliate in kind in Japan or elsewhere.

Instead, negotiations to end the war were intensified. In July 1953 a truce was signed that recognized the situation in the field. With slight modifications, the territories of North and South Korea remained largely what they had been before the war. That North Korea had been denied any territorial gain was the only consolation policymakers could claim for the heavy human costs of the war.

The Doctrine of Massive Retaliation

By the time President Eisenhower came into office in 1953, nuclear weapons were deeply embedded in U.S. military planning. The Eisenhower administration codified this military strategy in the doctrine of "massive retaliation." Massive retaliation meant that the United States, when faced with a Soviet threat to its interests, would threaten an all-out nuclear strike on the Soviet Union. It meant that the United States was willing to go to the brink of nuclear war to deter serious Soviet aggression.

The term "massive retaliation" captured in one phrase the essence of U.S. nuclear planning since Hiroshima. It also provided the justification for accelerated development of nuclear weaponry. On the eve of the 1952 election the United States exploded the first hydrogen bomb, a weapon a thousand times more powerful than the atomic bomb that had revolutionized warfare.

Under the doctrine of massive retaliation the United States developed new ways to deliver nuclear weapons. Added to the bombers that the Truman administration had to rely upon were ballistic missiles, a new method of getting weapons to their targets. Ballistic missiles could be launched from the ground or from submarines. Under Eisenhower the doctrine of a triad of nuclear delivery systems was developed—bombers were to be supplemented by ground and sea launched missiles.

The political success of the doctrine of massive retaliation was ironic in light of the failure of nuclear threats to significantly alter the division of Europe or the course of the Korean War. U.S. bluffs to use nuclear weapons over secondary issues had not made the Soviet Union compliant in the period when the United States had a nuclear monopoly. It was not clear why nuclear brinkmanship would be more successful now that the Soviets had their own nuclear arsenal.

The best case for the doctrine of deterrence was that it had prevented general war in Europe. It was widely believed that nuclear threats had deterred the Soviet Union from launching an all-out conventional attack on western Europe. If bluffs to use nuclear weapons over minor conflicts could be called, the Soviets had to take seriously such threats when vital U.S. interests were at stake. But there was little evidence that the Soviet Union either had such a grand design or were ever in a position to carry one out if they did.

The doctrine of massive retaliation was more a reflection of insecurities in the nuclear age. American fears of Soviet military power had intensified after the Soviet Union acquired the atomic and hydrogen bombs. America's self-image of righteous invincibility had been wounded by the stalemate in Korea. Massive retaliation expressed a kind of prenuclear thinking. If the Soviets now had the bomb, Americans needed to have more of them than they did.

Eisenhower, Congress, and the National Security State

Eisenhower, the former general, shared his predecessor Truman's estimation of the communist threat and an expansive notion of presidential war powers. But Eisenhower, a Republican president facing a Democratic Congress, developed a more consultative strategy for the use of military power. This can be seen in the expansion of treaty commitments and the use of prior congressional resolutions to legitimate possible presidential use of military power. On the other hand, Eisenhower also relied on covert operations by the CIA when the inevitable publicity of congressional consultation would be damaging to policy.

Treaty commitments and congressional resolutions had several purposes. First of all, in a crisis situation, they demonstrated national unity and resolve. They allowed the president to act quickly and decisively, using force if he deemed it necessary, knowing that Congress was on record as approving such action under specified circumstances. They also provided political cover for the executive if the intervention went wrong by putting Congress on record as approving the action.

The Truman administration had codified the U.S. alliance with Britain, France, and western Europe into the NATO treaty which was ratified by the Senate in 1949. The Eisenhower administration followed this precedent and expanded the range of noncommunist countries under the U.S. military umbrella. In 1954 the Southeast Asia Treaty Organization committed the United States (along with France and Britain) to the aid of South Vietnam, Laos, Cambodia, Thailand, the Philippines, Pakistan, Australia, and New Zealand. The Central Treaty Organization followed, covering Iran, Pakistan, and Turkey. Each of these treaties was ratified by a two-thirds vote in the Senate, thus placing Congress as well as the president behind the commitments.

The Eisenhower administration also drew Congress into a secondary, supporting role in decisions during military crises. When trouble flared in a foreign hot spot, the Eisenhower administration came to Congress requesting passage of a resolution that would empower the president to act however he saw fit to meet the crisis.

One example of this was the Suez crisis of 1956. Arab nationalism was running high, and pro-Western regimes in the Middle East were threatened by reaction to the heavy-handed actions of the British, French, and Israelis in seizing the Suez Canal. The resolution gave the president the authority to "employ the armed forces of the United States as he deems necessary to secure and protect the territorial integrity of any such nation or group of nations requesting such aid against overt armed aggression from any nation controlled by international communism."[5]

By votes of 355 to 61 in the House and 72 to 19 in the Senate, the resolution passed. In 1958 this authority was used to justify the sending of U.S. marines to bolster the pro-Western, minority Christian government of Lebanon against an Islamic rebellion. The mission was a success, and once again the prestige of the imperial president was bolstered.

Because of his political position Eisenhower had to involve Congress in many foreign policy actions. In other cases, however, he used the CIA and executive secrecy to carry out anticommunist operations. When popular uprisings unseated pro-Western governments in Guatemala in 1954 and Iran in 1955, the national security ideology prescribed counterinsurgency campaigns to restore Western influence. But Eisenhower wanted to avoid the international publicity that congressional consultation would inevitably bring. In these cases he successfully opted for covert action. When communists headed by Fidel Castro led a revolution against the corrupt but pro-Western Batista regime in Cuba, similar tactics were tried with less success. Castro remained in power as Eisenhower turned the reins of American government over to John Kennedy.

KENNEDY AND THE CUBAN MISSILE CRISIS

Kennedy, Counterinsurgency, and the Bay of Pigs

John Kennedy came to power promising to be a more vigorous cold warrior than his predecessor. Kennedy was concerned that the Eisenhower administration had relied too much on America's overwhelming superiority in nuclear weapons to counter the Soviet threat. In place of the Eisenhower doctrine of massive nuclear retaliation to Soviet aggression, Kennedy proposed that the United States develop greater conventional capability, that it be able to meet Soviet challenges with "flexible responses." One of the key elements in this flexible response strategy was greater counterinsurgency capability. Kennedy had been impressed with the CIA successes in Guatemala and Iran. One of his early initiatives was the formation of an elite military counterinsurgency unit that became known as the Green Berets.

Whereas counterinsurgency had been successful in some cases, Castro still held power in Cuba, heading the first pro-Soviet government in the western hemisphere. The Eisenhower administration had developed a plan to use Cuban exiles and U.S. forces to invade Cuba and overthrow Castro under the pretext of a popular Cuban counterrevolution. But it had not acted, leaving that decision to Kennedy.

The Kennedy administration approved the plan, and in the spring of 1961 the invasion was launched. When the Cuban exiles were quickly surrounded by Castro forces at the Bay of Pigs, Kennedy refused to turn the invasion into a massive U.S. operation. The Bay of Pigs was a colossal failure, neither undermining Castro nor covering up U.S. involvement.

The Cuban Missile Crisis

Cuba was the also the focus of the most important crisis of the Kennedy administration and probably of all the years since the first atomic explosion: the Cuban missile crisis. In 1962 the Soviet Union began installing nuclear missiles in Cuba. At the time the United States held a massive lead in nuclear weaponry. It was able to hit the Soviet Union with hundreds of atomic bombs and was thus assured of destroying the Soviet Union as a society. The Soviets were able to deliver only a few dozen nuclear weapons with assurance. This meant that they could kill tens of millions of Americans and wreak havoc, but they could not be sure of destroying the United States as a society or a military force.

In trying to catch up, the Soviet Union saw short-range missiles in Cuba as a definite advantage. Short-range missiles were cheaper and did not need to be as accurate. Placing missiles in Cuba also had the benefit of making clear the Soviet commitment to the survival of the Castro regime against any future U.S. campaigns like the Bay of Pigs.

The Soviets probably did not anticipate the virulence of the U.S. response to the Cuban missiles. The United States had placed similar missiles in Turkey and Italy, as part of a general strategy of encircling the Soviets with hostile bases.

But the Kennedy administration, reflecting the power of the national security ideology, did not see the Cuban missiles as the equivalent of U.S. missiles in Turkey. The Soviet Union was viewed as the evil aggressor, whereas U.S. missiles were thought of as merely part of the strategy of containment. Latin America was viewed as a U.S. protectorate, so Soviet power in this region was particularly distasteful. In addition, whatever realism there might have been in the administration about the motives for Soviet action, Kennedy knew the Democratic Party would suffer major electoral losses and most likely be chased from office if the missiles remained.

Recognizing the importance of devising careful but effective policies in the crisis, Kennedy set up a special committee within the executive branch, later referred to as ex-comm, to formulate the U.S. response. He knew that if policy-making were left to normal bureaucratic and congressional channels, the options developed would be predictable and unimaginative, reflecting the limited perspectives and historical stances of each agency. The missile crisis was too dangerous and unprecedented for policy to be the product of the special interests and old ideas of the bureaucratic apparatus.

Most members of the ex-comm originally favored air strikes to destroy the missiles and/or an invasion of Cuba to remove the missiles and restore a pro-Western regime. Kennedy resisted this advice, hoping to find a policy that would not lead to direct military conflict with Soviet forces. Kennedy was uncompromising on the basic issue of missiles in Cuba, but he hoped to avoid general war. Eventually a plan was worked out to show force and resolve without initiating conflict. The United States would blockade Soviet shipments to Cuba, hoping to keep the missile base from being completed and signaling American determination without immediately striking a military blow.

Kennedy also sought to give the Soviets a way out of the crisis that allowed them to save face, so they would not be perceived as simply backing down. While he was publicly refusing to make concessions under the gun, privately negotiations were vigorously pursued. In return for Soviet agreement to withdraw the missiles, Kennedy publicly pledged that the United States would never again invade or de-stabilize the Castro regime. While publicly denying it, Kennedy also agreed to withdraw U.S. missiles from Turkey.

The Cuban crisis was the closest the superpowers ever came to direct conflict between their own military forces. While the United States and the Soviet Union engaged in proxy wars around the globe, neither was willing to contemplate the effects of directly attacking the forces of the other. In the Cuban crisis, the United States and the Soviet Union at first appeared willing to risk nuclear annihilation to pursue some small military and political advantage. But in the end both powers showed enough sense to extricate themselves from the crisis.

In the United States the reflexive anticommunism of the national security ideology almost blinded policy-makers to ways out of the confrontation. But even as they exercised military power, key members of the administration were also determined to show the flexibility of a great power and to seek a nonmilitary solution to the crisis. After facing the realities of nuclear holocaust, the Kennedy administration was more determined than ever to seek to lessen tensions between the United States and the Soviet Union. It was no coincidence that the first major arms control treaty between the two powers, the test ban treaty, was signed less than a year after the Cuban missile confrontation.

HEGEMONIC FLEXIBILITY AND VISIONS OF WORLD ORDER

In the postwar era, the national security ideology based on confrontation with communism was politically victorious. It defeated challenges by Progressives on the left and isolationists and advocates of all-out war with communism on the right. But the national security philosophy does not capture the full range of presidential thinking and rhetoric about postwar America's role in the world. The militaristic national security ideology was sometimes tempered by the flexibility of a hegemonic power and visions of a more orderly, peaceful world.

During the modern era, the international system has often been dominated by a single hegemonic power. This plays a key role in ordering the world system. Since the hegemon benefits more than any lesser power from the status quo, it tends to act not only in its own narrow national interests but also to preserve the overall system.

In the nineteenth century the British were such a hegemonic power. The Industrial Revolution catapulted Britain ahead of other world powers and allowed it to conquer an empire on which "the sun never set." The British came to see the preservation of the global status quo as key to the maintenance of their predominant position in world affairs. They developed the theories of balance of power and free trade that equated the interests of the world capitalist system with those of the British Empire.

In the twentieth century, however, the costs of two world wars ended British hegemony. In the postwar world the United States stepped into the role the British had previously played. Now that the United States was the predominant military and economic power, it began to take on the task of organizing the world capitalist system.

U.S. policy-makers were now committed to preserving the status quo, making stability in the world system an overarching national goal. NATO, other military alliances, and even the early United Nations were attempts to maintain stability through organizing the major nonsocialist powers into a cohesive bloc. On the economic level, the dollar became the key currency of international trade. The United States pressed hard to integrate the economies and political systems of its allies in western Europe and to open the less-developed world to Western economies.

The American view of the responsibilities of world leadership sometimes led policy-makers to act in ways that favored the development and maintenance of the world system over a more narrow view of U.S. interests. The United States encouraged the recovery of Germany and Japan and the integration of western Europe even though this meant aiding potential rivals. The United States bore the costs of global military commitments that probably could not be justified on a narrow cost-benefit calculation of immediate national gain. The United States articulated a theory of free trade even though this sometimes meant penetration of U.S. markets by foreign competitors. These are some instances of what can be called hegemonic flexibility, of putting international stability over narrow U.S. interests.

The position of hegemonic flexibility also led in somewhat different directions than the national security ideology in steering the U.S. approach to the Soviet Union. A hegemon wants to maintain its position and is willing to use military force to do so. It did not become the hegemon by being pacifistic. But a hegemon also recognizes that it has the most to lose from general war, and this is, of course, even more true in the nuclear age. A hegemon recognizes it has many tools to influence the behavior of its rivals, military force being only one.

Policy-makers who were confident about America's hegemonic position tended to take a less confrontational approach to the Soviet Union. They emphasized the carrot as well as the stick in dealing with the communist world. A hegemon is aware of its predominant power position and thus is willing to make limited concessions to rivals, as long as these concessions do not threaten its predominance. A hegemon recognizes situations when it is less costly and even preferable to co-opt rather than to decisively defeat major rivals. Every president at one time or another tried to overcome the massive differences between the American and Soviet political systems and national interests and to realize their shared stake as world powers in the nuclear age.

Postwar Presidents on World Peace

Eisenhower at Geneva

The problems that concern us are not inherently insoluble. . . . They seem insoluble under conditions of fear, distrust, and even hostility, where every move is weighed in terms of whether it will help or weaken a potential enemy. If those conditions can be changed, then much can be changed. . . . We know that a mutually dependable system for less armament on the part of all nations would be a better way to safeguard peace and to maintain our security.

Kennedy on World Peace

Some say that it is useless to speak of world peace or world law or world disarmament—and that it will be useless until the leaders of the Soviet Union adopt a more enlightened attitude. I hope they do. I believe we can help them do it. But I also believe we must re-examine our own attitude—as individuals and as a nation—for our attitude is as essential as theirs.

Too many of us think [peace] is impossible. . . . But that is a dangerous, defeatist belief. It leads to the conclusion that war is inevitable—that mankind is doomed—that we are gripped by forces we cannot control.

Let us re-examine our attitude toward the Soviet Union. Both the United States and its allies, and the Soviet Union and its allies, have a mutually deep interest in a just and genuine peace and in halting the arms race. . . . For in the final analysis, our most common link is that we all inhabit the same planet. We all breathe the same air. We all cherish our children's future. And we all are mortal.[6]

Every postwar president made dramatic proposals to reduce cold war tensions. Every U.S. president of the postwar era met with Soviet leaders at summits. Truman proposed sharing atomic technology and eventual atomic disarmament. Eisenhower proposed the "open skies" plan to deal with the problem of verifying compliance with nuclear and other military accords. Kennedy signed the limited nuclear test ban treaty.

None of these plans changed the fundamental nature of the cold war or the commitment of these presidents to the national security ideology. But they did show that even as the national security ideology held sway, other ideas about how the United States should approach the world were circulating. All presidents had to contemplate the limits of U.S. power and the realities of what a new world war would mean. The American people were restless at the ever-growing commitments to foreign trouble spots and the growing specter of nuclear annihilation.

Of all the postwar presidents, perhaps John Kennedy expressed American hopes for world peace most eloquently. Kennedy had run for president as a more militant cold warrior than his predecessor. He had taken the country to the brink of nuclear holocaust over Soviet missiles in Cuba. But the Cuba confrontation had demonstrated the danger of endless confrontation in a nuclear age. Kennedy's remarks around the time of the test ban treaty show a willingness to reexamine the premises of the cold war and the national security ideology.

THE VIETNAM WAR AND THE NATIONAL SECURITY IDEOLOGY

The period of good feeling between the superpowers that the test ban treaty engendered was short-lived. Even as they were signing the test ban, the United States and the Soviet Union were deepening their commitments to their respective allies in Vietnam.

Vietnam had been part of the French colony of Indochina. During the second world war it had fallen to the Japanese. After the war the French tried to regain control aided by the United States. The anticolonial forces, led by Ho Chi Minh and the Communist Party, were able to prevent the French from succeeding. In 1954 the Geneva accords divided French Indochina into four territories: Laos, Cambodia, North Vietnam, and South Vietnam. North Vietnam was under the control of the communists. South Vietnam was put under control of pro-Western forces.

The division of Vietnam was never intended as a final political outcome but as a means for separating hostile forces and preparing for national reunification. Elections to reunify Vietnam were promised but never held because the South Vietnamese and their Western backers knew that the communist hero of decolonization, Ho Chi Minh, would have won. Stymied by the failure of the Geneva accords, communist forces in South Vietnam, aided by the North, began a guerrilla campaign to overthrow the pro-Western regime.

The Truman and Eisenhower administrations had backed the French attempt to regain control of Indochina. The Eisenhower administration had considered sending U.S. troops when the French withdrew in 1954. However, with the memories of Korea still fresh, the United States chose not to intervene directly. But the United States refused to sign the Geneva accords. The Eisenhower administration sent aid to the South Vietnamese regime and backed its refusal to implement the Geneva agreement. When Kennedy came to power, he saw Vietnam as a case amenable to his doctrine of flexible response to communist expansion. Here was a conflict where new tactics of counterinsurgency could be tested. The Green Berets, the new elite counterinsurgency forces Kennedy had created, were sent to advise and train South Vietnamese forces. Slowly the numbers and the role of U.S. forces expanded. Advisers began going out on combat missions. When, not surprisingly, they came under attack, they were given permission to carry weapons and return fire. By the time of Kennedy's death, 15,000 American troops were conducting regular combat missions.

But the major escalations of the Vietnam War came under Lyndon Johnson. In the 1964 campaign Johnson ran as the peace candidate, while his opponent Barry Goldwater called for stronger U.S. military action. However, even as he talked peace, Johnson was preparing for a wider war. In the summer of 1964, he used a minor clash between U.S. and North Vietnamese ships in the Gulf of Tonkin to build support for escalation of the war. Portraying this incident as a major act of aggression by the North Vietnamese, Johnson requested from Congress the authority to use whatever means he deemed necessary to protect the U.S. forces in Vietnam.

The Gulf of Tonkin Resolution passed the House unanimously and drew only two dissenting votes in the Senate. Not until the 1970s was it revealed that Johnson had lied about key details of the Gulf of Tonkin incident. At the time he treated the Gulf of Tonkin Resolution as only a precautionary measure. But when in 1965 Johnson decided to commit major U.S. combat forces to the conflict, he used this resolution as a virtual declaration of war giving him authority to escalate the war as he saw fit. From 1965, U.S. forces in Vietnam rose rapidly, reaching over 500,000 at their peak.

The justifications Johnson used for U.S. involvement in the war bore a remarkable similarity to those used by Truman to explain American commitment in Korea. Both presidents were driven by the national security ideology. Each characterized the communists as the aggressors and pro-Western regimes as innocent victims. Both men saw a larger international communist design of world conquest behind the conflict. In both cases the president claimed U.S. national security was at stake, that the loss of this war would bring on a wider conflict. Of course, the outcomes of the Korean and Vietnam wars were different. The tragedy of Korea was that so much blood was spilled and so many people suffered only to maintain the status quo ante. Still, the tragedy of Vietnam was even greater for Americans. So many lives were lost and so many sacrificed so much, only for the United States to suffer a humiliating defeat.

Lyndon Johnson on the Vietnam War

International Communist Aggression

North Viet Nam has attacked the independent nation of South Viet Nam. Its object is total conquest. . . . Over this war—and all Asia—is . . . the deepening shadow of Communist China. . . . It is a nation which is helping the forces of violence in almost every continent. The contest in Viet Nam is part of a wider pattern of aggressive purposes.

Global Containment

We fight because we must fight if we are to live in a world where every country can shape its own destiny, and only in such a world will our own freedom be finally secure. . . . Around the globe, from Berlin to Thailand, are people whose well being rests in part on the belief that they can count on us if they are attacked. To leave Viet Nam to its fate would shake the confidence of all these people in the value of an American commitment and in the value of America's word. . . . Let no one think that retreat from Viet Nam would bring an end to conflict. The battle would be renewed in one country and then another. The central lesson of our time is that the appetite of aggression is never satisfied. To withdraw from one battlefield means only to prepare for the next.[7]

CONCLUSION

In the middle third of the twentieth century internationalism triumphed over isolationism as the basis of U.S. foreign policy. In the wake of the second world war the United States emerged as the strongest military, economic, and political power in the world. But the United States did not feel secure in its newly won status. The Soviet Union arose as a major rival to U.S. power. In addition, the appearance of nuclear weapons had changed great power politics forever. The response of U.S. policy-makers to these new conditions was the development of the doctrines of the national security state. The United States embarked on a global mission to contain communism with the Soviet Union. Central to this strategy was the accumulation of massive stockpiles of nuclear weaponry. The United States conducted a cold war against the Soviet Union, counterinsurgency in the Third World, and conventional wars in Korea and Vietnam. However, the failure of the national security ideology in Vietnam led to new questions about the ideological foundations of U.S. foreign policy.

NOTES

1. Harry Truman, *Public Papers of the Presidents, 1947* (Washington, DC: U.S. Government Printing Office, 1948), pp. 176-180.

2. Donald B. Johnson and Kirk H. Porter, eds., *National Party Platforms* (Urbana: University of Illinois Press, 1972).

3. Harry Truman, *Public Papers of the Presidents, 1951* (Washington, DC: U.S. Government Printing Office, 1952), pp. 223-227.

4. Arthur M. Schlesinger, *The Imperial Presidency* (Boston: Houghton Mifflin, 1973), p. 133, Taken from *Department of State Bulletin*, July 31, 1950.

5. *Congressional Quarterly Almanac, 1957* (Washington, DC: Congressional Quarterly, 1958), p. 57.

6. Dwight Eisenhower, *Public Papers of the Presidents, 1955* (Washington, DC: U.S. Government Printing Office, 1956), p. 708; and John Kennedy, *Public Papers of the Presidents, 1963* (Washington, DC: U.S. Government Printing Office, 1964), pp. 459-464.

7. Lyndon Johnson in Janet Podell and Steven Anzovin, eds., *Speeches of the American Presidents* (New York: H.W. Wilson, 1988), pp. 642-645.

8

THE DECLINE OF U.S. POWER AND THE CRISIS OF THE NATIONAL SECURITY STATE

THE FAILURES OF THE NATIONAL SECURITY STATE

The preceding two chapters recounted the ideologies by which presidents up through Lyndon Johnson justified their policy behavior. They examined the public statements of many presidents, emphasizing the role of ideology in shaping the actions of administrations.

But as was noted in the Chapter 1, ideology serves another purpose: to obscure uncomfortable realities about the political system and the policies that administrations pursue. Chapters 8 and 9 take a more critical view of presidential ideologies. They recount how presidential ideologies failed to deal effectively with the real policy problems the nation faced and thus bear much of the responsibility for the policy failures that culminated in the political crises of the 1970s.

The United States had emerged from World War II as the dominant world power. While every other major power had been ravaged by the war, the continental United States had been untouched. In the immediate aftermath of the war, the United States was the overarching economic power, producing nearly half of the world's total goods and services. It was able to construct a series of political, economic, and military alliances that tied most of the former great powers together against its only rival, the Soviet Union. This unique postwar situation could not last forever, and in the 1960s and 1970s the "American Century" began to unravel.

The Vietnam War

The most obvious sign of the end of the postwar Pax Americana was the American humiliation in Vietnam. The myth of the invincibility of U.S. military might was forever laid to rest by a small, underdeveloped, minor power. Unlike other U.S. wars in the twentieth century, the loss of lives and the heavy material costs of the war did not lead to the achievement of any political objectives. Instead, after the death of 58,000 Americans and the suffering of over 200,000 wounded, and millions of Vietnamese killed and the tens of millions injured or uprooted, in 1975 the United States was forced to withdraw in defeat.

The Arms Race

The growth of the military power of the Soviet Union was another factor in the relative decline of U.S. power. At the end of the World War II, the United States was the only great power unscathed; the Soviet Union, in particular, had been decimated by the Nazi invasion. In the immediate aftermath of the war, the United States enjoyed a monopoly on nuclear weapons. But in the 1950s the Soviets developed the capacity to devastate the United States with nuclear weapons. By the 1970s the Soviets had attained rough parity in nuclear forces and Americans had to live in the shadow of MAD, mutual assured destruction.

The decision to go to war had always been one that had determined the fate of nations. But now war meant risking not only national power but also national suicide, and perhaps the end of the human race itself. Yet as Einstein had said about the explosion of the first nuclear weapon, "Everything has changed except the way we think and thus we drift toward unparalleled catastrophe." Military realities had changed, but political institutions were slow to catch up. In the postwar world, the cold war rivals acted much like the great powers of Europe before the world wars. The national security state was modeled on the failed empires of the past rather than on the realities of the nuclear age.

New International Economic Realities

U.S. economic power was also under challenge in the 1970s. The European and Japanese economies had recovered from the destruction of the war and were reemerging as major competitors with the United States for world markets and even in the American domestic market. In the immediate postwar period the U.S. economy represented nearly half of the world's total economic production. By the 1970s this figure had shrunk to less than 25 percent.[1] In the postwar period the U.S. dollar became the international currency. By 1971 the dollar was devalued and taken off the gold standard. But the worst had yet to come. In the wake of the 1973 Arab-Israeli war, the Arab oil embargo dealt a crippling blow to the Western economies. The emergence of OPEC as the dominant force in oil markets brought a steep increase in oil prices that triggered the two deepest recessions in the United States since the Great Depression.

POLARIZATION ON FOREIGN POLICY AND THE BREAKDOWN OF THE BIPARTISAN CONSENSUS

From the late 1940s through the 1960s the national security ideology dominated thinking in both major parties. In the immediate postwar period there were those within the Truman administration and Congress who counseled continued cooperation with the Soviet Union or a return to isolationism. But by the election of 1948 the national security ideology was triumphant in both major parties. While the national security ideology held sway, the greatest conflict in policy-making was generally on how tough to act toward the Soviets. There were always elements, usually in Congress or the military, who advocated all-out holy war against the communists, who criticized the incumbent administration for not being tough enough. Since anticommunism was the defining feature of U.S. foreign policy, those who were not responsible for the consequences could always advocate tougher measures against the Soviets. The incumbent president, who would be held responsible for the outcome of policy, had to weigh the potential Soviet reaction and thus could rarely match the most militant fire eaters. Tough or tougher—this was the dominant issue in the era of the foreign policy consensus.

But Vietnam and other crises broke down the bipartisan consensus on the national security ideology. In the 1970s many policymakers began to question the assumptions that had driven U.S. foreign policy for a quarter of a century. A real debate about the goals and methods of foreign policy emerged. Different concepts about America's role in the world and relations with the Soviet Union and the Third World began to gain credence, and the range of options which policymakers considered legitimate was expanded. A new set of ideas and assumptions about foreign policy emerged that I have labeled the theory of hegemonic flexibility. These themes had always been present to some degree in foreign policy-making. But under the impact of the defeat in Vietnam, American vulnerability to nuclear annihilation, and the decline of U.S. economic power, they took on new influence over policymakers. The assumptions of the national security ideology were under attack, and the theory of hegemonic flexibility was the ideology of centrist political opposition.

Richard Nixon had to preside over the U.S. defeat in Vietnam. Under intense pressure from a growing antiwar movement and its liberal Democratic supporters in Congress, he was also the first president to articulate a comprehensive theory of hegemonic flexibility. After Nixon left office, foreign policy differences began to take on an even greater partisan dimension. The Democratic Party became the home of the philosophy of hegemonic flexibility, while the Republican Party tended to return to the positions of the national security ideology.

The rising anti-Vietnam War movement had penetrated much more deeply into the Democratic party. In 1968 peace candidates Minnesota Senator Eugene McCarthy and Robert Kennedy got the vast majority of votes in the Democratic primaries. In 1972 the peace movement's candidate, Senator George McGovern of South Dakota, won the Democratic nomination.

The congressional Democratic Party was changing as well. Congressional Democrats became the center of opposition to the war. Each year liberal Democrats introduced bills to cut off funding for the war or restrict the power of the president to conduct the war as he saw fit. Even as Nixon gave ground on the substantive question of the Vietnam War and the larger questions of foreign policy philosophy, he was adamant in asserting his prerogative as president to set the course of foreign policy.

The conflict between congressional Democrats and the Nixon White House over foreign policy intensified over the years. The culmination of this struggle was the War Powers Act of 1973, which for the first time since World War II tried to put some meaningful congressional restrictions on presidential war-making. The War Powers Act had some Republican support but was largely the child of the Democratic Congress.

But the Democrats were not alone in turning foreign policy into a partisan political issue. Ronald Reagan nearly won the 1976 Republican presidential nomination away from incumbent Gerald Ford in large part through his attacks against Nixon-Ford policies in Vietnam and on arms control. The Reagan candidacy was the focal point of the counterattack of the supporters of the national security ideology. In 1980 Reagan made a major issue not just of the policy failures of the Carter administration but also of Carter's basic foreign policy philosophy.

Figure 8.1 represents the breakdown of the bipartisan foreign policy consensus schematically. From the end of World War II through the 1960s, the national security ideology held sway. In the 1970s, the doctrine of hegemonic flexibility emerged from the nether zones to become part of the political center.

Figure 8.1
The Breakdown of the Bipartisan Foreign Policy Consensus

WORLD ORDER	HEGEMONIC FLEXIBILITY	NATIONAL SECURITY	HOLY WAR
		[1946-1968 Bipartisan Consensus]	

[1972 to 1980 Political Center]

RICHARD NIXON AND THE STRATEGY OF HEGEMONIC FLEXIBILITY

Vietnamization

The most politically painful failure of the national security state was the Vietnam War. It was the dominant issue in the first term of Richard Nixon.

Nixon came to power as an unreconstructed cold warrior. He had made his early political reputation by hunting for domestic subversives. As vicepresident he had confronted Nikita Khrushchev in the famous "kitchen debate." He had campaigned as a hard-line anticommunist in both 1960 and 1968. He made the failure of the Johnson administration to bring the Vietnam War to a successful conclusion a major part of his 1968 campaign. He claimed he had a secret plan to end the war.

Now in power, Nixon recognized that he had to extricate the United States from the quagmire Vietnam had become. Throughout his first term Nixon looked for a way to strike a decisive military blow without increasing the domestic costs of the war or drawing the Chinese or Soviets into the conflict. He escalated the air war, increasing the frequency of bombing missions and widening the range of targets hit. In the spring of 1970 he invaded Cambodia to strike at communist forces taking sanctuary in officially neutral territory. In 1972 he mined the major Vietnamese harbors of Hanoi and Haiphong.

But the escalated bombing did not significantly alter the situation on the ground. The invasion of Cambodia failed to find the supposed central command post coordinating the war in South Vietnam, much less alter the course of the ground war. Sustained efforts to close North Vietnamese ports ran the constant risk of killing Soviet sailors and provoking a major Soviet response.

There simply was no way the United States could win the war when its South Vietnamese clients had so little political support in the countryside. Certainly there was no way the military tide could be turned without massively increasing U.S. casualties and risking inducing Chinese or Russian counterescalation.

The essence of Nixon's strategy was his Vietnamization plan. Vietnamization was a return to the position LBJ had taken before the commitment of U.S. ground forces. In the midst of the 1964 campaign Johnson had said that American boys should not be sent to do the job that should be done by Asian boys. Vietnamization proposed to turn the primary responsibility for the war back to the South Vietnamese.

Vietnamization had several appeals. Most important, it would reduce rising American casualties. It squarely faced the basic political reality of the war: that the United States could not impose a government on a people who would not accept it. It smoothed the way for an eventual U.S. withdrawal, reducing the exposure of U.S. forces to potentially heavy casualties in a final communist offensive.

The Nixon Doctrine as Hegemonic Flexibility

Vietnamization was only the most visible aspect of a more fundamental shift in U.S. foreign policy under Nixon. John Kennedy had said in his inaugural address that Americans would pay any price, bear any burden to defend liberty around the world. Vietnam proved this was not so. Nixon had to show the flexibility of a world power facing the fact that it had made commitments it could not keep. To justify retrenchment of the U.S. position in the world, the administration developed the Nixon Doctrine. Nixon did more than simply articulate a new doctrine. In the election year of 1972 he made bold pilgrimages to Beijing and Moscow to negotiate new relationships with the communist world and to try to minimize the international and domestic impact of final disengagement from Vietnam.

The Nixon Doctrine

Peace must be far more than the absence of war. Peace must provide a durable structure of international relationships which inhibits or removes the causes of war.

Peace requires partnership. Its obligations, like its benefits, must be shared. . . . To insist that other nations play a role is not a retreat from responsibility, it is a sharing of responsibility.

Our commitment to peace [must] be convincingly demonstrated in our willingness to negotiate our points of difference in a fair and businesslike manner with the Communist countries. We are under no illusions. . . . But any nation today must define its interests with special concern for the interests of others. If some nations define their security in a manner that means insecurity for other nations, then peace is threatened and the security of all diminished. This obligation is particularly great for the nuclear superpowers on whose decisions the survival of mankind may well depend.[2]

The Opening to China

The opening to China was the biggest shock. Since the communist victory in 1949 in the civil war with the U.S.-backed forces of Chiang Kai-shek, the United States had refused to recognize the communist government of China as legitimate. Instead, the United States preferred the legal fiction of recognizing the Chiang Kai-shek forces, which had been exiled to the offshore island of Formosa (Taiwan) as the government of all of China. Within two years of the communists taking power in China, the United States was at war with them in Korea. As other Western nations slowly adjusted to reality in the years following the Korean War, the United States maintained its hard line. It repeatedly used its veto power at the United Nations to keep the communists from taking China's seat on the Security Council. Probably the American politician most associated with this hard-line position was Richard Nixon. As Eisenhower's vicepresident and as a presidential candidate in 1960 and 1968, Nixon had repeatedly reiterated his rejection of any accommodation with the Chinese communists.

But the deteriorating position of U.S. forces in Vietnam had a salutary effect on the Nixon administration. In order to divert attention from the withdrawal from Vietnam, and in hopes of stabilizing the southeastern Pacific so that U.S. losses were confined to Indochina, Nixon traveled to Beijing and treated with his former nemesis.

Arms Control and the Soviet Union

However, China was neither the most powerful communist nation nor the most important military backer of the North Vietnamese. The Soviet Union was the communist country holding the high cards in the international power game. It was the power with the nuclear arsenal that could annihilate the United States. It was the military giant that could project forces into Europe, east Asia, the Middle East, and even Africa and Latin America. If there was to be a structure of world peace, it would have to begin with relations between the superpowers.

Even before its commitment of ground troops to Vietnam, the United States had been seeking agreements with the Soviet Union to control the nuclear arms race and stabilize regional conflicts. Eisenhower had met with the Soviets in Geneva. Kennedy had signed the nuclear test ban treaty. Johnson had carried on nuclear arms control talks even as he escalated the Vietnam War. But again, it was the staunch anticommunist Nixon who made the most dramatic moves, finalizing negotiations on nuclear arms limits and then flying to Moscow to sign the historic agreement.

The Strategic Arms Limitation Treaty (SALT) was truly a momentous treaty. The United States had developed the first atomic bomb during World War II. In the 1950s it enjoyed a huge advantage in nuclear capacity. At the time of the Cuban missile crisis in 1962, the United States could deliver more than 1,000 nuclear weapons against the Soviet Union. The Soviet capacity was closer to 100, enough to wreak devastation on the United States, but still a militarily meaningful disadvantage. However, in the 1960s Soviet nuclear capacity began to catch up with that of the United States. By 1972 both superpowers had thousands of missiles and were rapidly proceeding to arm them with multiple warheads. Each side had attained the ability to wreak assured destruction on the other even after absorbing a surprise first strike. This situation is called nuclear parity or essential equivalence.

The provisions of the SALT treaty recognized this nuclear parity. Each side agreed to limit its nuclear missile launchers to the numbers it had at the time of the treaty signing, roughly 2,500 launchers each. If either power wanted to deploy new systems beyond the treaty numbers, it had to destroy existing systems to keep within the totals. Just as important were the agreements on strategic defenses. Under the theory of mutual assured destruction (MAD), the U.S. and Soviet Union agreed to limit antimissile systems to two sites per country. This meant that each side could be assured its missiles could reach their targets, making further buildups militarily unnecessary.

SALT went into effect once it was ratified by the Senate in September 1972. It established the crucial precedent that the United States and the Soviet Union could reach and abide by arms control agreements. But there were also massive loopholes in the treaty. Although the number of missile launchers was limited, the number of warheads put on each missile was not. Therefore, each side could continue to increase the number of deliverable weapons by putting multiple warheads on each missile. This is exactly what each side did in the 1970s. SALT I negotiators also could not agree on more difficult issues like bombers and short-range and medium-range missile systems, so their development was totally unimpeded. SALT I was an important precedent, but it was only a marginal restraint on the arms race.

The War Powers Act, the Imperial Presidency, and the National Security State

While the Nixon Doctrine called for a more peaceful, orderly world, it was not a general retreat into isolationism. On the face of it, Nixon appeared to be searching for a new foreign policy that would fundamentally change the U.S. role in the world. But in many ways the Nixon Doctrine can be seen as an attempt to lower the costs of achieving traditional goals.

The doctrine of hegemonic flexibility as it emerged in the 1970s was, after all, a strategy to maintain U.S. hegemony even as the world was changing. Only now the United States would be calling on its resurgent European and Asian allies to pick up more of the costs and take more of the risks of maintaining the global system. The rich western Europeans and Japanese would be pressured to provide a higher proportion of the forces and the financing of Western military operations. Nixon's vision of regional Third World powers like the Shah of Iran or Ferdinand Marcos of the Philippines was that they would act as their own forces of counterinsurgency in their region of the world. The United States would provide financing, hardware, and training, but would be spared the need to shed American blood to achieve its goal of containing socialist and other radical Third World forces.

One thing the Nixon Doctrine did not envision was a decrease in the power of the imperial president over the national security and warmaking machinery.

The Nixon Doctrine was a grand policy strategy devised by a White House that saw itself in the tradition of the great imperial powers of nineteenth century Europe.

Nixon's foreign policy guru, Henry Kissinger, consciously patterned himself after Prince Metternich, who helped engineer the "concert of Europe" by which the European empires tried to keep their competition confined to the colonial periphery and away from the vitals of their homelands. Like the diplomats in Metternich's world, Kissinger valued secrecy and deception as great assets in the foreign policy chessgame. Nixon and Kissinger did not like either members of Congress or the general public meddling in their calculated maneuvering.

Failure in Vietnam intensified executive and congressional battles over war powers. Nixon eventually yielded to domestic pressure on the substance of Vietnam War policy, but he fought bitterly to maintain executive control over foreign policy decision making. The siege mentality in the White House that led to Watergate was conceived largely in the divisive struggles with Congress over escalation and deescalation of the war. The cold war faith in both the efficacy and the righteousness of covert action abroad eventually spilled over into the democratic process at home.

One of the tactics that congressional opponents of the war adopted was trying to use congressional power over government spending to end or limit the conflict in southeast Asia. Opponents of the war introduced bills forbidding the spending of funds for all or selected operations in southeast Asia. At first such fund cutoff bills got few votes, but as the war dragged on, the percentage of House and Senate supporters grew until it began to approach a majority. While the one funding cutoff bill that actually became law passed only after the Nixon had committed to withdrawing all U.S. fighting forces, the growing possibility that such legislation would pass placed strong pressure on the administration to bring the war to a conclusion.

A broader strategy adopted by congressional opponents of presidential warmaking was war powers legislation. The War Powers Act of 1973 was designed to rectify the changes in the balance between congressional and presidential war powers wrought by the cold war. On a policy level, it was designed to make it more difficult for the president to unilaterally commit U.S. forces to a combat situation. Thus the War Powers Act had the effect of undermining not only the imperial presidency but also the ability of the national security state to conduct counterinsurgency campaigns.

The War Powers Act was based on Congress' constitutional powers to declare war and control the funding of military operations. It requires the president to have explicit congressional endorsement when committing U.S. forces to combat. The War Powers Act tacitly recognizes the president's power to act decisively in a crisis by allowing the him the latitude to conduct military operations without prior congressional consent. But whenever the president commits U.S. forces to a combat situation, he must get a congressional resolution approving the decision. If Congress does not approve within 90 days, the troops must be withdrawn.

President Nixon bitterly fought any congressional restrictions on the president's control over foreign policy. When the War Powers Act passed Congress after years of debate, Nixon vetoed it. But even many Republicans supported some new restrictions on presidential warmaking, and his veto was overridden by a two-thirds vote in the House and Senate, and the War Powers Act became law.

The impact of the War Powers Act on foreign policy-making has been more symbolic than real. As the conflict in the Persian Gulf showed, it is very difficult for Congress to openly oppose decisive presidential action in a real crisis situation when American lives are at stake and the president is commanding the airwaves to call the American people to bold action. In actual practice congressional control over the funding of government operations has proven to be a more effective tool in limiting presidential warmaking, as the Reagan administration learned in its battles with Congress over funding the Nicaraguan contras in the 1980s. But the War Powers Act was an expression of growing public skepticism over unlimited presidential authority to commit U.S. forces to combat, and as such it captured the shifting politics of U.S. foreign policy in the 1970s.

Of course, the war powers conflict was only one of Nixon's troubles in his later years in office. While the Watergate scandals that eventually led to his downfall were driven primarily by the administration's political misdeeds, one of the original articles of impeachment considered by the House Judiciary Committee concerned Nixon's secret war in Cambodia and the concealing of this war from Congress. The siege mentality in the Nixon White House and the ever more bitter relationship with Congress were also effects of the polarization of the country over the Vietnam War.

Ford, Kissinger, and the Nixon Doctrine

Henry Kissinger had been a key architect of the Nixon Doctrine. During Nixon's first term, Kissinger, as national security adviser, had handled the secret negotiations leading to the China and Moscow trips. In the second term Kissinger was rewarded with the post of secretary of state. When Nixon resigned in 1974, the new president, Gerald Ford, retained Kissinger as his leading foreign policy adviser. Ford and Kissinger carried forward the policies of the Nixon years.

Ford and Kissinger continued the arms control process. In 1974 Ford traveled to Vladivostok, on the Pacific coast of the Soviet Union, to sign another set of arms agreements. The Vladivostok accords clarified some of the issues left unresolved in the SALT treaty. Both sides were limited to 2,400 missile launchers. For the first time the number of launchers that could carry multiple warheads was limited, to 1,300 per side.

JIMMY CARTER AND THE POLITICAL FAILURE OF HEGEMONIC FLEXIBILITY

The Inordinate Fear of Communism and New Global Realities

In the early years of his administration, Jimmy Carter pursued the path of hegemonic flexibility. In 1977, at Notre Dame, Carter made his first major foreign policy speech since becoming president. He openly rejected many of the premises of the national security ideology. He argued that America's inordinate fear of communism had undermined its ability to conduct a just and successful foreign policy. He championed human rights and self-determination in U.S. policy toward the emerging nations of the Third World.

> Being confident of our own future, we are now free of that inordinate fear of communism that once led us to embrace any dictator who joined us in that fear. . . For too many years, we've been willing to adopt the flawed and erroneous principles and tactics of our adversaries, sometimes abandoning our own values for theirs. We've fought fire with fire, never thinking that fire is better quenched with water. This approach failed, with Vietnam the best example of its intellectual and moral poverty.[3]

The Panama Canal and Latin America

Carter's new policies were best exemplified by the Panama Canal treaties and his human rights campaign. In the United States the Panama Canal was generally touted as a triumph of American vision and technology. In much of Central America, U.S. sovereignty over the Canal Zone served as a symbol of U.S. arrogance and imperialism, and a reminder of U.S. willingness to use its military superiority to impose its will on the region.

Tension had been growing between the United States and Panama over issues of sovereignty for many years. There had been periodic anti-American demonstrations and even riots by Panamanians seeking to regain control over the Canal Zone. Previous administrations had sought better relations, but none had been willing to face the domestic fallout of lessening U.S. control over the Canal Zone. However, as part of his administration's new flexibility in relations with Third World nations, Carter negotiated the treaties that returned legal sovereignty over the territory while maintaining de facto U.S. control over military use of the canal and military control of the area.

Carter's new stance in Latin America could also be seen in his cutoff of military aid to military dictatorships in Nicaragua, Chile, and Argentina. Previous administrations had been willing to look the other way while Latin American and Asian dictators had slaughtered their domestic opposition, as long as they retained friendly military and commercial relations with the United States. As part of his new emphasis on human rights and his deemphasis of anticommunism, Carter put some distance between the United States and the most brutal dictatorships in Latin America.

Carter's human rights policies were highly selective. Military dictatorships in strategically contested regions of the world like Iran and South Korea were not held to the same standard as less strategically important nations. But for the first time in postwar U.S. foreign policy, concern for international protection of human rights became more than a tool with which to bash the Soviets and their allies.

Arms Control Under Carter

The Carter administration was committed to detente with the Soviet Union and the arms control process begun by the Nixon-Ford administration. In February 1977 Carter proposed a dramatic new departure in the SALT talks. He called for deep cuts in existing weapons systems and strict limits on qualitative improvements of nuclear forces. At the same time he proposed these initiatives, Carter expressed a willingness to continue more cautiously along the lines of previous SALT negotiations.

The Carter proposal would have cut the allowable number of launchers from the 2,400 agreed to in Vladivostok to somewhere between 1,800 and 2,000. The cuts were to be focused on the more accurate land-based missile systems that could be used in a first strike against the other side's forces, thus crippling the opponent's retaliatory capacity and undermining the principle of mutual assured destruction. The restrictions on testing and deployment of new systems would overcome the limitations of previous agreements that controlled only some systems while allowing the arms race to accelerate in others.

The Carter proposals were very one-sided. They focused particularly on the Soviet advantage in very large, land-based missiles that were so central to the Soviet forces. The Soviets based most of their missile forces in the interior of their country, reflecting their history and geography as a land power. The United States had split its nuclear forces more equally between land, sea, and air delivery systems, reflecting its history as a sea and air power. Thus, to focus cuts on land based systems was to favor the United States. In their response to the Carter proposals, the Soviets chose to highlight their one-sided nature, and rejected them out of hand.

However, negotiations premised upon previous SALT agreements continued. In June 1979 a SALT II agreement was signed by Carter and Soviet leader Leonid Brezhnev at a summit in Vienna. The SALT II accord cut the total number of launchers from 2,400 to 2,250. It reduced the number of allowable multiple-warhead launchers from 1,320 to 1,200, and limited the number of land-based, multiple-warhead launchers to 820. It restricted each side to one new land-based missile system.

But SALT II never became law because it was never ratified by the Senate, as required by the Constitution. The Senate's refusal to ratify SALT II reflected the growing political failure of the strategy of hegemonic flexibility.

The Resurgence of the National Security Ideology

The policy failures of Vietnam and the spiraling arms race had brought discernible movement away from the national security ideology. But in the late 1970s it was the ideology of hegemonic flexibility that came under increasing political attack. By midterm, the Carter administration was sending mixed signals about its commitment to the ideas articulated in its first year. By its last year, the Carter administration had returned to most of the cold war doctrines that had guided U.S. policy in the 1950s and 1960s.

Several factors motivated this shift. The memory of the tragedy of Vietnam was beginning to fade. Already a historical revisionism was developing that blamed the debacle in Vietnam not on the national security ideology that justified the commitment of U.S. power, but on a failure of some mystical American will to win. The continued war and suffering in southeast Asia after the U.S. withdrawal lent superficial credence to the claim that the U.S. involvement had served some purpose, namely, to keep repressive communist regimes from coming to power.

Recognition was growing in the United States that its power to influence world events had declined. The rise of the OPEC oil cartel and its devastating effects on the U.S. economy were the most obvious signs of decline. The inability of the United States to halt the emergence of new socialist regimes in Africa and the Middle East was another. The fall of the Shah of Iran and the rise of Islamic revolution was yet another, particularly since building up the Shah as a regional power had been one of the central components of the Nixon Doctrine. Just as the predominant national security ideology bore the blame for the policy failures of the 1960s, so detente began to bear the blame for the setbacks of the 1970s.

Domestic politics also played a part in the shift away from hegemonic flexibility. Once LBJ left office in 1969, many Democrats who had been supporting his Vietnam policy out of party loyalty or pragmatic caution refused to do the same for Republican Nixon. In the same manner, once the Democrats recaptured the White House in 1976, many Republicans who had held doubts about detente came into open political opposition. The strong showing of Ronald Reagan in the 1976 Republican primaries revealed that opposition to detente was not only tenable but also, perhaps, even expedient.

The political pressures on detente increased in 1978. The Democrats lost 16 seats in the House of Representatives and 3 in the Senate in the midterm election of 1978. Carter foresaw the possibility of a strong challenge on the right in 1980 from Reagan or someone like him. In 1979 he began to position himself for the

1980 election by moving toward the political center. This shift affected relations with the Soviet Union.

The euphoria of the early years of detente was fading. Detente had borne many unrealistic expectations of immediate harmony between the superpowers. Many Americans believed detente required the Soviet Union to conform to the U.S. position on every issue of conflict. Anything less was often interpreted as a lack of Soviet commitment to detente. When the Soviet Union continued to back friendly regimes and revolutions, to use their military power for their political ends, and to pursue advantages around the world, opponents of detente seized on these actions as proof that it was not working. It did not matter to American critics of detente that, if measured by these standards, the United States was not very committed to detente either.

The Crises in Iran and Afghanistan

SALT II ultimately fell victim to the resurgence of the national security ideology. The early Senate debates on the treaty centered on growing concern about the decline of American power. But the death knells of detente were the Iranian hostage crisis and the Soviet invasion of Afghanistan.

In November 1979 militant Iranian students seized the U.S. embassy and held more than 50 American personnel hostage. Even more serious was the commitment of massive Soviet military forces to the aid of the failing communist government in Afghanistan. Detente was dead. In his 1980 State of the Union message the president articulated what came to be known as the Carter Doctrine: that the U.S regarded the continued flow of Persian Gulf oil as a vital national interest that would be defended with military force.

At this time in Iran, 50 Americans are still held captive, innocent victims of terrorism and anarchy. Also at this moment, massive Soviet troops are attempting to subjugate the fiercely independent and deeply religious people of Afghanistan. . . . The implications of the Soviet invasion of Afghanistan could pose the most serious threat to the peace since the Second World War. . . . Let our position be absolutely clear: An attempt by any outside force to gain control of the Persian Gulf region will be regarded as an assault on the vital interests of the United States of America, and such an assault will be repelled by any means necessary, including military force.[4]

The Carter administration reacted to the invasion of Afghanistan with several concrete measures. It withdrew the recently negotiated SALT II treaty from consideration by the Senate. Legislation to renew registration for the draft was initiated. Commercial ties were cut: grain sales were blocked and high-technology equipment was embargoed. American athletes were not sent to the Olympic

Games held in Moscow in 1980. High level diplomatic contacts with the Kremlin were severed.

The Carter administration's foreign policy ended on a very different note than it began. The criticism of the "inordinate fear of communism" had given way to a new cold war. In 1981 Ronald Reagan would make the new cold war the central philosophy of his early foreign policy.

NOTES

1. Joseph Nye, *Bound to Lead* (New York: Basic Books, 1990), pp. 74-77.

2. Richard Nixon, *Public Papers of the Presidents, 1970* (Washington, DC: U.S. Government Printing Office, 1971), pp. 116-122.

3. Jimmy Carter, *The Public Papers of the Presidents, 1977* (Washington, DC: U.S. Government Printing Office, 1978), pp. 954-962.

4. Jimmy Carter, *The Public Papers of the Presidents, 1980* (Washington, DC: U.S. Government Printing Office, 1981), pp. 196-197.

9

IDEOLOGICAL POLARIZATION AND THE CRISIS OF THE ACTIVIST STATE

THE INTENSIFYING CRISIS OF THE 1960s AND 1970s

From the late 1960s through the 1970s the United States experienced an ever more serious ideological crisis. The presidency of Lyndon Johnson began with great energy and enthusiasm, with the passage of the Civil Rights Act of 1964, the war on poverty, and other Great Society legislation. But it ended tragically, with the United States bogged down in a futile war in southeast Asia and the domestic policy consensus Johnson had so carefully crafted shattered by racial and social strife. The Great Society had not lived up to its billing as a solution to social problems. The political system was polarizing as newly militant political groups called for more radical change and conservatives blamed increasing racial and political tensions on the changes unleashed by liberal Democrats. In 1968 the Republicans regained the White House behind the candidacy of Richard Nixon. But the Democrats retained control of Congress. Relations between Nixon and the Democratic Congress steadily worsened, culminating in the beginning of impeachment proceedings and Nixon's resignation.

Further, in contrast with the prosperity of the Johnson years, as the country moved into the 1970s, the U.S. economy underwent a series of shocks. Inflation rose steadily, prompting Nixon to place the country temporarily under wage and price controls and to take the dollar off the gold standard. As Gerald Ford succeeded Nixon in 1974, the skyrocketing price of imported oil sent the country into what at that time was the worst recession since the Great Depression. The prosperity of the 1960s, which had been the glue of the policy consensus crafted by Johnson, was gone, and ideological conflict intensified.

THE FALL OF LYNDON JOHNSON AND THE SHATTERING OF THE DEMOCRATIC COALITION

The New Politics of Social and Racial Issues

In the election of 1964, Lyndon Johnson reunited the broad Democratic coalition that had swept FDR into power and held the White House for the Democrats throughout the 1930s and 1940s. Johnson won wide support from the whites and blacks; Protestants, Catholics, and Jews; trade unionists, city machines, and liberal reformers. He won the electoral votes of every region of the country except the deep South, where racial tensions were highest. This coalition that produced the landslide in 1964 also provided the votes for the Civil Rights Act of 1964 and the Great Society programs that passed in 1965.

But this grand coalition could not be sustained over the course of the Johnson presidency. The Johnson administration, which had begun with so many major achievements, was increasingly undermined by the heightening conflicts within society and the Democratic Party. The war in Vietnam dragged on with U.S. casualties rising but with no victory in sight. Larger and larger demonstrations against the Vietnam War mushroomed across the campuses of the land. Racial tensions erupted into riots in the Watts ghetto of Los Angeles in the summer of 1965 and spread to dozens of cities across the nation in subsequent summers. Johnson's popularity ratings began to plummet. In the midterm elections of 1966 the Democrats lost 47 seats in the House. The ideological majority that had spawned the Great Society was gone, and the period of innovation in domestic policy was over.

New political forces were mobilizing on both the left and the right and polarizing political life. The success of the civil rights movement led to the emergence of new political forces and new demands for change. Among blacks, a new set of leaders arose demanding not only civil rights but "Black Power." Opposition to the Vietnam War was growing among liberal intellectuals, students, and young people. And the women's movement was an increasingly powerful force to be reckoned with. Environmental activists were demanding that more be done to preserve the global ecosystem. The emergence of these new political forces represented a serious challenge to the Democratic political establishment that had dominated national politics for over 30 years. The Black Power, student, women's, and environmental movements all raised fundamental questions about the traditional roles and values of American society. Each presented fundamental challenges not only to prevailing political and economic practices but also to the very way Americans thought of their personal identities. In this sense they were all countercultural movements, movements that challenged the dominant political groups.

While the more radical elements of these countercultural movements demonstrated in the streets, the more moderate elements sought influence in the Democratic Party. But these challenges to prevailing doctrines did not go unanswered within either the Democratic Party or the larger political system.

The Black Power and women's movements ran into increasing opposition from other elements in the Democratic coalition. Blacks demanding political power in the North clashed bitterly with the Democratic machines and their ethnic supporters who had traditionally controlled city politics. Black and women's groups' demands for economic redistribution as well as political equality frequently conflicted with the narrow economic interests of white males. It was no longer without cost for a northern white politician to support the demands of black and women's groups. In foreign policy, the countercultural forces clashed with the national security state apparatus. Democrat Truman had been the architect of the national security state and the cold war system. Democrats Kennedy and Johnson had only applied the national security doctrines long accepted by the foreign policy establishment in escalating the Vietnam War.

The Democrats in the 1968 Election

As the 1968 election approached, Johnson faced growing opposition from antiwar and other dissident movements within the Democratic Party to his bid for another term. Antiwar Senator Eugene McCarthy of Minnesota announced his candidacy. Waiting in the wings was Robert Kennedy, brother of the martyred president. In the first test of strength, the New Hampshire primary, the nationally unknown McCarthy ran almost even with Johnson, who as the incumbent president had been expected to win easily. Robert Kennedy decided Johnson was vulnerable and entered the race. Rather than face a protracted struggle for the nomination of a party that would be hopelessly divided, Johnson chose to withdraw from the race. Hubert Humphrey, Johnson's vicepresident, stepped in to lead the Democratic establishment against the new political forces. Although he never put his name directly before voters, Humphrey utilized his strength with the party leaders who still controlled the presidential selection process. Humphrey held on to a precarious lead in delegates over Kennedy going into the final test, the California primary. Kennedy won California, but was assassinated the night of his primary victory.

At the Democratic convention in Chicago, the conflicts between the new political forces and the Democratic old guard boiled over. As demonstrators and police clashed in the streets, Democrats clashed on the convention floor. Humphrey won the nomination, but the historic Democratic coalition was in shambles. The beleaguered Democrats also faced defections from the right. Without the Southerner Johnson at the head of the ticket, the party that had imposed the civil rights revolution on the South had little chance of winning the support of segregationists. Governor George Wallace of Alabama bolted from the Democratic Party and ran the first major third-party campaign in 20 years. Wallace emphasized growing white opposition to activist government and to black and student demonstrators.

Nixon and Social Issues in the 1968 Election

The Republican Party was the ultimate beneficiary of the shattering of the Democratic coalition and the debacle in Chicago. The Republican strategy for dealing with the new social issues emphasized traditional values, in opposition to the new politics of the countercultural left. Nixon's southern strategy openly sought the votes of white Southerners and urban ethnics opposed to the gains blacks had won in recent years. A key element in Nixon's campaign in 1968 was the theme of law and order. It was not only Democrats who heard in Nixon's call for law and order a coded message of racism. The Nixon campaign skillfully exploited popular resentment against the growing Black Power and student peace movements. Nixon selected as his running mate Maryland Governor Spiro Agnew, whose main claim to national recognition had been a bitter confrontation with Black Power leaders in Baltimore.

Nixon won the White House in 1968 by the Sunbelt strategy of uniting the South and West against the eastern liberal establishment, a coalition that still dominates presidential elections today. But even as they were losing the White House, the Democrats retained their hold on Congress, a factor that would loom large in the fate of the Nixon presidency.

NIXON IN IDEOLOGICAL CONFLICT WITH THE DEMOCRATIC CONGRESS

Conflict and Compromise in the First Term

Conflict between the Republican executive and the Democratic legislature was the defining characteristic of the Nixon presidency. At times Nixon chose tactics of moderation, compromise, and accommodation. But the more prevailing mode was confrontation, particularly in the later years of his tenure.

The most significant early battles with Congress were over Nixon's nominees to fill Supreme Court vacancies. Reaction to the activist decisions of the Warren Court in the area of civil rights, rights of criminal defendants, and separation of church and state had been growing throughout the 1960s. Once in office, Nixon continued to work his southern strategy.

Nixon's first two nominees to the court were conservative Southerners of the old traditions, Clement Haynesworth and Harold Carswell. But the Senate must approve presidential judicial nominations. Northern Democrats and moderate Republicans in Congress were not going to allow the reemergence of segregationist doctrines as legitimate. Both these nominees were defeated. For the remainder of his term Nixon chose to nominate northern and western conservatives who had no record of supporting segregation. But a message had been sent to southern conservatives about who was responsible for tough implementation of civil rights laws, and who was not.

The same pattern of mixed confrontation and compromise can be seen in Nixon's economic, social, and budgetary policies. The Great Society had opened the ideological gates for social groups to expect government responsiveness to their needs and had expanded the range of government programs. In the wake of the Great Society, and facing strongly Democratic Congresses, Nixon often tried to steal the Democrats' activist thunder.

Nixon's mixed messages between the social security state and the limited interest state can be seen in his 1970 State of the Union message. On the one hand he criticizes big government, blaming it for rising inflation. But on the other hand he accepts it and invokes it to achieve new ends.

In the same speech Nixon attacks big government yet proposes a dramatic expansion of the role of the national government in protecting the environment and in income support of the poor. Nixon's ecology proposals led to the passage

Nixon's Mixed Messages on the Role of Government

For Limited Government

Economic Policy: A stark review of the fiscal facts of the 1960s clearly demonstrates where the primary blame for rising prices should be placed. In the decade of the sixties the Federal Government spent $57 billion more than it took in in taxes. . . . A balanced budget requires some hard decisions. It means rejecting spending programs which would benefit some of the people when their net effect would result in price increases for all the people.

Federalism: It is time for a New Federalism, in which, after 190 years of power flowing from the people and local and state governments to Washington, D.C., it will begin to flow back to the states and to the people.

For Activist Government

Environment: Clean air, clean water, open spaces--these should once again be the birthright of every American. If we act now they can be. . . . The program I shall propose to Congress will be the most comprehensive and costly program in this field in America's history.

Welfare Reform: [W]e cannot delay longer in accomplishing a total reform of our welfare system. When a system penalizes work, breaks up homes, robs recipients of dignity, there is no alternative to abolishing that system and adopting in its place [a] program of income support, job training, and work incentives.[1]

of the National Environmental Protection Act, the establishment of the Environmental Protection Agency, and a new era of federal involvement in the regulation of air and water pollution.

While Nixon's public rhetoric suggests an antiwelfare, antigovernment stance, his welfare reform proposal would actually have increased the number of working poor eligible for income support and the role of the national government in the welfare system. But it did not pass a skeptical Congress.

Even Nixon's attempts to revive the role of state and local governments in the federal system bore the imprint of the Great Society. Nixon's "New Federalism" combined traditional Republican concerns with the role of states and localities with the new federal largess. The main product of the New Federalism was another set of national grants to state and local governments, this time with no troublesome national strings attached to their use. This conflict between conservative rhetoric and activist policies also can be seen in Nixon's decision to impose wage and price controls. As the 1972 election approached, Nixon worried about the effects of rising inflation on his reelection campaign. So despite his symbolic commitment to free markets and limited government, he used discretionary authority Congress had created and invoked a freeze on wage and price increases until he could win a second term.

In Nixon's second term, however, as economic and budgetary pressures mounted, political pressures shifted, and reelection concerns were eliminated, Nixon increasingly returned to a more consistent limited state stance. Now his rhetorical blasts at the "spendthrift" Congress were matched by executive refusal to spend money Congress had appropriated. Frustrated by his inability to influence congressional votes, Nixon took to the constitutionally dubious tactic of impounding, or simply refusing to spend, monies Congress had appropriated. Billions of dollars appropriated by Congress for water and sewage treatment projects and other programs were never released by the executive branch.

WATERGATE AS THE EXPRESSION OF IDEOLOGICAL POLARIZATION

Domestic Counterintelligence and the Nixon White House

In the tense times of the later Nixon years, confrontation between the president and the Democratic Party over budgetary policy and authority was overshadowed by their conflicts over war powers, executive secrecy, and administration dirty tricks against its political opposition. The systematic lawbreaking in the Nixon White House, which came to be labeled "Watergate," was based on much more than simple official venality. It reflected the mounting political conflict between the Nixon administration and the emerging countercultural forces in American society. It also was a product of the increasing ideological polarization between a Republican president and a Democrat-controlled

Congress as the Republican Party was moving to the right and the Democratic Party was moving to the left.

In 1968 the Johnson-Humphrey forces still controlled the Democratic Party. Despite growing skepticism about the Vietnam War, most Democratic members of Congress felt obligated to support the war effort. But once the Republicans won the presidency, Democratic leaders were freed from the bonds of party loyalty. Congressional Democrats and presidential contenders were increasingly responsive to the new countercultural forces that challenged the war, racism, sexism, environmental degradation, and the political and economic institutions that they believed were responsible for these ills.

The Nixon White House had skillfully played on the divisions within the Democratic coalition and made historic gains for the Republican Party with its southern strategy. But as the war dragged on and domestic reform slowed, the strength of the countercultural forces raising fundamental challenges to the policies in Vietnam and at home grew. The Nixon administration increasingly felt under pressure from the demonstrators in the streets and liberal opponents in Congress. Reflecting this siege mentality, the Nixon White House stepped up domestic counterintelligence operations. Although it is rarely openly admitted in established political circles, repression of dissident political groups has long been a practice in American politics. Historically, groups that raise fundamental ideological challenges to the dominant beliefs of the times have been the target of surveillance, infiltration, dirty tricks, persecution by the legal apparatus, and even political violence.

In the first half of the century, socialists and trade unionists had faced such repression, particularly during the "red scares" of the early 1920s and the McCarthy era. In the 1950s civil rights leaders were a new focus of domestic counterintelligence. Martin Luther King was under continuous FBI surveillance and the victim of vicious leaks from counterintelligence agents about his alleged sexual proclivities. In the Nixon years antiwar, Black Power, and women's groups, and eventually even Democratic Party presidential candidates, were the targets. Government agents infiltrated antiwar and Black Power groups. They spied on leaders, burglarized offices, and forged documents. Provocateurs initiated violence at political demonstrations, and in some cases incited organizations to make violent political attacks on opponents. Prominent opponents of the administration were targeted for special income tax audits. In addition to the FBI and other historic counterintelligence agencies, the White House staff increasingly developed its own dirty tricks apparatus. As 1972 approached, many of these White House operatives transferred to Nixon's reelection campaign and turned their attention to leading Democratic presidential contenders. The burglary at the Watergate complex was aimed at the headquarters of the Democratic National Committee, which had its offices there.

The McGovern Campaign and the New Liberalism

The Nixon administration's escalation of domestic counterintelligence operations reflected the growing ideological challenge posed by the countercultural political groups. Nixon was correct in sensing that new forces were gaining momentum across the country. The convergence of these movements in the Democratic presidential nomination process made the election of 1972 unlike anything seen in American politics since the 1930s.

As a concession to dissident forces, the Chicago Democratic convention had agreed to reform the rules of the presidential selection process. Antiwar Senator George McGovern of South Dakota chaired the committee that wrote the new rules which opened up the process, took control from party bosses, and guaranteed minorities, women, and youth representation in the process. McGovern then utilized his knowledge of the new rules to win the Democratic nomination. The 1972 McGovern campaign had elements of an insurgency against the establishment that had controlled the Democratic Party since the 1940s. The "new politics" or new liberalism of the McGovern campaign had real differences with the New Deal liberalism of FDR or LBJ.

The older liberalism had provided the philosophical impetus to U.S. internationalism. It had taken the United States into two world wars, launched the cold war, formed the national security state, and committed the nation to fight communism in Korea, Vietnam, and around the globe. The new liberalism of the McGovern campaign was less concerned about cold war objectives than about an immediate end to the Vietnam conflict. The new liberalism sought to attain peace not through military containment of communism but through negotiations with communist regimes and reduction of U.S. commitments around the world.

The new politics differed from the old liberalism on domestic policy as well. With the exception of the early days of the New Deal, the old liberalism was essentially distributive politics. It sought to expand government benefits to the politically well organized segments of society. FDR and LBJ practiced the politics of the social security state.

But the new politics was social democratic. The groups supporting McGovern sought to redistribute income to the poor and to empower groups historically excluded from positions of power. They believed that such ends could be achieved only over the opposition of corporate capitalism. So for the first time in decades, class-conscious rhetoric was reintroduced into the Democratic Party platform.

Full-employment—a guaranteed job for all—is the primary economic objective of the Democratic Party. . . . We are determined to make economic security a matter of right. This means a job with decent pay and good working conditions for everyone willing and able to work and an adequate income for those unable to work.

The Democratic Party deplores the increasing concentration of economic power in fewer and fewer hands. Five per cent of the American people control 90 per cent of our productive national wealth. Less than one per cent of all manufacturers have 88 per cent of the profits. Less than two per cent of the population now owns approximately 80 per cent of the nation's personally-held corporate stock.[2]

The historic Democratic coalition had been an amalgam of a wide variety of ethnic groups, a study in cultural pluralism. In contrast with the white, Protestant, conservative Republican base, the old Democratic liberalism had been supported by blacks, Puerto Ricans, Jews, Irish, Italians, Poles, and myriad other ethnic groups.

The McGovern campaign drew its support not from this historic Democratic coalition but primarily from the newly emerging countercultural groups that were less concerned with historic identities and more interested in defining new identities for themselves. The McGovern rules for delegate selection had for the first time guaranteed women and minorities full representation in the nomination process. The McGovern strategy of trying to build a coalition of new political forces historically excluded from political power was reflected in the party platform plank on women.

Women historically have been denied a full voice in the evolution of the political and social institutions of this country and are therefore allied with all under-represented groups in a common desire to form a more humane and compassionate society.[3]

While the McGovern forces were calling for an end to the Vietnam War and experimenting with social democracy and countercultural messages, the Nixon Republicans relied on the tried-and-true themes of traditional Americanism and the limited state. Nixon won the 1972 election in a landslide. But this moment of triumph was largely illusory, for the Nixon presidency was about the enter its most severe crisis.

The Watergate Scandals

Antiwar and Black Power groups had been crying foul over the violation of their political rights by domestic counterintelligence agencies for years. The McGovern campaign tried to make an election issue of the Watergate burglary and associated dirty tricks, but it could not upset the momentum of the Nixon reelection campaign. But after the election was over, the Democratic Party used its control of the investigative powers of Congress to strike back at the Nixon White House. A special committee of Congress was set up to probe the mounting charges against the Nixon presidency.

The glow of Nixon's reelection landslide was quickly dimmed as the news of 1973 was increasingly dominated by revelations of illegal activities at the White House. Day after day American citizens saw and heard television broadcasts of White House staffers admitting their involvement in dirty tricks and even asserting their right to engage in such practices.

Nixon tried to limit the damage by covering up as much of the White House involvement in the scandals as he could. He invoked the doctrine of executive privilege to try to keep White House documents from congressional investigators. Historically, many of the personal documents of presidents have been kept confidential in order to allow the White House to be able to conduct business frankly, without having the exact text of meetings readily made public. But Nixon asserted a much more global right to keep virtually every executive branch record out of the hands of congressional investigators.

More important, just as in the earlier dirty tricks operations, the White House coverup was unbounded by any legal restraints. Witnesses were coached in how to mislead investigators and were told to lie. Hush money was paid to buy the silence of key witnesses. But this strategy backfired, as the old crimes were only compounded by Nixon's personal involvement in the obstruction of justice.

Slowly the Nixon administration unraveled under the pressure. In April 1973 Nixon fired many of his top aides, including Chief of Staff H.R. Haldeman and leading domestic policy adviser John Ehrlichman. In the fall Vicepresident Agnew was forced to resign under charges of taking bribes and income tax evasion when he was governor of Maryland. In October several top members of the Nixon Justice Department resigned rather than carry out Nixon's demand to fire independent investigator Archibald Cox.

The most damaging revelation was that Nixon had secretly taped virtually all White House meetings. The tapes of these meetings were widely thought to contain the "smoking gun" that proved his personal involvement in illegal activities. Nixon tried to invoke executive privilege to keep the tapes from being released to investigators, but in the summer of 1974 the Supreme Court ruled unanimously that the tapes must be turned over to Congress. They did, in fact, reveal Nixon's direct involvement in illegal actions designed to coverup the truth about the scandals. The House Judiciary Committee voted 27-10 to begin the process of impeaching Nixon. In August 1974 Nixon resigned, the first president in American history to do so.

Watergate as Domestic Counterinsurgency

The collection of crimes and scandals dubbed Watergate can be understood as a form of domestic counterinsurgency. Covert action, lying, and lawbreaking had long been accepted practice in executive counterinsurgency operations. During the Vietnam War, the Nixon administration carried these practices to new heights by conducting secret bombing of much of Cambodia for several years

Excerpts from the Articles of Impeachment of Richard Nixon
(voted by the House Judiciary Committee)

Obstruction of Justice

Richard M. Nixon . . . has prevented, obstructed, and impeded the administration of justice, in that:

[A]gents of the Committee for the Re-election of the President committed unlawful entry of the headquarters of the Democratic National Committee . . . for the purpose of securing political intelligence. Richard M. Nixon . . . engaged personally and through his close subordinates and agents, in a course of conduct or plan designed to delay, impede, and obstruct the investigation of such unlawful entry; to cover up, conceal and protect those responsible; and to conceal the existence and scope of other unlawful covert activities.

The means used to implement this course of conduct or plan included:

—making false or misleading statements
—withholding relevant and material evidence
—counseling witnesses with respect to the giving of false or misleading statements
—[approving] the surreptitious payment of substantial sums of money for the purpose of obtaining the silence or influencing the testimony of witnesses
—[causing] defendants and individuals convicted to expect favored treatment and consideration in return for their silence or false testimony.

Abuse of Power

[Richard Nixon] has repeatedly engaged in conduct violating the constitutional rights of citizens
—He [caused] income tax audits . . . to be initiated or conducted in a discriminatory manner.
—He misused the FBI, the Secret Service, and other executive personnel . . . by directing or authorizing such agencies or personnel to conduct or continue electronic surveillance . . . for purposes unrelated to . . . any lawful function of his office.
—He [authorized] a secret investigative unit within the office of the President . . . unlawfully utilized the resources of the CIA [and] engaged in covert and unlawful activities.[4]

before publicly invading that country. In the wake of the Watergate investigation, another special committee created by Congress found systematic abuses of executive power in international counterinsurgency campaigns. The tactics used by the Nixon administration against domestic countercultural forces were borrowed from the methods of counterinsurgency campaigns abroad. The burglars who broke into Democratic headquarters at the Watergate were right-wing Cuban exiles who had learned their trade in operations against the Castro regime. Several of the White House staffers convicted of crimes like burglary were recruited from the international intelligence community. When it sought to strike more comprehensively at its domestic enemies, the Nixon administration tried to use the counterintelligence apparatus of the FBI, CIA, and other federal agencies.

If the counterintelligence operations of the Nixon administration had been confined to fringe groups, as similar actions had been in the past, they probably would have been tolerated by the larger political system. However, this repressive apparatus' operations increasingly targeted the major opposition party, which still controlled a majority in Congress. The White House burglars not only raided antiwar groups' offices, they also broke into the national headquarters of the Democratic Party. The "dirty tricksters" not only planted provocateurs in the Black Panther Party, they also planted them in the campaigns of leading Democratic presidential candidates. Unlike the Socialist Workers, the Democrats were a party strong enough to fight back effectively. This mistake, much more than the tactics themselves, was the root of Nixon's downfall.

It fell to Gerald Ford to try to pick up the pieces of the presidency after Watergate. Ford had been appointed vicepresident by Nixon after Agnew had resigned under a cloud. Because he bore the millstone of having been chosen by his disgraced predecessor, Ford had little real chance to make his own mark on the presidency. He had to confront Democratic congressional majorities swelled by the electoral repudiation of Nixon's party in the 1974 midterm election. Immediately upon taking office Ford had to cope with the worst economic and fiscal crisis the United States had faced since the Great Depression. Any significant leadership role was denied him when he failed to win election in his own right, despite running a much closer race than might have been expected under the circumstances.

STAGFLATION AND FISCAL CRISIS

Immediately on the heels of the political crisis of Watergate came the intensification of the economic crisis that had been building during the Nixon years. Table 9.1 shows the magnitude of the economic changes the nation faced in the 1970s. The 1960s had been boom times. But what goes up must come down. After the go-go 1960s, the economic cycle reasserted itself, and the economy went into recession in 1970. The expenditures in southeast Asia also

Table 9.1
Average Annual Performance on Key Economic Indicators, 1965-1981

	Unemployment	Economic Growth	Inflation	Deficit ($ Billion)	Deficit (% of GNP)
1965-1970	4.0	3.4	4.2	6.4	0.9
1971-1974	5.5	3.1	5.8	16.9	1.5
1975-1981	7.1	2.7	9.2	61.8	2.9

Sources: U.S. Census Bureau, *Statistical Abstract of the United States;* Council of Economic Advisers, *The Economic Report of the President;* Congressional Budget Office, *Report to the House and Senate on the Budget;* and Department of Labor, *Handbook of Labor Statistics.*

put increasing pressure on the dollar.

In 1971 the Nixon administration took a series of dramatic steps to keep the resultant inflation from impairing his reelection campaign. He took the dollar off the gold standard, effectively devaluing it. In order to check this and other inflationary pressures, Nixon used the discretionary authority Congress had granted and imposed wage and price controls on the economy. Once reelected he gradually lifted the controls. The inflation that had been caged for the 1972 campaign was unleashed. Then in 1974 OPEC asserted its control over oil markets, and the price of oil skyrocketed. The resultant "oil shock" fueled the inflationary fires. Inflation climbed from 3.2 percent under the controls in 1972 to 5.9 percent in 1973 to 9.9 percent in 1974.

The oil shock drained so much purchasing power from the domestic economy that the nation was thrown into what was at the time the worst recession since the Great Depression. This put heavy strain on the federal budget. During a recession, government revenues decline because individuals and businesses have less real income to tax. At the same time government expenditures climb because more individuals draw government benefits like unemployment compensation, welfare, food stamps, and Medicaid. The federal deficit, which had averaged $16.1 billion from 1971 to 1974 climbed to $43.6 billion in fiscal 1975 and $66.4 billion in 1976.

The economy recovered somewhat in 1976. But the damage had been done, and throughout the rest of the 1970s economic performance did not return to the glory days of the 1960s or even the more modest levels of the early 1970s.

THE GROWTH OF GOVERNMENT IN THE 1960s AND 1970s

The Dissipation of the Momentum of the Great Society

The growth of domestic programs begun during the Great Society continued into the Nixon years. However, the momentum for program expansion generated during the Great Society slowly dissipated. By the mid-1970s the period of innovation in domestic programs had come to a halt.

The ideological majority created by the Democratic victory in the 1964 election that had launched the Great Society had only been temporary. By the midterm election of 1966 white backlash against programs perceived as primarily benefiting minorities could be seen. But even after Nixon came to power in 1969, domestic programs continued to grow. Politically popular programs like Medicaid and Medicare expanded as new benefits were added to their coverage. Increased federal aid to education and job training programs had broad public support. Food stamps, which had been only an small experimental program in the Johnson years, was expanded to a national entitlement.

In his first term Nixon made the creation of the Environmental Protection Agency and expansion of federal aid to state and local governments major components of his domestic agenda. Then as he moved to the left on foreign policy, he covered his conservative flank by stiffening his opposition to domestic program growth. However, by then Nixon had largely lost control over public policy. Government spending for human resources, or people programs, averaged 4-6 percent of GNP in the Eisenhower and Kennedy years. It rose to over 7 percent during the Johnson presidency and continued to rise through the Nixon years until it averaged between 11-12 percent in the Ford and Carter years.

The economic crisis that followed the OPEC oil price shock brought an end to any major new domestic spending programs. The economic crisis meant a government fiscal crisis, as aid to the unemployed and impoverished automatically increased at the same time government revenues were falling. Just as the boom times of the 1960s were over, so was the creation of new government programs that were characteristic of those times. Money was tight, and even more significantly, big government came to be blamed for the political turmoil of the late 1960s and the fiscal crisis of the 1970s. Even the recapturing of the White House by the Democrats in 1976 had little effect, as the budgetary status quo largely prevailed throughout the Carter years.

Perspective on the Great Society and Domestic Program Growth

Figure 9.1 uses the typology of domestic program ideologies developed in Chapter 2 can help put the expansion of government during and after the Great Society into perspective. The Great Society built upon the limited interest state that had been the residue of the New Deal. Lyndon Johnson had employed the

Figure 9.1
The Impact of the Great Society on Domestic Policy

| SOCIAL | SOCIAL | LIMITED | LAISSEZ- |
| DEMOCRACY | SECURITY | INTEREST | FAIRE |

[1938-1963 Political Center]

[1964-1980 Political Center]

rhetoric of social democracy and social transformation to justify the passage of new programs. But in the long run, the domestic program changes unleashed by the Great Society can be seen more as a movement toward a broader social security state than toward social democracy or real social justice.

The idea that government was ultimately responsible for taking an activist response to certain economic and social needs was firmly established in the first term of FDR. But in the nearly 30 years that followed the New Deal, activist government was still limited in the roles it was allowed to perform. There was broad consensus that government should stabilize overall economic activity and insure the income of certain politically powerful groups. But there was no such consensus that other serious social problems were the responsibility of government.

Probably the most crucial issue left largely untouched by the post-FDR limited interest state was racial justice. The system of segregation that had grown up in the South after Reconstruction had relegated blacks to the margins of American society, belying all the pious Fourth of July speeches about political equality. Poverty was another social problem that escaped the sustained attention of the limited interest state. The New Deal had helped to insure the income of many workers against the fluctuations of the economic cycle and to protect them when they were too old to work. But it offered little help to the permanent underclass, those who were chronically unable to find or hold jobs.

The Mixed Record of the War on Poverty

Lyndon Johnson consciously saw his Great Society as an extension of the New Deal. The Great Society was designed to complete the liberal agenda, to address the problems of race and poverty left unresolved by the New Deal. It would fill in the gaps of the American welfare state, extending economic security and democratic rights more broadly throughout the society.

The Great Society was characterized by sweeping rhetoric about social transformation. This was not all hype. For blacks in particular, civil rights and the Great Society brought dramatic changes in their daily lives, allowing them to participate in politics and civil society where they had previously been excluded. But overall, the accomplishments of the Great Society were much more modest than its rhetoric.

Despite the increase in job training programs, unemployment began to increase in 1970 and averaged over 6 percent for the decade. Despite the extension of medical insurance to the elderly and the very poor, tens of millions of Americans remained without health insurance. Despite the expenditures on urban development, most inner cities remained racial and economic ghettos. Despite the increased expenditures on compensatory education, millions of students dropped out of school and tens of millions of adults remained functionally illiterate.

The war on poverty had mixed results with regard to the number of Americans who lived below the official poverty line. The number of Americans whose income put them below the official poverty line declined from roughly 19 percent when Lyndon Johnson took office to hover between 11 and 13 percent during the 1970s. But the number of Americans who could earn enough income to lift themselves above the poverty line without government assistance payments remained around 20 percent throughout the 1970s.

The Expansion of the Social Security State

In many ways the expansion of government in the 1960s and 1970s can be seen less as the government acting as an agent of social transformation than as a social security state. Even in the programs aimed at the poor, well-organized interests were often the greatest beneficiaries. Medicare and Medicaid payments went not directly to the poor but to doctors and hospitals. Increased expenditu res on education benefited schools and teachers as much as pupils. Aid to cities usually benefited downtown business interests much more than the local poor.

The community action aspect of the war on poverty was the most clearly social democratic element of the Great Society. It was designed to mobilize the poor so they could fight for their own interests in the democratic process. But in doing so, the community action groups quickly came into conflict with the established political machines of local government. Once this pattern became clear, Congress and the Johnson administration's enthusiasm for community action cooled rapidly. Funding and political support for community action agencies soon were quite limited. Left without the material and political resources to achieve major changes in local politics, many community action programs evolved into a very traditional form of politics. In many cases these organizations were ultimately used by emerging minority politicians to grant patronage and build their base for local election campaigns. The fate of community action programs revealed the real philosophy underlying the Great Society. The Johnson administration and northern congressional liberals had been willing to take real risks to establish basic political rights for southern blacks. But when forced to choose between social transformation and redistribution of political power or political peace with established interests in the North and West, congressional Democrats and the Johnson administration sided with the political establishment.

However, the declining support for programs targeted to the poor and minorities did not mean the end of this period of government expansion. Once the historic barriers to the role of government broke down, many new programs were created that had little or nothing to do with poverty or social justice.

One dramatic example is in federal guarantees of investments made by private parties. These are programs where the federal government promises to step in and pick up the tab if a private party defaults on a loan or other commitment. Probably the most publicized of these loan guarantees in the 1970s was the federal bailout of a failing military contracting giant, the Lockheed Corporation. Another widely known federal loan program begun in the 1970s guaranteed student loans, with the federal government promising to pick up the tab if students defaulted on covered loans for college expenses. Government loan guarantee programs had begun in the New Deal. But the range and amount of private transactions covered by such guarantees skyrocketed in the 1970s.

Another area where the federal government expanded dramatically was in the grants it made to state and local governments. After adjusting for inflation, the amount of these grants in 1975 had grown to ten times the amount of 1960.[5] With the minor exception of community action programs, decisions on how to spend these funds were made by existing governments and bureaucracies. While some of these funds went to poverty programs, the vast majority did not. More often the use of these funds reflected the priorities of state and local power elites.

For different reasons both Democratic liberals and Republican conservatives preferred to portray the expansion of government in the 1960s and 1970s as primarily benefiting the poor and minorities. Liberal Democrats wanted to claim credit for achieving social justice and to curry support among minority and women's groups. Conservative Republicans wanted to picture big government as benefiting only a few and to capitalize on the resentments of white middle-class voters. But this image of the activist government of the 1960s and 1970s is misleading. While there were real gains for poor and minorities, the expansion of government programs in this period did more to protect the income and lifestyles of the middle and upper classes than to help the poor or to achieve social justice.

THE IDEOLOGICAL CROSSPRESSURES ON THE CARTER ADMINISTRATION

The Nixon scandals, the economic crisis, and the strategic nomination of a southern governor with little record on national issues allowed the Democrats temporarily to put the New Deal coalition Humpty-Dumpty back together one more time in 1976. Jimmy Carter just squeaked by Gerald Ford, the man appointed to the vicepresidency by the disgraced Nixon. With the Republican Party still tarnished by the Watergate affair, the Democrats won the largest majorities in Congress since 1964. Yet despite holding a big majority in Congress and recapturing the White House, any impulse of the Democrats toward domestic reform was squelched by budgetary squeeze, growing distrust of government, and memories of the fate of the activist Lyndon Johnson.

Carter Policy Initiatives

Jimmy Carter consciously sought to avoid identification with any particular political-economic philosophy. In describing his position he recycled the Eisenhower line that he was "a liberal on social issues and a conservative on economic issues." This phrase revealed a lot. On the one hand, Carter felt the pressures of the various constituency groups in his party who expected new government programs for their members and expansion of the social security state. On the other hand, the combination of a sluggish economy and popular skepticism about government led in the direction of limiting the interest state.

Carter tried to avoid costly social program initiatives in the Johnson mold. The centerpiece of his domestic agenda was his energy package, which responded to the oil import crisis. But Carter's energy program stalled in the Senate, did not pass until nearly two years into his term, and in its final form bore little resemblance to the original proposal. Carter's welfare reform package, like Nixon's, never passed at all. Carter and his staff had little taste for the legislative process and, more significantly, not much of a programmatic agenda beyond the energy program. The choice of energy as the top-priority legislative agenda item reflected the seriousness of the crisis of the Democratic Party. As a Democrat, Carter felt pressure to produce an activist agenda, yet in the changed climate of the 1970s he wanted to avoid association with new social programs. But the strategy of focusing on energy policy proved to be a political liability. The fragile Democratic coalition was fragmented by differing regional interests. The energy-consuming Frostbelt wanted cheap energy, and new taxes and regulations on energy producers. But the energy-producing Sunbelt wanted high prices, low taxes and regulation, and protection of markets. The result was legislative stalemate and a weak final bill.

Some programs with considerable constituency support grew substantially during the Carter years. Teachers' unions had been a major force in the Carter campaign, and so aid to education grew by nearly $5 billion. CETA public jobs were supported by a coalition of unions, minorities, and local officials, and thus also grew. Social Security taxes were raised to protect the pensions of the elderly. But Carter's presidency was remarkable for a Democratic administration in that it offered few broad, expansive initiatives in social policy. Those which were submitted to Congress, like welfare reform and expanded health insurance, were defeated.

The Tactics of Symbolic Politics and Cultural Pluralism

The Carter administration was cross-pressured between its interest group constituencies and demands to limit the growth of government in the wake of the fiscal crisis. It also had to balance the competing claims of elements of its party. Carter tried to bridge the ideological gap between the counterculture wing of the party, which had produced the McGovern campaign, and the more traditional New Deal Democrats through the strategies of cultural pluralism and symbolic politics. He gave symbolic affirmation to the causes of minorities through his close ties to the King family and his frequent references to King's legacy. For the women's movement, he endorsed the ERA and elevated his wife Rosalynn to a more visible role in selected policy issues. He appealed to the environmental movement by putting solar energy collectors on the White House. But like JFK, his symbolic appeals largely substituted for programmatic action. Presidential budgets and legislative output gave few new material resources to these causes.

Carter's strategy of cultural pluralism took more substantive form in his appointment process. He was the first president to appoint two blacks to his cabinet. Andrew Young, former civil rights activist, was named U.N. ambassador, the first black to serve in a major foreign policy position. Patricia Harris was first named head of the small Housing and Urban Development Department, which has often been headed by blacks, and was later promoted to secretary of Health and Human services, the department with the largest budget. Carter's judicial appointments were also much more pluralistic than those of his predecessors. Roughly 15 percent of his appointments to the federal bench were black and 6 percent were Hispanic, contrasting with the 3 percent black and 1 percent Hispanic appointments in the Nixon-Ford years. Sixteen percent of his appointments were women, contrasting with 1 percent by Nixon and Ford.[6]

Carter's appointments strategy worked to turn the "new" politics of countercultural groups into the "old" politics of patronage. Like LBJ's war on poverty, it tended to co-opt the outsider groups through putting selected members in office, making the rewarded groups reluctant to bite the hand that fed them. At the same time it was a practice readily understood by more traditional New Deal Democrats. And best of all, unlike Johnson's war on poverty, appointments to federal offices added no expenditures to the budget and made no immediate programmatic commitments.

But ultimately the Carter administration was not able to steer the treachero us ideological crosscurrents of the late 1970s. In the 1978 congressional elections the Democrats suffered unusually large losses for a party with a first-term president. Inflation rose steadily throughout the Carter administration, reaching dangerous double-digit levels as the 1980 election approached. In late 1979 Iranian militants seized hostages from the U.S. embassy in Tehran and the Soviet Union invaded Afghanistan. The Carter administration seemed increasingly weak and unable to cope with domestic and foreign crises. The mounting policy failures of the Carter presidency paved the way for Ronald Reagan.

NOTES

1. Richard Nixon, *Public Papers of the Presidents, 1970* (Washington, DC: U.S. Government Printing Office, 1971), pp. 8-16.

2. Donald B. Johnson and Kirk H. Porter, eds., *National Party Platforms* (Urbana: University of Illinois Press, 1977), p. 786.

3. *Ibid.*, pp. 791-792.

4. *Congressional Quarterly Almanac, 1974* (Washington, DC: Congressional Quarterly, 1975), p. 884-885.

5. Palmer, John L. and Isabel V. Sawhill, *The Reagan Experiment* (Washington: Urban Institute Press, 1982).

6. Edwards and Wayne, *Presidential Leadership* (New York: St. Martin's Press, 1985), pp. 393-394.

PART IV

IDEOLOGY IN THE REAGAN-BUSH YEARS

10

THE REAGAN RESTORATION

THE RESTORATION OF PRESIDENTIAL LEADERSHIP

The Crisis of Confidence in Government

In the summer of 1979, as he prepared for his reelection campaign, Jimmy Carter reflected on the frustrations of his presidency in a televised address to the nation. Carter was already sensing the loss of support that would lead to his rejection at the polls in 1980. But he argued that the problems of government went deeper than his administration, that the nation was experiencing a "crisis of confidence."

Carter was largely accurate in his analysis, though this did not help him in his reelection campaign. The series of scandals commonly referred to as Watergate deeply shook popular confidence in government. Richard Nixon was the first president in American history to be forced to resign in disgrace. The image of the president as the altruistic leader of a virtuous government that had been cultivated through the twentieth century was shattered.

The decline in popular faith and trust in government in the 1970s could be observed in people's responses to public opinion polls. In the 1950s and early 1960s, when pollsters asked people whether they could usually trust the government in Washington to do what was right, roughly two-thirds would answer "yes." By the late 1970s the number of positive responses to this question was more like one-third.

Jimmy Carter on the Crisis of Confidence in Government

The symptoms of this crisis of the American spirit are all around us. For the first time in the history of our country the majority of people believe that the next five years will be worse than the past five years. . . . Two-thirds of our people do not even vote. The productivity of American workers is actually dropping.

We were sure that ours was a Nation of the ballot, not the bullet, until the murders of John Kennedy and Robert Kennedy and Martin Luther King Jr. We were taught that our armies were always invincible and our causes were always just, only to suffer the agony of Vietnam. . . .We respected the Presidency as a place of honor until the shock of Watergate. . . . We remember when the phrase "sound as a dollar" was an expression of absolute dependability, until 10 years of inflation began to shrink our dollars and our savings.

What you see too often in Washington and elsewhere around the country is a system of government that seems incapable of action.[1]

The decline in confidence in government directly affected the power of presidential administrations to lead the country. The Johnson and Nixon administrations began strongly but ended in political failure. Gerald Ford was a caretaker unable to win election on his own right. Carter was ineffective with Congress, was challenged for renomination within his own party, and was defeated in his reelection campaign. The defeat of two consecutive incumbent presidents showed that the president was no longer a transcendent figure in the American political system.

The Great Communicator

Into this atmosphere of growing political and economic crisis stepped Ronald Reagan. The decade of the 1980s began with a new president committed to restoring American economic health, U.S. power abroad, and traditional values at home.

Ronald Reagan almost seemed sent from central casting to play the hero who triumphed over adversity and crisis. In an age when most people get most of their political information from television, Reagan's skills in front of the camera, developed not only in his film roles but also in his years as a television spokes-man for General Electric, were invaluable. His ability to reduce complexities of modern bureaucracy to simple anecdotes and one-liners gave him the ability to communicate with ordinary people in a form they could understand. Once in office, his courage and humor in the face of an assassination attempt were endearing. He even joked with the surgeon, quipping, "I hope you're a Republican". He just seemed like a nice guy to most people.

This agreeable personality, rather than the ideology he was espousing, was the primary basis for his political success. But it is also true that Reagan's political philosophy tapped many of the resentments and frustrations of the American voter. In the beginning of his term, Reagan's ideological consistency was clearly an asset. Answering the common charge that his ideology was too simplistic for our complex world, he often repeated, "There are simple answers to many of our problems—simple but hard."[2] In place of the "malaise" of the Carter era, he offered optimism and elemental faith in America and its traditional values.

Reagan certainly restored much of the shattered credibility and faith in the presidency in his first term. In part because his strong ideology turned off liberal Americans, Reagan's approval rating among voters started lower than any recent president. It suffered serious decline during the severe recession of 1982-1983. But when prosperity was restored, so was the president's popularity with the voters. Like Republicans Eisenhower and Nixon before him, Reagan won a landslide reelection. Unlike Nixon, Reagan was able to retain his popularity throughout his second term.

Reaganism as Ideological Restoration

Reagan's political and policy successes led his more ardent supporters to talk of a "Reagan revolution." But it is certainly incongruous to think of such a militant social conservative and anticommunist as a revolutionary. A better characterization would be the "Reagan restoration." This term captures more accurately the spirit of the Reagan presidency. Ronald Reagan wanted to reverse the leftward movement of public policy in the 1960s and 1970s and to restore the policies that prevailed in a prior era. He rejected activist economic and social policies and sought to return to the philosophy of the limited state. He wanted to reverse the decline of U.S. power in the world by reviving the national security state and the cold war between the United States and the Soviet Union.

The Reagan era can be compared with other decades when Republican presidents came to power after turbulent times under Democratic leadership. In 1952, at the height of the cold war and in the midst of the Korean War, Dwight Eisenhower ended twenty years of Democratic control of the White House and presided over the conservative decade of the 1950s. Similarly, in 1920 Republican Warren Harding swept to power on the slogan "return to normalcy," playing on popular revulsion with the carnage of World War I and the Democrat Wilson's determination to keep the United States involved in European power politics. The 1980s, 1950s, and 1920s were all decades characterized by Republicans in the White House, the ascendancy of corporate power and the private pursuit of wealth, and social and political conservatism. Weary of government activism in either domestic problems or foreign conflicts, many sought to return to values they believed characterized a simpler, more idyllic American past. Republican presidents were politically successful by appealing to this desire to restore an imagined past when times were better.

Thinking of the Reagan presidency as a restoration also conjures up comparisons with other regimes that have sought to return their countries to some real or imagined former glory. There are some striking similarities between the spirit of the Reagan presidency and that of the DeGaulle presidency in postwar France, the empire of Napoleon II in mid-nineteenth century France, and the restoration of the emperor in nineteenth century Japan.

In each of these cases a country besieged by hostile outside forces and beset by internal turmoil turned to a leader who promised to return the country to its former greatness, security, and tranquillity. DeGaulle, like Napoleon II before him, came to power when France's status as a world power was in decline and internal dissent was rising. He, like Napoleon II, evoked in his countrymen memories of France's role as a world power and promised to return France to its former prominence by restoring its traditional values and institutions. Both men were able to solidify political coalitions that effectively governed France for decades. But neither was really able to slow significantly the decline of French power in the world.

The restoration of the Japanese emperor had some different twists. Like the French restorations, the emperor cult promised to bring back a prior golden era by returning the country to its traditional values and institutions. Like the French restorations, the emperor cult was successful as an ideology, creating a political system that governed for decades. But the twist was that the supposed golden era of previous emperors never really existed. The Japanese restoration promised a return to an imagined rather than a real past. Another irony is that under the emperor Japan rose to heights of world power undreamed of by previous emperors. The Japanese restoration was successful by invoking an imagined past, whereas French restorations were unsuccessful in restoring a real past.

From these cases it can be seen that restorations, like any ideological movement, rest partly on truth and partly on fiction. In some cases ideological restorations can succeed politically; they can renew the strength of a regime beset by internal and external crises. But it is rare for ideological restorations actually to return a country to a real past state of political grace. Ronald Reagan came to power in a period of economic crisis and decline of U.S. power. In the short to medium term he was able to restore prosperity and the perception of U.S. power. He was able to construct a political coalition that endured and ensured his political success. However, despite the surface prosperity, the Reagan years also brought the continued decline of the United States in the world economy, the weakening of key sectors of the economy, and the worsening of many social conditions in the United States. Although Reagan was politically successful while in office, it is too early to judge the place of his administration in history.

THE RESTORATION OF THE LIMITED STATE

The economic crises of the 1970s were major factors in the decline in confidence in government and the successive failures of incumbent presidents Ford and Carter to win reelection. In the 1980 television debates Ronald Reagan had asked the voters if they were better off after four years of the Carter administration. Many decided they were not. Reagan promised to restore prosperity by returning to the philosophy of limited government and putting faith in the "magic of the marketplace."

The Reagan administration moved quickly in its first year to set in motion its supply-side plan to revive the economy. Reagan skillfully utilized the traditional "honeymoon" period when a new president is generally given the benefit of the doubt by those in the political system who hope the new administration will prove successful. He used his considerable media skills in several appearances before Congress and the television cameras in 1981 to explain his economic program and sell it to Congress and the public. The assassination attempt in March that wounded the president also undoubtedly contributed dramatically to sympathy for the administration, just as the martyrdom of John Kennedy contributed to public sympathy for the Johnson administration in its first year.

Reaganomics consisted of two main elements: monetarism and supply-side fiscal policies. Monetarism was based on the belief that the rising inflation of the 1970s had been caused by too rapid expansion of credit by the Federal Reserve Board, which regulates the number of dollars circulating in the economy. Monetarism was an elaboration of the old theory of "tight money," that inflation could be limited by limiting the total number of dollars in the economy. Monetarism argued that the expansion of credit, or the money supply, should be slow and steady—that the money supply should grow only as fast as the overall economy.

The president has no direct control over monetary policy, which is made by the independent Federal Reserve Board (FRB). But the president does appoint new members to the board, and the FRB often does respond to presidential leadership. In his last year in office Jimmy Carter had appointed a new head of the FRB, Paul Volcker, who was committed to tight money policies, so the incoming Reagan administration got full cooperation in its monetarist philosophy from the FRB.

The president plays a much more direct role in fiscal policy. Each year he submits a recommended budget to Congress. While Congress has the final say on all taxing and spending decisions, a strong president can use his powers in the legislative process to shape the outcome of budgetary decisions.

Reagan's proposals to implement his philosophy in fiscal policy consisted of tax cuts, cuts in domestic spending, increases in military spending, and cuts in the federal apparatus regulating business. Most dramatic were the supply-side tax cuts. The president called for 10 percent across-the-board cuts in income taxes in 1982, 1983, and 1984, and for additional cuts in business taxes. In a televised

Reaganomics and the Federal Budget

The Philosophy of Limited Government

Government policies of the last few decades [are] responsible for our economic troubles. We forgot or just overlooked the fact that government . . . has a built-in tendency to grow. Now, we all had a hand in looking to government for benefits as if government had some sources of revenue other than our earnings.

But in all these years of government growth we've reached—indeed surpassed—the limit of our people's tolerance or ability to bear an increase in the tax burden.

The Budget Plan

First we must cut the growth of Government spending.
Second, we must cut tax rates so that once again work will be rewarded and savings encouraged.
Third, we must carefully remove the tentacles of excessive Government regulation which are strangling our economy.
Fourth, while recognizing the independence of the Institutions, we must work with the Federal Reserve Board to develop a monetary policy that will rationally control the money supply.
Fifth, we must move, surely and predictably, toward a balanced budget.[3]

speech, using colored charts as props, Reagan presented the fundamental argument of supply-side economics to the nation. The economic stimulus of the tax cuts would be so great that rapid economic growth would be unleashed. This growth in the private economy would mean that government would have a larger economic base from which to draw taxes, and thus tax revenues would increase even as tax rates were reduced.

In his budget message to Congress, Reagan also proposed a wide range of cuts in federal spending that would total $41.4 billion in 1982. Programs to be cut included subsidies to regional and local governments, federal subsidies to the arts and humanities, the synthetic fuels program, the space program, the postal service, and assistance to workers displaced by foreign competition. Programs for the poor were particularly targeted for cuts, including Medicaid, food stamps, welfare, and federal aid to education.

In a speech before a joint session of Congress, Reagan outlined several key exemptions from the budget cuts. Social Security retirees and veterans would not face cuts in their pensions. The safety net of programs for the "truly needy" would be preserved. The Pentagon would not share in the sacrifice; it would have its budget increased.

The president was assisted in his quest to pass his program through Congress by the fact that the 1980 election had produced Republican control of the Senate for the first time since 1954 and the largest contingent of House Republicans since the Nixon years. Combined with the "boll weevil" conservative southern Democrats in the House, the conservative ideological coalition passed a budget reflecting the president's priorities.

The final budget passed by Congress had spending cuts of $35 billion, an $18 billion increase for the military, and tax cuts for individuals and businesses cumulating at over $200 billion annually when fully implemented. Of the $35 billion cut from spending, nearly $25 billion came from programs to aid the poor, representing 70 percent of the total spending reductions.[4]

The legislative year of 1981 proved to be the high-water mark for Reagan budgetary policy. Reagan's dramatic success in getting Congress to pass his budget priorities was not matched in subsequent years. The supply-side tax cuts did not produce immediate economic recovery. Instead, the tight money policy produced the worst recession since the Great Depression. By mid-1982 the monthly unemployment rate hit 11.8 percent, the highest level since the 1930s. In the 1982 election the Democrats picked up 24 House seats, although they could not regain control of the Senate. But the gain of the votes in the House meant that the Democratic leadership now had effective control of the chamber, and any subsequent budgets would have to be negotiated with them.

Economic recovery did come in 1983, and not coincidentally the economy grew at a rapid 6 percent rate in 1984. But by then the fiscal and political climate had changed considerably. The honeymoon period was long gone. Congress had already made the easiest spending cuts; any subsequent cuts would be increasingly difficult politically. Annual federal deficits were climbing rapidly. The highest deficit in the Carter years was $74 billion, but the 1982 deficit was $111 and the 1983-1985 deficits averaged almost $200 billion annually.[5] Over the course of the Reagan years, control of economic and budgetary policy shifted away from the presidency and back to Congress.

THE RESTORATION OF THE NATIONAL SECURITY STATE

International Threats

In foreign policy, the election of Ronald Reagan meant the sustained attempt to restore the primacy of the national security ideology over the doctrine of hegemonic flexibility. It signaled a return to military force as the primary instrument of foreign policy, confrontation rather than detente with the Soviet Union, and pursuit of counterinsurgency in the Third World.

The 1970s had been a period of detente, of relaxing of tensions with the Soviet Union. Confrontation between the superpowers continued, but increasingly it was supplemented by negotiation on arms control and other issues of mutual interest. Conservative Republican president Richard Nixon had signed the path-breaking SALT I treaty with the Soviet Union and opened the door to relations with the communist government in China. Jimmy Carter had argued that it was necessary for Americans to give up their "inordinate fear" of communism in order to develop a constructive foreign policy. While military confrontation between the superpowers continued, rigid policies toward Soviet, Chinese, and other socialist regimes had been replaced by more flexible policies.

The 1970s had also brought disillusionment with the theories of containment and active counterinsurgency against revolutionary forces in the Third World. U.S. involvement in the Vietnam War had been based on the belief that it was America's responsibility to see that socialism did not spread through the Third World. But Vietnam had proved to be the wrong war in the wrong place at the wrong time, and thus it cast doubt on the strategy of counterinsurgency. Jimmy Carter's emphasis on human rights represented an attempt to establish new ways to project American values on the international scene beyond the use of military force.

But the 1970s was also a period of serious defeats for the United States in foreign policy. The Vietnam War was lost. OPEC manipulated the American economy, provoking major recessions. The decade ended on an ominous note with the Soviet Union invading Afghanistan and the Iranians holding Americans hostage in Tehran.

The Reagan administration came to power believing that the United States was in even deeper crisis in its international position than in domestic affairs. The Reagan campaign painted a picture of an alarming decline in U.S. power and prestige in the world. It attributed this decline to the policies of detente and the failure to maintain American military strength.

The Republican platform of 1980 argued that the Carter administration had allowed the Soviet Union to seize decisive military superiority, that

> Since 1977, the United States has moved from essential equivalence to inferiority in strategic nuclear forces . . . threatening the survival of the United States and making possible . . . political coercion and defeat.[6]

The Republicans pledged to return the United States to a position of "military superiority." The Republican platform expressed this anger at the weakening of the United States and outrage at terrorist incidents and hostage situations.

> Never before in modern history has the United States endured as many humiliations, insults, and defeats as it has during the past four years: our ambassadors murdered, our embassies burned, our warnings ignored, our diplomacy scorned, our diplomats kidnapped.[7]

Terrorism and the Revival of Global Counterinsurgency

The outrage of Americans at incidents of international terrorism was the basis of much of the Reagan campaign to take a more confrontational and militaristic approach toward selected hostile governments. The combination of fear of the Soviet military and apprehension over the spread of socialism and radicalism in the Third World provided the basis for the revival of the doctrine of counterinsurgency against revolutionary forces in the Third World. By focusing national attention on attacks on American civilians, the Reagan administration reinforced the perception that ordinary Americans were in imminent danger from hostile forces in the world. Terrorist violence was portrayed as the work of crazed fanatics senselessly aimed primarily at innocent victims. Since fanatics cannot be reasoned with, the use of military force could be justified.

The Reagan Counterinsurgency Campaign

A Confederation of Terrorist States

Iran, Libya, North Korea, Cuba, Nicaragua—continents away, tens of thousands of miles apart—but (they have) the same goals and objectives. Most of the terrorists who are kidnapping and murdering American citizens and attacking American installations are being trained, financed, and directly or indirectly controlled by a core group of radical and totalitarian governments—a new, international version of "Murder, Incorporated." And all of these states are united by one, simple, criminal phenomenon—their fanatical hatred of the United States, our people, our way of life, our international stature.

Sandinista Nicaragua as a Terrorist Nation and a Soviet Base

The Sandinistas are transforming their nation into a safe house, a command post for international terror . . . The Sandinistas have even involved themselves in the international drug trade. . . . There seems to be no crime to which the Sandinistas will not stoop—this is an outlaw regime.

With a billion dollars in Soviet-bloc aid, the communist government of Nicaragua has launched a campaign to subvert and topple its democratic neighbors. . . . Using Nicaragua as a base, the Soviets and Cubans can become the dominant power in the crucial corridor between North and South America. . . . They will be in a position to threaten the Panama Canal, interdict our vital Caribbean sea lanes, and ultimately move against Mexico. Should that happen, desperate Latin peoples by the millions would begin fleeing north into the cities of the southern United States.[8]

The vision of a worldwide terrorist conspiracy plotting the demise of the United States proved to be the 1980s version of the monolithic communist conspiracy that was at the heart of the cold war. In one speech on antiterrorism policy, Reagan referred to a "confederation of terrorist states." Like the vision of the monolithic communist bloc, the idea of state terrorism provided the justification for U.S. action against hostile regimes.

The counterterrorism campaign picked out small and weak countries, which were described as part of a worldwide network backed by the rival superpower, thus justifying using U.S. military power against much weaker nations. Because these regimes were portrayed as being in the Soviet orbit, they were by definition totalitarian and not legitimate governments with any popular backing. Thus, to destabilize or overthrow them could be justified in the name of democracy and self-determination.

In public, the Reagan administration took a tough line on terrorism. In some cases, rhetoric was matched by the direct use of U.S. military force, as in the bombing raids on Libya and the invasion of Grenada. Both these actions were justified as counterterrorism. The Libyan raid was called retaliation for terrorist bombings, and the invasion of Grenada was ostensibly to rescue captive American students. In other cases, aid to insurgents fighting left-wing regimes was begun, as in Nicaragua, Angola, Afghanistan, and Indochina. But in certain cases where the adversary was powerful, secret deals were made, as in trading of arms for hostages held by pro-Iranian forces.

Counterinsurgency in Nicaragua

The proving ground of the revived doctrine of counterinsurgency was Central America. In 1979 the Sandinista revolution overthrew the corrupt dictator Anastasio Somoza, whose family had ruled Nicaragua with an iron fist and with U.S. blessing for nearly fifty years. The Carter administration had tried different tactics to deal with the Sandinistas. It had cut off aid to the Somoza regime because of its human rights record, aid it restored in the early months after the revolution. But as Marxists gained controlling influence in the postrevolutionary government, the Carter administration distanced itself from the Sandinistas.

When the Reagan administration took power in 1981, it labeled the Sandinistas as Soviet clients and began a campaign to eradicate Marxist influence in Central America. The United States started to stage large-scale annual military maneuvers in Honduras, just miles from the Nicaraguan border, as a warning to the Sandinistas. Covert action to form a rebel force, popularly known as the "contras," was begun. In 1984 U.S. involvement in the mining of Nicaraguan harbors and CIA training manuals on assassination and terror tactics became public. These revelations led Congress to cut off funds for any intelligence activities directed against Nicaragua.

There ensued a running political battle between the administration and the

Democratic leadership in Congress over support for the contras. The administration sought to keep the aid flowing. When Congress cut it off, the Reagan administration returned each subsequent year to ask for renewal of the aid. In 1985 Congress did approve some military aid. But it is now known that members of the administration went to great lengths to maintain the aid even during the period when Congress had forbidden it. The secret, illegal diversion of profits from the secret, and probably illegal, sale of arms to the Iranians to fund the contras was just one example of the administration's attempts to evade congressional restrictions on its counterinsurgency campaign.

The Reagan administration felt justified in its support of the contras because it believed the Sandinistas were establishing a Soviet base on the Central American mainland. The Nicaraguans were portrayed as committed to both terrorist tactics and the ultimate triumph of the Soviet bloc over the West. Because the Sandinistas were defined as a serious military threat to the United States, a military response was justified. Because the Sandinista regime was seen as a totalitarian dictatorship, U.S. intervention into Nicaraguan internal affairs was called democratic.

However, there are other aspects of the Nicaraguan story that were absent from Reagan's public analyses of the situation. Nowhere in any Reagan speech was there mention of the U.S. occupation of Nicaragua for nearly two decades which only ended in the 1930s. Nowhere in any Reagan speech was there any admission that the United States was the Somozas' patron for forty years, thus earning the hostility of those who fought to overthrow his dictatorship. Reagan continually referred to Nicaragua as "on our doorstep," as if Central America belonged to the United States, an attitude more reminiscent of nineteenth century colonialism than of true concern with democracy in the region.

The New Cold War

In Reagan's first term his administration tried to restore another key element of the national security state: confrontation with the Soviet Union. He continued to give lip service to the calls for diplomacy and negotiation that had come to go hand in hand with the traditional anticommunism in foreign policy doctrine. Reagan had publicly opposed SALT II and every other major arms control agreement ever reached. But once in office he agreed to stay within its limits as long as the Soviets did. However, alongside the call for arms reductions was the fundamental hostility toward the Soviets that was characteristic of the cold war. In his first press conference, speaking without prepared text, Reagan reiterated his misgivings about the Soviets and his wariness of detente. The cold war was back.

One aspect of the new cold war was the issuing of a public document on Soviet military power that ultimately became institutionalized in a series of annual reports. These glossy brochures, full of pictures of Soviet military hardware, revived the image of the Soviet Union as an aggressive, warlike power seeking global military and political domination.

Reagan's cold war rhetoric was matched by action. The United States embarked on a massive military buildup. Adjusted for inflation, the Pentagon's budget increased by 8.1 percent in 1982, 8.6 percent in 1983, 5.0 percent in 1984, 8.6 percent in 1985, and 6.0 percent in 1986 for a cumulative increase of 41.8 percent. Reagan accelerated the arms programs planned in the later Carter budgets. A new generation of missiles was deployed in Europe, which gave the United States a new capability to make nuclear strikes deep into Soviet territory from bases in Europe. A new generation of more accurate nuclear missiles was deployed on the Trident submarines, making them much more useful as a first-strike weapon system. A new generation of cruise missiles was developed. The powerful land-based MX nuclear missile was revived, although controversy over its basing mode continued to delay deployment. Two new strategic bombers were put on line: the Stealth bomber, which was designed to evade Soviet radar detection, and the older B-1, which had been scrapped by the Carter administration. The navy was expanded to 600 ships.

The revival of the cold war drew opposition both at home and abroad. In the United States and western Europe, the peace movement was newly activated by fear of escalation of the arms race and heightened political tensions. NATO's deployment of a new generation of longer-range missiles that for the first time could strike into the Soviet interior from European bases was particularly controversial in Europe. In 1982 the Soviets canceled all arms control talks to pressure NATO to abandon such deployments. In western Europe opposition to the NATO strategy was manifested in the emergence of the antinuclear Green Party in West Germany, the prominence of disarmament forces in the British Labour Party, and similar developments in smaller states. The Reagan arms buildup also drew opposition in the United States. In the American midterm election of 1982, hundreds of ballot initiative campaigns were generated in towns, cities, and states proposing that the United States negotiate a freeze on the nuclear arms race. In November 1982, millions of Americans voted for a nuclear freeze, which carried virtually everywhere it was on the ballot.

Star Wars

It was in this situation of the breakdown of arms talks with the Soviet Union and growing opposition to the arms race in the United States and western Europe that Reagan offered his major innovation in nuclear doctrine, the Strategic Defense Initiative, or "Star Wars." Since the Soviet nuclear arsenal began to match the destructive capabilities of the U.S. arsenal in the 1960s, U.S. nuclear doctrine had been based on the principle of mutually assured destruction or MAD. Mutually assured destruction means that even if one superpower launched a devastating nuclear first strike, the other would be assured of having enough survivable nuclear capability to wipe out the aggressor in a second strike. This should deter either power from launching an attack. SALT I and II were based on this principle.

But in March 1983, President Reagan made a bold new proposal to break out of the reliance on holding the world's people hostage to nuclear obliteration in order to maintain the peace. He argued that strategic defense was possible, that new defensive technologies could be developed to destroy incoming Soviet missiles and thus provide a protective shield over the American population in case of any attack. Star Wars represented an alternative to arms control. In a televised address to the nation Reagan presented his vision.

> Wouldn't it be better to save lives than to avenge them? [We can] embark on a program to counter the awesome Soviet missile threat with measures that are defensive. . . . What if free people could live secure in the knowledge that their security did not rest upon the threat of instant U.S. retaliation to deter a Soviet attack, that we could intercept and destroy strategic ballistic missiles before they reached our own soil or that of our allies?[9]

The image of an effective defense against hostile missiles was certainly a reassuring one to Americans who lived daily with the threat of nuclear annihilation. But most analysts questioned whether such a defense could successfully be constructed. Opponents argued that Star Wars was not so much a real response to the threat of nuclear holocaust as symbolic reassurance to a frightened public. Most members of the scientific community expressed significant doubts about its feasibility.

The timing of the Star Wars initiative was instructive. The Reagan administration had been successful in getting Congress to approve the largest peacetime arms buildup in history. But political opposition at home and among the European allies was growing. The breakdown of the arms control process with the Soviet Union, which had been institutionalized over the prior 20 years, was reviving fears of U.S.-Soviet military conflict. It was in this atmosphere of heightened anxiety about nuclear war that the Reagan administration unveiled a proposed technological fix for U.S. vulnerability to Soviet nuclear capability.

THE SOCIAL AGENDA OF THE REAGAN RESTORATION

Early Caution

One of the most important themes of Ronald Reagan's campaign in 1980 was to return the United States to traditional social values. As a candidate Reagan had decried the erosion of the American family, the continuing secularization of American society, and the rise of crime and drugs in the streets. Political conservatives had particularly opposed federal court decisions such as those which had asserted a woman's right to obtain an abortion and those which had established the principle of affirmative action for minorities and women in employment. Conservatives wanted to restore the legal and social doctrines that prevailed before the liberal Warren Court expanded national protections of civil rights and liberties.

In the early Reagan administration, social issues generally took a back seat to economic and foreign policy. With the magnitude of his economic and foreign initiatives, Reagan was not willing to risk his finite political capital on bitter battles over explosive social conflicts. The Reagan administration did use some of his executive and legislative powers to pursue the conservative social agenda. Reagan gave token support to attempts in Congress to amend the Constitution to ban abortion. But this approach never came close to garnering the two-thirds vote in Congress necessary just to start the amendment process.

The Reagan Justice Department reversed more than a generation of practice and consistently entered civil rights cases in the federal courts on the side of white rather than minority litigants. But the more conservative elements of the administration were stymied when they tried to block renewal of the Voting Rights Act, which protects minority participation in the political process. Congressional Democrats and even some northern Republicans stood firm, and rather than be seen as opposing the right to vote, Reagan acceded to renewal of the act.

The Strategy of Judicial Appointments

However, over the course of his term Reagan made use of his considerable powers regarding the judicial branch to pursue his social agenda. The most useful of these powers proved to be the appointment of federal judges. The judicial branch of the national government often makes the controlling decisions on some of the most difficult social issues, the very ones elected officials generally try to avoid because of the controversy they engender. The president appoints Supreme Court justices and other federal judges whenever vacancies arise, subject to confirmation by majority vote of the Senate.

All presidents have taken political party affiliation into account when selecting federal judges. The recent Republican hold on the presidency meant that by the end of Reagan's term the majority of federal judges and six of the nine Supreme Court justices were Republicans. But historically, presidents have selected judges reflecting the diversity of views in their party. The Reagan administration's departure from past practice came in the degree of ideological screening of potential judicial appointees. Blocked in the attempt to pursue its social agenda in Congress, the Reagan administration made sure its judicial appointments furthered its social agenda.

The Democrats have been able to use their control of Congress to blunt the impact of conservative Republican presidents on the judiciary. For example, the Democrats waited until Jimmy Carter won office to increase the number of federal judges, thus giving him disproportionate impact on the lower federal courts even as he was denied a Supreme Court appointment.

Democrats in the Senate also have used their power to confirm Supreme Court nominations. Early in the Nixon term they used their ability to reject nominees to the Supreme Court in order to keep Nixon from appointing segregationist Southerners, forcing the appointment of such moderates as Harry Blackmun, who wrote the decision legalizing abortion and Lewis Powell, who wrote the key decisions endorsing affirmative action.

In his early years Reagan had one advantage over Nixon in his court appointments. The Republicans controlled the Senate, which must confirm nominees to the bench. Reagan's first Supreme Court appointment was masterful. By selecting Sandra Day O'Connor, Reagan diffused the most serious opposition to a conservative justice—that "he" would be insensitive to women's issues. Reagan got his second opportunity to name a Supreme Court justice when Chief Justice Warren Burger resigned in 1986. Burger's resignation came in time to allow Reagan to name a new justice, Antonin Scalia, and to elevate the very conservative justice, William Rehnquist, to chief justice while Republicans still controlled the Senate.

The Democrats recaptured the Senate in the elections of 1986, dramatically changing the politics of court appointments. When moderate justice Lewis Powell resigned in 1987, Reagan nominated the strong ideological conservative Robert Bork to fill the position. The Democratic Senate voted by a slim margin not to confirm Bork because he had such an activist agenda for reshaping legal doctrine. Only when Reagan nominated the more moderate Anthony Kennedy was the Senate willing to confirm.

CONCLUSION

The early Reagan presidency can best be characterized as an attempt at ideological restoration. Ronald Reagan was able to revive the flagging power of the presidency and to some degree reverse the leftward trends of public policy in the 1960s and 1970s. In domestic policy he returned to the philosophy of the limited state, cutting taxes and many social programs. In foreign policy he revived the doctrines of the national security state, embarking on a major military buildup, taking a cold war stance toward the Soviet Union, and launching several counterinsurgency operations in the Third World.

However, as his first term progressed, Reagan's hold on public policy began to weaken. Although Reagan was able to win a landslide reelection, the ideological dynamics of his second term were different from those of the early Reagan restoration.

NOTES

1. Jimmy Carter, *Public Papers of the Presidents, 1979* (Washington, DC: U.S. Government Printing Office, 1980), pp. 1235-1247.

2. This line goes back as far as 1968 and appears in campaign speeches and presidential statements. Ronald Reagan, *The Creative Society* (New York: Devon-Adair, 1968), p. 20.

3. Ronald Reagan, *Public Papers of the Presidents, 1981.* (Washington, DC: U.S. Government Printing Office, 1982), pp. 79-83, 221-222.

4. Congressional Quarterly, *Reagan's First Year* (Washington, DC: Congressional Quarterly, 1982).

5. Office of Management and Budget, *The United States Budget in Brief, Fiscal 1985*, (Washington, DC: U.S. Government Printing Office, 1985), p. 84.

6. Ibid., pp. 207, 205.

7. Donald B. Johnson and Kirk H. Porter, *National Party Platforms of 1980* (Urbana: University of Illinois Press, 1982), p. 177.

8. Ronald Reagan, *Public Papers of the Presidents, 1985* (Washington, DC: U.S. Government Printing Office, 1986), pp. 894-900, and *Public Papers of the Presidents, 1986* (Washington, DC: U.S. Government Printing Office, 1987), pp. 352-357.

9. Ronald Reagan, *Public Papers of the Presidents, 1983* (Washington, DC: U.S. Government Printing Office, 1984).

11

FROM REAGAN TO BUSH: THE PULL OF THE POLITICAL CENTER

IDEOLOGY IN THE LATER REAGAN PRESIDENCY

The Persistence of Divided Government

From Eisenhower in 1954 through Nixon, Reagan, and now Bush, every Republican president has had to face a Congress controlled at least in part by Democrats. And with the brief exception of the heady days of the early Reagan restoration, when the Republicans captured control of the Senate for the first time since 1954, Republicans presidents have had little reason to think their party would win control of Congress anytime soon.

Republican presidents can use the symbolic props of the ceremonial presidency without the cooperation of congressional Democrats. Republican presidents can skillfully articulate their philosophies and policy positions without the cooperation of Congress. They can go on TV and appeal directly to the American people without the cooperation of Congress. But they cannot pass legislation or appropriate funds without congressional approval. Presidents are limited in their ability to shape public policy unless they can win congressional assent.

The advantages of the majority party in Congress go beyond simply having the most votes on budgets and other legislation. The American political system gives great advantages to the party that holds a majority in a house of Congress. The majority party names the chair of every committee in that house. It controls the flow of legislation to the floor of that house. It takes the lion's share of the staff and other resources.

The dilemma Republican presidents thus face is between conflict and cooperation with Democrats in Congress. If a Republican president is going to have any impact on public policy, he must have the support of at least some congressional Democrats. Yet if the Republican Party is to ever regain control of Congress, it must draw clear lines of conflict between its policy stances and those of congressional Democrats.

All recent Republican presidents have oscillated between these two choices over the course of their administrations. Dwight Eisenhower leaned more toward cooperation with congressional Democrats and bipartisan policy-making. Ronald Reagan favored ideological confrontation more often. But all Republican presidents have had to find ways to work with Congress and yet to draw distinctions between their party and its philosophy and that of congressional Democrats.

In his first two years in office Ronald Reagan largely opted for the strategy of ideological polarization and confrontation with the Democrats in Congress. He passed his economic and budget policies by putting together a coalition of Republicans and a handful of conservative southern Democrats.

After this coalition lost the votes to control the House of Representatives, in the 1982 midterm election, Reagan continued to articulate his conservative philosophy but showed some willingness to move toward the political center, particularly in his opening toward the Soviet Union. The Reagan administration showed some willingness to compromise on budgetary policy as well, although generally it was congressional Republicans who took the lead in working out agreements with congressional Democrats on budgetary matters.

However, at the same time the Reagan administration moved more toward the political center in foreign and economic policy, it continued to pursue a strategy of ideological polarization with regard to many aspects of social policy, particularly in its judicial appointments. Like Nixon before him, while abandoning the cold war policies favored by the Republican right, Reagan covered his right flank by taking a confrontational stance toward congressional Democrats on key domestic issues.

The Reagan Restoration had peaked as a political phenomenon by the middle of Reagan's first term. Several developments in domestic politics, the economy, and world affairs put the ideological conservatives in the administration increasingly on the defensive in the later Reagan presidency, particularly in the second term. While Reagan remained one of the most personally popular presidents in a generation, the ability of his administration to chart a consistent conservative direction in public policy lessened considerably over the course of his incumbency. The Reagan presidency prospered, but the Reagan restoration increasingly stalled.

The Loss of the Ideological Majority in Congress

Probably most important in checking the Reagan restoration were the congressional elections of 1982, 1984, and 1986. The election of 1980 had given the impression of a broad mandate for Reagan's conservative policies. The Republicans won control of the Senate for the first time in 26 years and had one of their largest House delegations since the 1950s.

But in 1982 the Democrats recaptured 24 House seats, and thus effective control of the House of Representatives, although they failed to recapture the Senate. The ideological coalition between Republicans and a handful of conservative southern Democrats, which had provided the votes to pass Reagan's first-year budget plan in the House, was rendered ineffective. Now the Reagan administration would have to bargain with the Democratic leadership in the House to pass legislation and get funds appropriated for programs.

The Cycle of Presidential Power

The congressional elections of 1984 and 1986 reinforced this reality. In 1984, even as Reagan won a landslide reelection, the Democrats held onto their House majority, losing only 15 seats. In the midst of the Reagan landslide the Democrats picked up two Senate seats, although control of the Senate remained in Republican hands.

From 1985 on, Reagan faced the fate of all presidents since the passage of the Twenty-second Amendment, which limits the president to two terms. After 1984 Reagan's name would never be on a national ballot. Democratic members of Congress would never fear his active opposition, and Republican members of Congress would never seek his favor to the same degree that they did when he was the likely standard-bearer of his party in the next presidential election. Second-term presidents are increasingly irrelevant to the electoral calculations of members of Congress, "lame ducks" in the electoral competition.

Reagan was now further on the downhill slide of the cycle of presidential power. Most presidents have the most influence on Congress and domestic policy in their first year or two, when they are still in their "honeymoon" period with Congress and the public. By the first midterm election presidents usually have lost some of their popularity with voters, and their party usually loses some seats in Congress.

While most incumbent presidents win reelection, they rarely get a second honeymoon. Instead, as lame ducks, their influence wanes and usually their popularity fades considerably. The second midterm election of a president's administration generally brings more serious losses for his party in Congress and the final blow to a president's ability to influence domestic policy. Often presidents have long since turned to foreign affairs as their most likely arena for policy success.

Reagan was surprisingly immune to the usual decline in a president's personal popularity, but this did not spare him the loss of influence over policy in the second term. The midterm election of 1986 was a further blow to both Reagan and congressional Republicans, as the Democrats regained control of the Senate for the first time in the Reagan years. Like Eisenhower before him, Reagan found that his personal popularity could not be translated into permanent gains for his party in Congress. Also like Eisenhower, Reagan would have to compromise with Democrats in Congress in order to govern.

The Chronic Fiscal Crisis

However, political factors were not the only problems the Reagan restoration faced. The very success that Reagan had in getting his economic policies adopted in his first years in office meant that his administration was held responsible for the costs and benefits of these policies. When some of the costs of the policies of the Reagan restoration became apparent, resistance to administration policy leadership stiffened in Congress and the broader political system.

Reaganomics had some immediate adverse consequences. The tight money policies adopted to check the inflation of the later Carter years pushed the country into a deep recession, the worst since the Great Depression. The annual rate of unemployment for 1982 and 1983 neared 10 percent, the highest level in over 40 years. Reagan was partially successful in blaming these conditions on the "mess" he had inherited from the Carter administration, particularly when the country began to recover in 1982, in time for the congressional elections. But the losses of congressional Republicans in 1982 were largely due to the country's skepticism about Reaganomics.

However, the recession of 1981-1982 was followed by a strong recovery and several years of sustained economic growth. Reagan's personal popularity recovered along with the economy. Yet economic growth did not solve all the problems of Reaganomics. The 25 percent cut in income taxes and the other tax cuts of Reaganomics were never matched by spending cuts of the same magnitude, creating a permanent budget deficit. The supply-side theory that lower tax rates would spur such rapid economic growth that in the long run greater total tax revenues would be reaped proved incorrect. The combined effects of the Reagan tax cuts and the recession pushed the deficit to over $200 billion in 1983. Even the rapid economic growth of the mid-1980s did not ease the problem. Budget deficits remained in the hundreds of billions of dollars throughout the Reagan presidency and into the Bush administration.

Related to the budget deficits were the trade deficits. Until the 1980s, in almost every year since the end of World War II, the United States had run a trade surplus with the rest of the world. That is, it sold more goods abroad than it bought from abroad. But this changed dramatically in the Reagan years as the United States began to run a chronic trade deficit of more than $100 billion a year. The causes and effects of the budget deficit and the trade deficit will be explored more completely in succeeding chapters. But it is clear that the chronic trade and budget deficits undermined the ability of the Reagan administration to exercise leadership in economic policy. In the later Reagan years Congress increasingly took control of economic policy away from the administration.

In 1983 it was a coalition of congressional Republicans and Democrats who engineered the reform of the Social Security system and a small increase in excise taxes. In 1985 its was another coalition of congressional forces that developed and passed the Gramm-Rudman Deficit Reduction Act, the most serious attempt to control the budget deficits of the Reagan years, and the tax reform package that attempted to make the tax system fairer by closing some of its loopholes. As the trade deficit grew along with the budget deficit, congressional leaders, particularly Democrats, also tried to exercise leadership in foreign economic policy.

If the Reagan tax cuts had brought the national books into balance, the supply-side advocates in the administration would have been in the position to continue to direct national economic policy. But as the red ink mounted and the administration continued to prove unable or unwilling to meet the challenge, control of budgetary policy shifted to Congress.

In contrast with the first economic messages of the Reagan administration in 1981, which had charted the course of national policy, the running joke on Capitol Hill was that later Reagan budgets were "dead on arrival," lifeless exercises that had little real impact on congressional decisions. The Reagan administration could block any new taxes with its veto threats, but it provided little positive leadership out of the deficit quagmire.

The Iran-Contra Scandal

The Iran-contra scandal was another political and policy failure that reduced the Reagan administration's ability to influence public policy in its later years. The origins of this scandal will be examined more closely in Chapter 13. Early in Reagan's second term, news began to leak of secret deals and arms shipments to Iran in order to obtain the release of American hostages held by pro-Iranian forces in Lebanon.

These deals were in direct contradiction of the official White House policy of never negotiating with terrorists and probably violated laws forbidding certain forms of assistance to terrorist nations. Ronald Reagan had made Jimmy Carter's lack of toughness is dealing with the Iranians who held American hostages a major campaign issue in 1980. But now it was revealed that the Reagan administration had sent American arms to Iran to obtain the release of hostages.

It was soon also revealed that some of the profits from the arms deals had been diverted to aid the contra rebels fighting to overthrow the government of Nicaragua. This was clearly in direct violation of laws passed by Congress cutting off U.S. aid to the contras. The Reagan administration's attempts to overthrow the government of Nicaragua had always been controversial in Congress, and in 1983 Congress had forbidden the use of any more government funds to support the contra rebels. Once the diversion of some of the profits of the Iran arms sales to the contras became known, congressional investigators discovered a series of secret government actions to fund the war in Nicaragua despite the congressional ban on aid.

The Iran-contra situation was potentially the Reagan administration's Watergate. The parallels were many. Once again a Republican administration, frustrated with political opposition in a Democratic Congress, resorted to secret government, secret slush funds, and even secret war to pursue policies rejected by Congress. Once again an administration had unilaterally made war and conducted foreign policy without regard to Congress' war powers. Once again a president had espoused one set of values in public but had acted in exactly the opposite manner in policy-making. Once again the misdeeds of the executive branch were paraded into Americans' living rooms through marathon televised congressional hearings.

However, there were some important differences between Watergate and Iran-contra. The Reagan administration had used secret government against foreign, not domestic, opponents. It had not made the same kind of direct attack on political opponents and directly subverted the electoral process as had the Nixon White House. Reagan was an immensely popular president who still enjoyed strong support throughout the country, while Nixon had never really enjoyed the trust or affection of large segments of the American population.

Perhaps most important, there was no convincing evidence linking Ronald Reagan personally to the misdeeds of his advisers. There was no "smoking gun," no record of the president's involvement in illegal activities on tape. Instead, the Tower Commission, which the president appointed to investigate the controversy, concluded that Reagan did not have any personal knowledge of the misdeeds of his administration. The congressional committee investigating the scandal was also unable to prove any direct involvement of Reagan in illegal activities.

However, the congressional and Tower Commission reports painted a picture of a president uninvolved in the daily decision making of his own administration. Even though they cleared Reagan of any direct responsibility, it damaged the president severely to be seen as a hands-off executive, not really in charge of his own house. The separation of Reagan's personality from the difficult decisions of governing had proven politically useful in insulating the president from damage when policy failed, in creating the "teflon presidency" where no policy failure stuck to the president himself. But it was almost as damaging for Reagan to be seen as unaware of crucial decisions of the administration he was supposed to be leading.

The Iran-contra affair undermined the credibility of the Reagan administration and further reduced the president's power to affect public policy. For much of the second term the White House had to spend a large proportion of its staff resources putting out the political fires the scandal had caused, diverting attention from other issues. Like most presidents before him, Reagan found his ability to influence events fading ever faster as his second term progressed.

New Directions in Foreign Policy

However, even as the Reagan presidency felt its influence on events in Washington slipping away, it was able to turn to foreign affairs to score policy successes. Like many prior presidents facing seemingly insurmountable obstacles in domestic politics, in his second term Reagan turned more and more to summitry to repair his sagging public image.

Perhaps the most dramatic changes in the policies of the Reagan administration in its second term were the changes in its attitudes toward the Soviet Union. In his first term Reagan had rejected the detente of the 1970s and returned the country to the hard-line cold war policies of the national security state. The one major exception to Reagan's budget cuts was the Pentagon, which was flooded with funds to pursue weapons projects from MX missiles to Star Wars space defenses.

The new cold war met with resistance both in the United States and in western Europe. Peace movements mobilized hundreds of thousands to demonstrate against the deployment of a new generation of missiles in Europe and other escalations of the arms race.

But probably the most significant development that led to the reversal of the cold war policies of the early Reagan administration was the rise of Mikhail Gorbachev as the leader of the Soviet Union. Gorbachev was a new kind of Soviet leader who charted bold new courses in both the internal and international policies of the Soviet Union. Under Gorbachev's leadership the Soviet communists made radical reforms in their economy, dramatically democratized their political system, significantly loosened their control over eastern Europe, and made sweeping and sincere initiatives for arms control and reduction of tensions between East and West.

Under these conditions it became increasingly difficult for the Reagan administration to portray the Soviet Union as the "evil empire." Instead, the Reagan administration showed the flexibility to deal with the new Soviet leadership. Reagan and Gorbachev met at four summits in Reagan's second term, and in 1987 they concluded an arms control treaty that reduced the level of nuclear forces in Europe. Like Nixon before him, Reagan, the career cold warrior, found that new international and domestic realities meant that military power was not the only effective means of dealing with the Soviet Union, that political and diplomatic tools were sometimes better means of achieving U.S. objectives.

Reagan's Reversal on Arms Control and the Soviet Union

The Evil Empire

Reagan's First Press Conference: So far detente's been a one-way street that the Soviet Union has used to pursue its own aims. . . .
The only morality they recognize is what will further their cause, meaning they reserve unto themselves the right to commit any crime, to lie, to cheat, in order to attain that. . . . I think when you do business with them, even as in detente, you keep that in mind.

Speech to Evangelical Ministers: I urge you [not] to ignore the facts of history and the aggressive impulses of an evil empire, to simply call the arms race a giant misunderstanding and thereby remove yourself from the struggle between right and wrong and good and evil. . . . While they preach the supremacy of the state, declare its omnipotence over individual man, and predict its eventual domination of all people on the Earth, they are the focus of evil in the modern world.

For Arms Control

Reykjavik Summit: We proposed the most sweeping and generous arms control proposal in history. We offered the complete elimination of all ballistic missiles—Soviet and American—from the face of the Earth by 1996. While we parted company with the American offer still on the table, we are closer than ever before to agreements that could lead to a safer world without nuclear weapons. . . . We proposed a 10-year period in which we began with the reduction of all strategic nuclear arms . . . [by] 50 percent in the first five years. During the next five years, we would continue by eliminating all remaining offensive ballistic missiles, of all ranges.

The INF Treaty: This treaty represents a landmark in post-war history because it is not just an arms control, but an arms reduction, agreement. Unlike treaties of the past, this agreement does not simply establish ceilings for new weapons; it actually reduces the number of such weapons. In fact, it altogether abolishes an entire class of U.S. and Soviet nuclear missiles. . . . I believe this treaty will not only lessen the threat of war but can also speed along a process that may someday remove that threat entirely. Indeed, this treaty . . . signals a broader understanding between the United States and the Soviet Union.[1]

Partisan Polarization over the Future of the Judiciary

While the second Reagan term saw a dramatic reversal of his conservative stance in international relations and the reassertion of the political center in congressional leadership in budgetary policy, there was one significant exception to the general drift toward the political center in the later Reagan years: the continuing attempt of the administration to achieve its social agenda through transforming the federal judiciary.

In the early Reagan years, the conservative social agenda of the Christian right had been deferred as economic and foreign policy initiatives were given highest priority. However, as the Reagan administration abandoned ideologically conservative positions in foreign policy and gradually lost control of economic policy, it returned to the social agenda that had been postponed in the early days of the Reagan restoration.

Perhaps the most lasting legacy a president leaves is his judicial appointments, who serve on the federal bench for life. Over the course of his term Reagan appointed a majority of federal judges and three of the nine Supreme Court justices.

All presidents have chosen almost all their judicial appointees from their own political party. But the Reagan administration departed from precedent in the degree to which it used not only political party but also political ideology as a litmus test of judicial candidates. All of Reagan's appointments to the federal judiciary were ideological conservatives, and the vast majority were affluent white males. In his first term Reagan made 167 judicial appointments. Of these only 17, or just 10 percent, were women, and only 2, or just 1 percent, were black.[2]

Reagan's first two appointments to the Supreme Court were relatively uncontroversial. Going against the pattern that he showed in lower court appointments, Reagan skillfully defused possible opposition to an ideologically conservative appointment in his first selection by choosing a woman, Sandra Day O'Connor, thus muting feminist opposition. His second appointment was to replace Chief Justice Warren Burger, a strong conservative force on the court. Picking another conservative to take Burger's seat and elevating another conservative to the largely symbolic role of Chief Justice would have little immediate impact on the balance of votes on the court. Therefore, Reagan's choice of Antonin Scalia to join the court and the promotion of William Rehnquist to Chief Justice drew little fire.

But when moderate Republican Lewis Powell resigned, the situation was different. Powell had been a swing vote on the court and had written key opinions in support of civil rights and affirmative action. Now another conservative appointment would shift the ideological balance of the court, giving the hard-line conservative faction a decisive majority.

The struggle over the confirmation of Robert Bork highlighted the issues at stake in the ideological composition of the federal judiciary. Bork was a law professor before he became a judge. It was as a professor that Bork stated most clearly an activist conservative theory for systematically reversing the direction of the Supreme Court.

Bork consistently followed the conservative line on all major issues. He espoused the Christian right's principles on abortion and religion in schools. He advocated the economic theory of laissez-faire in his writings on antitrust. He espoused the national security state's view of executive power in foreign affairs. His writings provided the philosophical justification for the positions a new militantly conservative majority in the judicial branch would pursue.

Bork did moderate his positions in his confirmation hearings, trying to dispel the image that he was an activist who wanted to radically reformulate legal doctrine. But most supporters as well as opponents took Bork's writings before being nominated as a better gauge of his philosophy and probable behavior than his testimony before a committee controlled by the political opposition.

At the heart of Bork's judicial philosophy was the doctrine of original intent, which argues that issues of constitutional law should be decided almost solely on the basis of what the framers of the Constitution intended. The doctrine of original intent is ostensibly a theory of limited government. It has been used to argue that the framers never intended to grant Congress or the courts the power to deeply regulate economic activity and political life. For example, in his writings on antitrust he was highly critical of government overregulation of business, espousing a laissez-faire preference for market decision making.

Bork also favored restricting court scrutiny of racial and gender discrimination in the workplace, schools, and other institutions. Bork had opposed the civil rights acts of the 1960s. He was very critical of court decisions implementing these acts, repeatedly arguing that the courts had overstepped their bounds and had become too interventionist in interpreting the Constitution and civil rights statutes.

On the other hand, since Bork's doctrine of original intent meant he did not recognize rights not specifically enumerated in the Constitution, original intent was used as a theory of virtually unlimited government regarding reproductive behavior, police powers, the actions of the military and national security agencies, and the rights of political dissent. Perhaps the thorniest issue the doctrine of original intent raised was the issue of the right to privacy, which was the legal basis of the *Roe v. Wade* decision that legalized abortion. The Constitution never specifically addresses a right to privacy. But prevailing legal doctrine inferred from the Bill of Rights protections of person and property that the Constitution provides a general protection of an individual's right to privacy. From this the Supreme Court in *Roe v. Wade* ruled that government could not interfere with a woman's private decision whether to have a child.

But the theory of original intent does not recognize rights that are not specifically enumerated in the Constitution. Bork's position was that the courts should not invent an unenumerated right to privacy. By this reasoning *Roe v. Wade* was wrongly decided and thus, presumably, should be overturned.

Bork also sided with big government on national security issues. He argued that legislation to put some nominal legislative and judicial controls on the behavior of the CIA and other intelligence agencies was unconstitutional interference in the prerogative of the executive to conduct foreign policy. Bork also had a very restricted view of Congress' right to limit presidential warmaking. About President Nixon's decision in 1971 to invade Cambodia without consulting Congress, Bork wrote that the attempts by Congress to limit the president's conduct of the war "constitutes a trespass upon the powers of the Constitution reposes exclusively in the President."[3]

After a bitter battle, the Senate refused to confirm the Bork nomination. Reagan's next choice had to withdraw because of personal indiscretions. Only when Reagan selected a relatively unknown quantity, Anthony Kennedy, did the Senate finally confirm a new justice.

CONTINUITY AND CHANGE IN THE BUSH ADMINISTRATION

In 1988 George Bush won the presidential election with 54 percent of the popular vote, carrying 41 states, the fifth presidential victory for Republicans in the last six elections. The Republican presidential majority first put together by Richard Nixon and solidified by Ronald Reagan survived one of the toughest tests of American politics. The Republicans won a third consecutive presidential election, the first time either party had done so since the 1940s.

Yet as had been their pattern for most of the last 40 years, the same voters elected a majority of Democrats to Congress. So George Bush faced the same dilemma as all recent Republican presidents. Like his predecessors, in his first term Bush exhibited a mix of partisan polarization and bipartisan cooperation. Budgetary policy and social issues such as abortion continued to divide Congress and the president. But on the other hand, on foreign policy and in certain cases of domestic policy, bipartisan cooperation was possible. Later chapters will detail the policy struggles of the first Bush term. This section provides a general overview that puts the Bush presidency in comparative perspective.

In his campaign and in his early administration, Bush distanced himself somewhat from the Reagan approach and endorsed the principle of the activist state in such areas as the environment, education, child care, and the minimum wage. Once in office he worked with congressional Democrats to put together a package to bail out the ailing savings and loan industry. The "war on drugs" also generally received support from congressional Democrats, whose response was mainly to try to outbid the president on how tough they could be and how much more they could spend than the administration recommended.

However, any significant movement to a more activist approach to other domestic problems remained checked by the deficit. Bush and the congressional Democrats were able to reach compromise budget agreements, but with a few minor exceptions Bush stuck to his campaign promise of no new taxes. Ideological conservatives flayed him for the budget agreements he entered that included small tax increases, but, like Reagan before him, Bush blocked any major tax increase which would have had significant impact on the deficit. Bush subtly altered Republican presidential rhetoric on the role of government. But on taxes he wanted to sharpen the polarization between the parties, hoping to retain the Republican image as tax cutters while painting the Democrats as the "tax and spend" party.

Thus the man who campaigned to be the "education president" offered few resources for education in his budgets. The man who called himself the "environmental president" compromised with congressional Democrats on a new Clean Air Act, but refused to sign an international treaty on gases polluting the environment. Despite the Republicans' rhetorical commitment to family issues, no significant new funding for child care or parental leave from work was forthcoming. As the election of 1992 approached, both Bush and congressional Democrats were less inclined to compromise. In 1991 Bush twice vetoed legislation that would have extended unemployment benefits before acquiescing on a third such bill. Bush also twice vetoed bills that would have required employers to offer unpaid leave for workers who had young children or family emergencies.

On abortion and other social issues the Bush administration also preferred polarization over bipartisanship. Bush continued the Reagan strategy of pursuing the conservative social agenda through court appointments. In his first term Bush was able to nominate two Supreme Court justices, David Souter and Clarence Thomas. Souter was a relative unknown with little public record, but he was known to be philosophically conservative. Although his opponents tagged him the "stealth" nominee, Congress had little basis for rejecting him and he was confirmed easily.

When the first black on the Supreme Court, civil rights stalwart Thurgood Marshall, resigned, Bush made a much more controversial choice. He nominated Clarence Thomas. Thomas, like Marshall, is black, but as Ronald Reagan's choice to head the Equal Employment Opportunity Commission, he had bitterly attacked affirmative action and other components of the historic black political agenda. Thomas appeared to be headed for a close confirmation when one of his former staffers accused him of sexual harassment on the job. However, lacking convincing evidence of such wrongdoing, opponents could not block Senate confirmation.

Thomas made the fifth of the nine Supreme Court justices named by either Reagan or Bush. With Marshall gone, only one historic liberal remains on the court. The cumulative impact of these appointments can be seen in recent court decisions in abortion, affirmative, and other cases. The court began to back away from the strong guarantees of access to abortion it had established in *Roe v. Wade*. A judicial revolution like the one spurred by the liberal Warren Court in the 1950s and 1960s was not yet in sight, but the direction of the court had clearly been changed.

While partisan polarization was the rule in social policy, bipartisanship was strongest in foreign policy. More than at any time in the last twenty years, the development of a new bipartisan consensus on foreign policy seemed like a realistic possibility. There remained considerable uncertainty about what should guide U.S. policy as the cold war, which had defined the nation's international position for half a century, was coming to an end. But in the short term, the reduction of tensions with the Soviet Union received broad political support from both parties.

President Bush also generally garnered bipartisan support for his military interventions in the Third World. The invasion of Panama drew little criticism and much support from congressional Democrats. Bush's decision to send troops to the Persian Gulf also won broad support. Most congressional Democrats did oppose the resolution authorizing the president to begin the war with Iraq, but Bush won enough Democratic votes to pass it through both houses of Congress. Once the war began, virtually all congressional Democrats declared their support for the troops and the president's policy. Since the policy was so painless and successful, congressional criticism was largely silenced.

CHARACTERIZING THE ECONOMIC AND FOREIGN POLICY SHIFTS SINCE 1981

The 1980s began with the conservative ideological offensive of the Reagan restoration. The Reagan restoration did have a significant impact on public policy, but it was never as dramatic as the bold rhetoric of the great communicator. Democrats in Congress were able to blunt many of the policy initiatives of the Reagan restoration. As the decade wore on, first Reagan and then his successor, George Bush, moved more toward the political center on certain key issues, although both men also took staunch conservative positions on other important issues. The ideological dynamics of economic and budgetary and foreign policy in the 1980s are shown in Figures 11.1 and 11.2. These are very rough generalization about a complex set of issues, but they serves to clarify the overall movement of policy.

Ronald Reagan carried on a sustained rhetorical campaign against big government throughout his presidency, propounding the themes of laissez-faire and the free market. But even his own policy proposals were less harsh on government spending than was his rhetoric. Reagan's first two budget proposals had a significant impact on the kinds of programs the government spent its money on, and did slow the growth of government spending characteristic of the 1960s and 1970s. But from 1983 on congressional Democrats and more moderate Republicans had greater control over budgetary policy than did the Reagan administration, so policy outcomes were more a continuation of the status quo than a revolution in public policy.

Figure 11.1
Economic Policy Positions and Outcomes Since 1981

SOCIAL DEMOCRACY	SOCIAL SECURITY STATE	LIMITED INTEREST STATE	LAISSEZ-FAIRE

[Policy Outcomes: 1938-1963]

[Policy Outcomes: 1964-1980]

[Reagan Rhetorical Stances]

[Reagan Budget Proposals]

[Bush Rhetorical Stances]

[Policy Outcomes 1983-1992]

Figure 11.2
Foreign Policy in the 1980s

PEACE MOVEMENT	HEGEMONIC FLEXIBILITY	NATIONAL SECURITY	HOLY WAR

[1946-1968
Bipartisan
Consensus]

[1970s-1980s Political Center]

[Reagan Rhetoric: 1981-1984]

[Policy: 1981-1984]

[Reagan-Bush Rhetoric
and Policy: 1987-1990]

In the 1988 election and his first term in office, George Bush sent more mixed messages about the role of government than had Reagan. On the philosophical level Bush endorsed such activist government programs as an increase in the minimum wage, expansion of child care and education programs, and toughening of the Clean Air Act. However, like Republicans Nixon and Eisenhower before him, at the same time Bush endorsed particular expansions of government programs, he still talked about limited government and was reluctant to provide funds for new programs.

In foreign policy the changes between the early Reagan restoration and the later Reagan and early Bush years were even more dramatic. The Reagan restoration attempted to return to the practices of the national security state that had dominated American foreign policy in the 1950s and 1960s. In his first term Reagan's rhetoric was even more hard-line than that of most of his cold war predecessors. Again, some of his policies were blocked by congressional Democrats, but because the president has more constitutional and political powers in foreign policy-making, the Reagan restoration had more impact on foreign policy than on budgetary policy.

But in his second term, faced with the Gorbachev phenomenon, Reagan reversed course. From the Reykjavik summit on, he adopted the stance of hegemonic flexibility, increasingly sounding more like Jimmy Carter than the earlier Ronald Reagan. Swept along by the dramatic changes in eastern Europe and the Soviet Union, George Bush went further than any previous president in contemplating the end of the cold war and a new U.S. foreign policy. The world system has changed so much in recent years that foreign policy in the 1990s is unlikely to fit the categories of thought that have dominated policy-making for more than 40 years.

NOTES

1. Ronald Reagan, *Public Papers of the Presidents, 1981* (Washington, DC: U.S. Government Printing Office, 1982), p. 57; *1983*, pp. 359-364; *1986*, pp. 1411-1415; 1987, pp. 1455-1456.

2. George Edwards III and Stephen Wayne, *Presidential Leadership* (New York: St. Martin's Press, 1985).

3. Robert Bork, "Comments on Legality of U.S. Action in Cambodia," *American Journal of International Law* 65 (1971), p. 79.

12

THE CHRONIC FISCAL CRISIS

ECONOMIC PERFORMANCE IN THE REAGAN-BUSH YEARS

Policy Dynamics

To paraphrase Charles Dickens, the Reagan-Bush years have been both "the best of times and the worst of times." The longest peacetime expansion in contemporary American history was sandwiched between the worst recession since the Great Depression and a prolonged period of stagnation and recession, spiced with the sweet-and-sour sauce of an income tax cut and a chronic fiscal crisis. The Dow Jones Industrial stock average more than tripled, from around 1,000 when Ronald Reagan entered office to over 3,300 in 1992. On the other hand, a leading newsmagazine estimated that more than one in five American workers were out of a job at one time or another during the recession of the early 1990s.

Domestic policy-making in the Reagan-Bush years can be divided into three basic periods: the Reagan restoration (1981-1982), the later Reagan years (1983-1988), and the Bush presidency. The time lag of economic conditions on political and ideological dynamics produced some interesting contradictions during these periods. Politically and ideologically, Reaganism was riding high at the very time the economy was entering the worst recession since the Great Depression. The political fallout of the recession of 1981-1982 allowed the Democrats to regain tight control of the House of Representatives. Thus even as the boom of the middle 1980s was unfolding and assuring Reagan's reelection, control of fiscal and other domestic policies was slipping from Reagan's hands.

By the time George Bush had taken office, the boom of the mid-1980s had largely spent itself. Economic growth was slow in the early Bush presidency, and the economy slipped into a recession in 1991. With regard to domestic policy-making, the first Bush term most resembled the later Reagan administration. There was a general immobilism of public policy, with congressional Democrats exercising as much or more power over policy as the executive but with no one really in control. However, there were significant differences in the ideological tone of the Reagan and Bush administrations. Even as Ronald Reagan lost political control over domestic policy he continued on the ideological level to espouse consistent conservative doctrine. George Bush, on the other hand, was more of an ideological as well as political pragmatist whose positions on the role of government in domestic affairs were never as fixed as Reagan's. Like Republican presidents before Reagan—Ford, Nixon, and Eisenhower—Bush gave mixed messages about the role of government. At the same time he appealed for limited government, Bush endorsed government activism on a range of issues. This gave him more flexibility with congressional Democrats, and thus marginally more influence over budgetary policy than Reagan had in his later years.

After the significant, if overdramatized and misunderstood, policy shifts of the Reagan restoration, there were few major changes in social programs in the second Reagan term or the first Bush term. Domestic policy seemed to drift without direction. Democrats in Congress blocked any further major program cuts. Republicans in the White House for the most part blocked major innovations or expansions in domestic programs, and the growing budget deficit made any major new programs seem out of touch with fiscal reality. The "war on drugs" and Head Start for poor preschool children received more funding, but overall there was little change in social policy during the Bush years.

Performance on Economic Indicators

The mixed economic record of the Reagan and Bush presidencies is shown in Table 12.1. They can claim one unadulterated success—cutting the inflation rate. By the end of the 1970s people had come to expect that the dollars they made would be worth considerably less in a few years. But by the 1990s inflationary expectations had been wrung from the economy and people expected their dollars to retain their purchasing power from year to year. The average inflation rate from 1960 to 1981 was 5.1 percent and climbed to 9.2 percent from 1975 to 1981. But in the Reagan-Bush years it has been 4.1 percent. Inflationary pressures have slowly crept back into the economy in the 1990s, but they are still low compared to those of the 1970s.

Other macroeconomic indicators were more mixed during the Reagan-Bush years. Economic growth was impressive in the mid-1980s, but wrapped around that boom were a very deep recession and a period of general stagnation.

Table 12.1
Average Annual Performance on Key Economic Indicators, 1965-1991

	Unemployment	Economic Growth	Inflation	Deficit ($ Billion)	Deficit (% of GNP)
1965-1970	4.0	3.4	4.2	6.4	0.9
1971-1974	5.5	3.1	5.8	16.9	1.5
1975-1981	7.1	2.7	9.2	61.8	2.9
1982-1990	7.0	2.9	4.1	181.3	4.4
1991*	6.7	-.7	3.1	268.7	4.7

*1991 numbers are approximations based on best available data
Sources: U.S. Census Bureau, *Statistical Abstract of the United States*; Council of Economic Advisors, *The Economic Report of the President* and *Economic Indicators*; Congressional Budget Office, *Report to the House and Senate on the Budget*; and Department of Labor, *Handbook of Labor Statistics.*

Overall, in the Reagan-Bush years economic growth averaged 2.5 percent and unemployment averaged nearly 7 percent. In comparison, in the 1960s and 1970s economic growth averaged 3.4 percent and unemployment averaged 5.5 percent. Unemployment rates also reflect the boom-bust cycle. Unemployment hit a post-Depression high of 9.7 percent in 1982. In the late 1980s it returned to a more typical level of 5+ percent, although it was still high compared with other boom periods. However, in the recession of 1991-1992 it began to rise, climbing over 7 percent again.

On certain other economic indicators performance during the Reagan-Bush years was dismal. Adjusted for inflation, the average wages and weekly earnings of workers actually declined in this period. From 1982 until the end of 1991 wages fell 3.1 percent. When Ronald Reagan took office, the United States had 21 million workers in manufacturing industries; when he left office there were only 18 million. Fully 15 percent of all manufacturing jobs were gone. Some industries suffered even greater losses. The steel industry lost about 240,000 jobs, or 60 percent of its work force, in the Reagan years. The loss of manufacturing jobs continued into the 1990s. In late 1991, for example, General Motors alone announced plans to cut 74,000 jobs.

Problems of poverty also worsened in the Reagan-Bush years. The percentage of people whose incomes fall below the official poverty line fluctuates with the economic cycle, but in this period it rose more rapidly during the recessions than it declined during the boom. Social program cuts meant that the number of poor people lifted above the poverty line by the government also fell. Full statistics on the increases in poverty caused by the 1991-1992 recession are not yet available, but the figures from the 1980s are chilling enough.

From 1975 to 1979 the percentage of people whose income put them below the poverty line was 11.8, but from 1982 to 1989 the poverty rate climbed to an average of 14.1 percent. In the 1970s the percentage of American children living below the poverty line averaged 15.5 percent. From 1982-89 it averaged 20.2 percent. Even in the expansionary year of 1987 more than half of all children being raised in a household where the mother was the sole adult were in poverty.

Underlying the economic indicators were two economic problems that have become more severe in the Reagan-Bush years: the fiscal crisis of the American government and the changing position of the United States in the world economy. These basic changes in the American economy deserve sustained attention.

THE DEFICIT CRISIS

Suppose that when Ronald Reagan had been running for president in 1980, in contrast with his general desire to cut programs, he had proposed to expand a little-watched federal program. This program did not provide any services to any citizens. However, it did make payments that went almost exclusively to wealthy individuals and large financial institutions, and increasingly to foreign individuals and institutions. When Ronald Reagan came into office this "no services" program already cost roughly 10 percent of the national budget. But in contrast with cuts in other spending, under Reagan this program would grow. From costs of $53 billion in fiscal year 1980, it would expand by the end of fiscal 1990 to $184 billion, totaling over $1.2 trillion in the period from 1984 to 1991. When Reagan's successor was campaigning for reelection in 1992, this program without services would consume 15 percent of the annual budget, with commitments still expanding rapidly.

It is hard to believe any political candidate would make such a proposal to the American people and even harder to believe he would survive politically if he did. But this is not a hypothetical case. It is the story of payments on the national debt, which provide no services to anyone and no benefits to the vast majority of citizens.

Table 12.2 shows that the largest budget deficit in the Carter administration was $73.8 billion. Budgets from 1983-1991 averaged deficits of nearly $200 billion. The deficit for fiscal 1992 is officially estimated to be close to $400 billion. All presidents prior to Reagan had accumulated a total of a trillion dollars of debt. By 1986 Congress and the Reagan administration had more than doubled that amount. In 1990 the total passed $3 trillion. As Lloyd Bentsen charged in his 1988 vicepresidential debate, it was not hard to create the illusion of prosperity by writing $200 billion of hot checks each year. However, by the 1990s the

Table 12.2
Budget Deficits in the 1970s and 1980s

	$ (billions)	Percent of GNP		$ (billions)	Percent of GNP
1970	2.8	.3	1981	78.9	2.6
1971	23.0	2.2	1982	127.9	4.1
1972	23.4	2.0	1983	207.8	6.3
1973	14.9	1.2	1984	185.3	5.0
1974	6.1	.4	1985	212.3	5.4
1975	53.2	3.5	1986	221.2	5.3
1976*	73.7	4.3	1987	149.7	3.4
1977	53.6	2.8	1988	155.1	3.2
1978	59.2	2.7	1989	152.0	3.0
1979	40.2	1.6	1990	220.4	4.1
1980	73.8	2.8	1991**	268.7	4.7

*does not contain the transition quarter when the budget year was changed.
**approximations based on the best available data.
Source: U.S. Census Bureau, *Statistical Abstract of the United States* (Washington, DC: U.S. Government Printing Office, 1991).

bill on that debt made even the illusion of prosperity impossible to maintain.

There are two dimensions of the deficit crisis—the cyclical and the structural. The economic cycle has a dramatic effect on the federal deficit. In the hard times of 1982-1983 and 1990-1991, the budget deficit jumped more than $100 billion with two years. When unemployment rises, people out of work make heavy demands on social programs like food stamps, medical aid, and welfare, pushing up government spending. At the same time, unemployed people and failing corporations pay less in taxes, cutting government revenues. Furthermore, during a recession, the government cannot raise tax rates because that would only push more businesses into bankruptcy and put more people out of work. It would also appear particularly heartless to cut spending when workers are losing their jobs through no fault of their own.

A rising deficit in a recession is not necessarily a bad thing. Government spending can help stimulate the economy and be part of the recovery process. What was different about the deficit in the Reagan-Bush years was its structural dimension. Usually when the economy is recovering from recession, the deficit falls back to a more normal level. But in the Reagan years, even as the economy moved from a terrible recession into a sustained boom period, the deficit remained in the range of $150-$220 billion, two or three times the highest recessionary deficits before Reagan. The massive Reagan tax cuts coupled with no real cuts in overall government spending meant that even during good times, the government was operating at a huge loss. This is the structural component of the deficit.

When in the late 1980s economic growth slowed and the economy entered another recession in 1991, the deficit skyrocketed again. From Reagan-era "lows" of around $150 billion from 1987 to 1989, the deficit climbed back over $200 billion in 1990 and was projected to be close to $400 billion in 1992.

ECONOMIC POLICY IN THE LATER REAGAN ADMINISTRATION

Economic and social policy in the Reagan-Bush era were dominated by the overarching fact of the federal deficit. The 1981 tax cuts were the most popular thing Reagan had done. Neither Reagan nor Bush was willing to risk his popularity by admitting that the tax cuts had been too large.

In its first term the Reagan administration kept preaching the supply-side gospel that economic growth would expand the tax base and soon bring the deficit down to manageable proportions. The administration also argued that the deficit should be controlled by cutting government spending rather than raising taxes. But supply-side theory proved erroneous because even as the economy recovered and expanded from 1983 on, massive deficits remained. Cutting government spending also proved to be a mirage. Congress had made the easiest spending cuts in the 1981 budget and was not likely to approve further large-scale cuts, particularly after the Democrats regained effective control of the House of Representatives in the 1982 elections.

By Reagan's second term it was clear that economic growth coupled with further spending cuts was not a realistic formula for solving the deficit problem. Over time the administration's argument shifted to making the case that the economy continued to prosper despite the deficits, so the deficits must not be so bad.

It is also clear that in some ways the deficit worked to the advantage of other Reagan policies. In the face of growing demands that social program cuts be reversed or that new initiatives be taken in social policy, the administration could point to the deficit situation and say that new spending or new initiatives were unrealistic at this time. In one of his first speeches before the nation, Reagan had argued that the best way to cut government spending was to "cut its allowance," that is, to cut the taxes that funded government programs. Certainly economic and social policies in the 1980s were formulated in an environment in which major innovations in the approach to economic or social problems were ruled out by the pervasive fiscal crisis.

Congressional leaders of both parties were never as optimistic as Reagan that the deficit situation could just be ignored. But in the absence of presidential leadership, Congress was unable to cope with the crisis. In 1983 Congress tried to respond to the budget crunch, passing a modest tax increase coupled with projected spending cuts. But the tax increase was tiny compared with the tax cuts they had voted in 1981, and the spending cuts were never really implemented.

The year 1983 also brought reform of the Social Security system, which had been thrown into a fiscal crisis of its own by the deep recession of the early Reagan years. Current benefits went largely untouched, although benefits were indirectly cut by raising the retirement age in future decades and by taxing the benefits of the wealthy. Future tax increases were also accelerated. These actions, coupled with the economic recovery, put the Social Security system on a sound financial basis. By the end of the decade it was running large surpluses that wily politicians quickly learned to count in calculating the overall budget deficit.

Major changes in economic policy were impossible in the election year of 1984, but Reagan's landslide reelection put him in the position to exercise leadership in economic policy in 1985. However, instead of tackling the difficult deficit issue, the Reagan administration made new changes in the tax code the centerpiece of its legislative program for its second term.

The most popular thing Reagan had done in his first term was to reduce income taxes. Not surprisingly, the administration wanted to do it again. But the large deficits made it impossible to cut income taxes again without raising new revenues to compensate for the cuts. Therefore the top economic priority was tax reform. Income tax rates would be cut again, but loopholes in the tax code would be closed.

The Reagan administration explicitly ruled out tax reform as a way of coping with the deficit situation. The administration's stance was that tax reform should not be used to raise government revenue. Tax reform had to be "revenue neutral"; that is, for every dollar raised by closing a loophole, a dollar would have to be cut from income tax rates. The administration held firm to its position that it would veto any tax reform bill that raised overall tax revenues, and eventually it got its way.

Tax reform cut the tax rate for the top bracket from 50 percent to 28 percent. It also raised the minimum income that had to be made before income was taxed, taking several million low-income families off the tax rolls. While the very rich and the poor benefited most from these changes, the gains for the middle class were few. Business taxation was increased by numerous changes in the code, most importantly a minimum tax that required corporations to pay a certain rate regardless of how many deductions they could accumulate.

More directly related to the deficit crisis was the other major change in economic policy made in 1985, the Gramm-Rudman Deficit Reduction Act. Gramm-Rudman was a device to force the administration and Congress to face the deficit problem. It set a deficit reduction target for each fiscal year that was a percentage of the prior year's deficit. If the president and Congress could not agree on a package of spending cuts and tax increases that met the deficit reduction target, spending for all government programs would be cut across the board by whatever percentage would be necessary to reach the target. Half of the cuts would come from the military, the other half from other government programs. Only Social Security benefits, payments on the national debt, and a handful of poverty programs were exempt from these automatic cuts. Gramm-

Rudman did have some impact on the budget deficit. In order to avoid the automatic cuts, Congress was able to produce budgets that met the target figures. The official deficit numbers came down from the $200 billion level to around $150 billion in 1987-1989.

However, Gramm-Rudman was also subject to political manipulation. When the original target deficit reductions proved too difficult to meet, Congress simply changed the targets. Some of the reductions shown in the official budget had more to do with creative accounting than real spending changes. Social Security trust fund surpluses were counted against the deficit, even though they were earmarked for future benefits. One-time sales of government assets were used to help balance the books for one year. But finally in 1989, when stymied in negotiations with the Bush administration, Congress allowed the automatic Gramm-Rudman spending cut provisions to go into effect to bring down the 1989 deficit. The total amount involved was small by government standards, but the outcry from bureaucrats and constituents was enough to convince Congress not to allow this to happen again. As economic growth slowed, spending on social entitlements such as food stamps grew at the same time that revenues leveled off, putting increasing pressures on the budget. After the experience of the automatic cuts of 1989, in 1990 Congress eviscerated Gramm-Rudman. Gramm-Rudman had made it technically more difficult to raise spending or cut taxes, but manipulation of its deficit targets and other maneuvering had kept its bark much worse than its bite.

THE BUSH ADMINISTRATION AND THE FISCAL CRISIS

Before he even took office, George Bush had taken positions that made it hard to deal with the fiscal crisis. One of his central campaign themes in 1988 was his pledge of no new taxes. Tax cuts had been the most popular element of Reaganomics, and the Bush campaign wanted to continue to exploit the tax issue. Furthermore, the "no new taxes" pledge solidified Bush's standing with the ideological wing of the Republican party that had never fully trusted his conservative credentials.

Many pundits thought that upon assuming office Bush might quickly abandon his tax pledge. If Bush thought a tax increase was necessary, it might have been politically wise to move immediately and give himself four years for the voters to forget, while implicitly blaming his actions on his predecessor. However, despite pressures from the press and congressional Democrats, Bush stuck to his tax pledge in his first year in office.

But the fiscal crisis created by the Reagan tax cuts would not go away. In the budget negotiations of 1990 the Bush administration agreed with congressional Democrats to a tax increase of $137 billion over the next five years. Changes were made in the income and payroll tax codes, and excise and user taxes were raised. However, these modest tax increases had only a marginal effect on the massive federal deficit. As the economy weakened further and the 1992 election approached, both Democrats and Republicans shelved any talk of further deficit reduction or tax increases. Like Ronald Reagan before him, George Bush used the ideological power of the media presidency and his veto power over legislation to set a political climate that made it impossible to raise the kind of revenues that would significantly cut the deficit. Like Reagan, Bush allowed some modest tax increases, but only under the kind of political circumstances that put him in the position to blame them on the Democratic Congress. Not surprisingly, under those conditions the deficit crisis was not solved. The slowing of economic growth and the recession of 1991 pushed the deficit out as the top economic priority while adding hundreds of billions to the debt bill.

The Savings and Loan Crisis

A new kind of fiscal crisis had been building in the Reagan years, and it broke into the open after George Bush took office—the collapse of the savings and loan industry and the potential for similar collapses in the banking and insurance industries. The failure of hundreds of savings and loans (also called thrifts) was in part a result of their inability to adapt to changing economic circumstances, exacerbated by outright fraud. But government policies had a role in initiating the crisis and in making things much worse as the crisis unfolded.

Savings and loans were created during the Depression when the Roosevelt administration reorganized the national banking system. They were a type of bank that would specialize in loans to families for buying homes and to developers for undertaking real estate projects. They were an attempt by the national government to direct funds to the housing industry so that ordinary families would have the chance to buy their own homes. As part of the New Deal reforms, individuals' deposits in savings and loans were insured by the government. If a thrift went bust the government would replace the lost savings of depositors.

Thrifts were safe if unspectacular financial institutions as long as interest rates were regulated to ensure a comfortable margin between the interest paid on funds collected and the interest paid on loans. But when the Reagan administration set interest rates free to meet market demands as part of its larger deregulation of financial services, the "mom and pop" savings and loans were not equipped to compete with international financial tigers. Most thrifts held on during the boom years of the mid-1980s but in the late 1980s the industry began to lose billions of dollars a year and bankruptcies began to climb. A 1988 congressional report found 505 thrifts, over 15 percent, on the verge of bankruptcy, and another 435 at high risk, putting nearly a third of all thrifts in danger of collapse.[1] Because of the deposit insurance system, each thrift bankruptcy costs the government. When a thrift fails, the government tries to find a buyer who will reopen the institution with insured accounts intact. But often buyers cannot be found or the government ends up losing huge sums of money in putting together deals to attract skeptical buyers. The deposit insurance system was not geared for systemic failure. By the time George Bush took office, a new system was necessary to deal with such a massive problem.

The Bush administration and Congress made the thrift bailout a top legislative priority of his first year. The regulatory system overseeing thrifts was totally overhauled, and a new deposit insurance fund was created to replace the empty one. Further, $20 billion in general funds was pumped into the system immediately and general funds were promised for costs after 1992. The Reconstruction Finance Corporation was to borrow $30 billion by selling bonds and was given the authority to borrow more if needed. Estimates varied widely depending on economic assumptions, but few thought the initial $50 billion would do the job. Most estimates ran in the hundreds of billions of dollars in long-term costs.

While the savings and loan crisis got the headlines, the larger banking system was also deeply troubled. More than 200 banks failed or needed major assistance in both 1988 and 1989. In those years the banking insurance system operated at a loss, and reserves were drawn down to the lowest ratio to deposits in history. As part of the thrift bailout the government also took on the commitment to pump general treasury funds into the banking system if that crisis worsened. The government estimated that by 1993, 5 percent of the entire national budget would be spent on deposit insurance for financial institutions.

The Economic Recovery Plan

Overall, the economy was stagnant during the Bush's first three years in office. Annual growth averaged only around 1 percent and the economy slipped into recession in 1991. These conditions were in part cause and in part effect of the continuing fiscal crisis and the deepening crisis of financial institutions. As he prepared for his reelection bid, George Bush knew the state of the domestic economy would be the overarching issue in the 1992 campaign. He billed his year-opening State of the Union message as his most important statement on economic policy.

The centerpiece of the recovery program was another series of tax cuts. Bush proposed tax cuts for families with children, new home buyers and the real estate industry, people who purchase health insurance, companies engaged in research and development, corporations that invest in plant and equipment, and those who make profits from selling capital assets.

In contrast with his specific tax cut proposals, Bush relied on vague generalities with regard to activist government programs. He called for negotiations to open world markets to U.S. goods, more choice and flexibility in educational programs, tough measures against street crime, reform of the banking and legal systems, and a conference on urban families. But the speech was lacking specifics, and more important, new resources to tackle these difficult issues.

The Bush Economic Recovery Plan

We must have a short-term plan to address our immediate needs and heat up the economy. And we need a longer-term plan to . . . guarantee our place in the world economy.

Tax Cuts

—I have [changed] the federal tax withholding tables . . . to have the government withhold less from . . . paychecks.

—I am proposing . . . a new 15 percent investment tax allowance.

—My plan would . . . provide a $5,000 tax credit for the first purchase of [a] home.

—I am asking [Congress] to cut the capital gains tax to a maximum of 15.4 percent.

—For people who will explore the promise of emerging technologies my plan is to make the research and development tax credit permanent.

—I ask [Congress] to pass my [tax free] enterprise zone legislation [and] extend tax incentives for mortgage revenue bonds and low income housing.

—My plan [makes] basic health insurance affordable for all low income people not now covered . . . by providing a health insurance tax credit of up to $3,750.

—[To] ease the burden of rearing a child [I plan] to raise the personal exemption by $500 per child for every family.

Deficit Control

We must get the federal deficit under control. . . . I call upon Congress to . . . give me the same thing 43 governors have—the line item veto—and let me help you control spending.[2]

Bush continued a decade of Republican symbolism on the issue of the deficit. There was one area where the president did propose serious spending cuts—the military. Bush called for the cancellation of the mobile Midgetman nuclear missile, termination of the B-2 bomber and Seawolf submarine production lines, and other real cuts in military spending.

But except for the military Bush avoided taking on powerful constituencies in an election year. Instead, he tried to pass the blame to the Democratic Congress and "pork barrel" spending. Bush called for elimination of 246 programs but did not elaborate, except to single out the Lawrence Welk Museum. Again, the president could be sure that Congress, which had rejected most of these cuts in the past, would not pass them now.

Bush also asked for a line-item veto, which would free the president from the need to accept or reject congressional legislation as a whole and allow him to pick and choose which parts of a bill he would veto. Like the balanced budget amendment of the Reagan years, this proposal was offered with the certain knowledge that there was no way Congress would cede its constitutionally mandated power over the budget. The Bush administration knew that the line-item veto issue makes for a good sound bite but is a nonstarter as public policy.

THE DECLINE OF THE UNITED STATES IN THE WORLD ECONOMY

The Significance of the Trade Deficit

In the Reagan-Bush years in addition to the budget deficit the United States began to run another critical deficit—the trade deficit. Americans were increasingly buying more from abroad than they were selling, over $100 billion a year in the later Reagan and early Bush years. As technology advances, it becomes cheaper and cheaper to exchange goods, services, and information across national boundaries. The political and economic integration of Europe and the economies of the Pacific Rim have also spurred the development of global markets and corporations able to operate on a global scale.

The rising trade deficit reversed the pattern the United States established early in the twentieth century and consistently maintained after World War II, of selling more abroad than it bought. Its perpetual trade surpluses in the postwar world were taken as a sign of the strength of the U.S. economy. The chronic deficits of the 1980s shown in Table 12.3 could only be taken as a sign of the erosion of U.S. economic power. Americans were losing not only low technology, low wage jobs, but increasingly also losing high tech, high paying jobs to

Table 12.3
The U.S. Trade Balance, 1960-1991

	$ (billions)		$ (billions)
1960	2.8	1984	-99.0
1965	5.4	1985	-122.3
1970	2.3	1986	-145.4
1975	18.1	1987	-162.3
1980	1.1	1988	-128.9
1981	6.9	1989	-110.0
1982	-5.9	1990	-99.3
1983	-40.1	1991	-66.2

Source: U.S. Census Bureau, *Statistical Abstract of the United States* (Washington, DC: U.S. Government Printing Office, 1991).

foreign competition. The decline of the U.S. in the world economy was the main reason for the loss of 15 percent of all manufacturing jobs in the U.S. economy during the Reagan years.

Ironically, the shrinking of the trade deficit in the late 1980s and the early 1990s was as much a sign of weakness as strength. It was true that U.S. exports were up. But more important, due to the recession, the ability of American consumers to buy any goods, foreign or domestic, was severely restricted, and thus imports fell along with sales of domestic goods.

In order to finance the huge budget and trade deficits and to maintain current standards of living, the United States has been borrowing massively from foreigners and increasingly selling American assets to foreign interests. When the Reagan administration took office, the United States was the largest creditor nation in the world. Americans were owed $140 billion more by foreign institutions and individuals than they owed to foreigners, more than any other people in the world. By the time the Reagan administration left office, the United States was the largest debtor nation in the world. On net, Americans owed roughly $400 billion to foreigners, more than any nation in history. Besides borrowing, another way to finance a deficit is to sell one's assets, and Americans have increasingly been selling their properties to foreign buyers. Highly publicized purchases like those of Columbia Pictures and the Rockefeller Center complex in New York are just the most visible cases of the U.S. liquidating its capital assets in order to pay for current consumption.

The domestic economy is severely impacted by the trade and budget deficits in another way. If foreign investors were to find other markets more attractive, the United States would face a severe financial crisis. Therefore U.S. interest rates must be kept relatively high to attract foreign capital. But high interest rates make it more expensive for domestic corporations to borrow money to expand their plant, equipment, employment, and other operations. In the late 1980s the high interest rates necessary to attract foreign capital stifled domestic growth. The recession of the early 1990s brought interest rates down to 20-year lows, but once the recession passes, the U.S. will again feel building pressure to match interest rates abroad.

Trade Policies in the 1980s

As pressure from foreign competition in U.S. markets has grown, so has domestic pressure for protection of U.S. markets from foreign goods. In the postwar era the United States had generally been a strong force for free trade of goods around the world. As the dominant industrial and political power in the postwar world the United States initially benefitted greatly from the integration of the world's capitalist economies. Free trade meant increasing access of strong U.S. firms to foreign markets. Economic integration of the capitalist economies also supported the political alliance systems the United States created.

However as the European and Japanese economies recovered from their wartime devastation and as the costs of U.S. global military commitments, such as the Vietnam war, climbed, free trade increasingly became a two edged sword. More and more free trade meant not only U.S. sales to foreign markets, but also Japanese and European sales in American markets. European and Japanese automobiles and steel began to take ever more significant shares of the domestic market. The U.S. consumer electronics industry withered and faded under competition from Japan and low-wage Asian countries. Trade policy became an ever more salient element of American politics and the doctrine of free trade began to come under challenge.

The United States had never been totally consistent in its free trade policies. Even in its period of ascendancy it had protected domestic textile manufacturers and key agricultural producers from foreign goods at the same time it called for greater liberalization in other goods. As foreign goods increasingly penetrated U.S. markets, more inconsistencies appeared. For example, in 1978 the Carter administration placed significant restrictions on steel imports. The textile, footwear, and other industries also benefited from protection under Carter.

The Reagan administration came into office as a strong advocate of free trade, consistent with its general opposition to government intervention in economic affairs. However, Reaganomics produced an escalating trade deficit, spurring political pressures for protectionist policies. The tight money policies of Reaganomics increased the value of the dollar, making U.S. exports cost more abroad. At the same time, the budget deficit encouraged domestic consumption, and thus the demand for imports made cheaper by the high dollar.

The mounting trade deficit spurred calls in Congress for revision of trade policies. In the postwar environment, the president has usually been the strongest advocate of free trade, reflecting his concern with the broader economic, political, and military impacts of trade policy. But members of Congress, who are focused on representing the leading economic interests in their districts, have been more inclined to press for protection of the industries of their region. This tension between the executive branch's commitment to free trade and Congress' desire to protect certain industries increased dramatically as the trade deficit climbed in the Reagan years.

While the Reagan administration continued to preach free trade, in practice it sometimes bent to congressional demands for protection. In its first year in office, in order to head off more drastic congressional action, the Reagan administration negotiated restraints on Japanese sales of automobiles in the United States that remain in effect. Protection of the steel and textile industries were extended in the Reagan years. New protection was extended to the semi-conductor industry. At the same time the Reagan administration pressed for freer trade in agricultural goods, hoping that greater access for American farmers to European and Japanese markets would improve the U.S. trade position and ease the farm crisis.

In its second term the Reagan administration brought down the value of the dollar, particularly against the Japanese yen. This made U.S. exports cheaper and Japanese and other imports relatively more expensive. In a couple of years the value of the yen doubled compared with the dollar. But the devaluation of the dollar only slowed the growth of imports; it did not reverse the trend. At the same time the stronger yen made Japanese purchases of U.S. assets easier, spurring acquisitions of U.S. companies by Japanese buyers.

As the trade crisis persisted, congressional demands for more aggressive and systematic trade policies increased. The perception grew that the United States was open to foreign goods but that foreign markets were not allowing U.S. goods fair access, that the playing field of international trade was not level. The slogan "fair trade" was coined to contest the idea of free trade, and to assert that the U.S. market could not remain wide open if foreign markets were not opened up. Several Democratic presidential candidates, most notably Missouri's Richard Gephardt in 1988 and Iowa's Tom Harkin in 1992, made the growing trade deficit a central issue in their campaigns.

Like Ronald Reagan, George Bush continued to advocate the virtues of free trade. But also like Reagan, he felt the pressure to improve the U.S. trade position. By the 1990s the trade deficit did begin to decline, not so much as a result of the devaluation of the dollar, but because during recession, consumers have less income to spend.

One of the first actions of the Bush administration was to initiate talks with the Japanese government to open the Japanese market to a wider range of U.S. goods. Roughly one-third of the U.S. trade deficit was with Japan, and the perception was growing that the Japanese did not allow U.S. goods fair access to their markets. In early 1992 President Bush traveled to Japan with the leaders of many U. S. corporations, including the CEOs of the auto companies who had just laid off tens of thousands of workers. The United States was able to gain the agreement of Japanese auto companies to double their purchases of U.S. auto parts to $19 billion annually, and of the Japanese government to buy more U.S. computers. But few analysts thought that these agreements alone would reverse the trade imbalance.

LAISSEZ-FAIRE OR THE LIMITED INTEREST STATE

The economic policies of the Reagan and Bush administrations can best be characterized as partially successful attempts to restore the philosophy and practices of the limited interest state. The term "limited interest state" is appropriate because it captures both the concern with the size and reach of government that dominates the rhetoric of recent Republican presidents, and the ultimate acceptance of big government when it protects or promotes certain powerful political and economic interests.

While much of Reagan's and Bush's public rhetoric evoked images of the laissez-faire government believed to have characterized the nineteenth century, the public policies of the Reagan-Bush years were far from any such standard. Military contractors had their coffers filled in the Reagan years. Under the Bush administration the savings and loan industry won a bailout expected to cost the treasury hundreds of billions of dollars. The largest social insurance program, Social Security, with its more than 30 million beneficiaries, was largely spared from the budget ax. While Republican administrations preached the virtues of the market, farm subsidies rose to unprecedented heights. While Republican presidents talked free trade, key industries were extended trade protection.

There were some real cuts in federal spending in the Reagan-Bush years. Funds for programs to aid the poor, the unemployed, and low-skill workers were cut. Money for enforcement of environmental laws was reduced. Federal aid to cities, states, and local governments and schools was axed.

There is a pattern to be seen, but it cannot be explained purely on ideological grounds. Instead, the groups that had their programs cut were groups that have traditionally been tied to the Democratic Party. Industrial workers, the urban poor, teachers, and environmentalists have historically given greater political support to the Democratic than to the Republican Party. City and state governments are more often in the hands of the Democrats. These were the losers during the Reagan restoration. On the other hand, military contractors, financial companies, and farmers have historically been more Republican constituencies, particularly in recent decades. These groups generally saw their programs expand, although the end of the cold war has made military cuts inevitable.

Clearly, if a constituency group was big enough, powerful enough, and potentially Republican enough, there was room for its programs in the Republican budget. David Stockman, budget director in Reagan's first term, documents in *The Triumph of Politics* the policy inconsistencies of the administration in which he served.[3] Stockman joined the administration committed to reducing the size of government and returning to the principles of laissez-faire economics. But his experiences in four years of preparing Reagan administration budgets convinced him that his colleagues were not willing to take the political risks of putting their rhetoric about cutting the size of government into practice. Supply-side tax cuts were politically popular and thus were the center of everybody's attention. But cutting spending meant offending powerful constituency groups, and few in the administration wanted to face the political heat. Stockman concludes that if the most ideologically conservative administration in 50 years was not willing to fight entrenched interest groups, no future administration is likely to truly practice laissez-faire economics.

The limited interest state therefore is a state restricted more in scope than in size. Fewer interests lay claim to shares of government spending while overall spending remains roughly constant. Federal budgets in the Reagan-Bush years have not reduced overall spending but, rather, have changed its composition. These outcomes can be justified in the name of the higher national priority these interests represent. Or they can be explained as the result of a more homogeneous and less expansive Republican Party coalition. But it is a pattern that has survived throughout the 28 years of the past 40 when control of government has been divided between a Republican president and a Democratic Congress. It was true of the Eisenhower, Nixon, Ford, Reagan, and Bush years. Reagan pursued a harder rhetorical line on big government than his Republican predecessors, but the outcome was similar in terms of the size and scope of public spending.

Defenders of the ideological purity of Republican administrations point out that Congress has more power over national budgets and national spending than does the president. This is true, and no one knows what policies Republican presidents would adopt if they had consistent party or ideological majorities in Congress. But we do know the budgets Reagan and Bush have recommended and the choices Republican presidents have made under conditions of divided government. They have chosen to implement the politically popular element of their philosophy—tax cuts. Except for the early Reagan years they have avoided implementing the unpopular side of their creed—spending cuts. The result has been the chronic fiscal crisis.

NOTES

1. *Congressional Quarterly Almanac, 1988* (Washington, DC: Congressional Quarterly, 1989).

2. George Bush, *Congressional Quarterly Weekly Report* (Washington, DC: Congressional Quarterly, Inc., February 1, 1992), pp. 264-268.

3. David Stockman, *The Triumph of Politics* (New York: Harper & Row, 1986).

13

A BRAVE NEW WORLD

A WORLD IN CHANGE

The late 1980s and early 1990s ushered in the most dramatic changes in world politics since World War II. The later Reagan years and especially the Bush years saw the most favorable developments for U.S. foreign policy since the beginning of the cold war. America's chief rival for nearly half a century, the Soviet Union, literally passed out of existence. The Iron Curtain, which had separated Europe into two hostile war blocs, disappeared virtually overnight. Nations that had been formally independent but controlled by the Soviet Union regained their political freedom, and even nations that had been incorporated into the Russian empire for centuries were gaining their independence. Historic arms control agreements followed one upon the other, but seemingly could not keep pace with the withdrawal of the Red Army from eastern European states and the former Soviet republics. Not even the most ardent holy warrior against communism could have imagined such a quick and painless end to the cold war. These historic changes in the face of Europe brought talk of a new world order to replace the polarized world of superpower conflict.

Certainly the decade of the 1980s did not begin on a very promising note. It began with the demise of detente. In early 1980 the Soviet Union was embarking on its invasion of Afghanistan, the United States was locked in a bitter confrontation with Iran over hostages, the SALT II treaty was failing in the U.S. Senate, and NATO was preparing to deploy a new generation of longer-range missiles in Europe.

Ronald Reagan, who had opposed detente and arms control, was rising to power in the United States, calling for a restoration of the doctrines of the national security state, a new hard line toward the Soviet Union, and a massive military buildup. The aging oligarchy that led the Soviet Union seemed equally unable to make the changes in its international behavior and domestic politics that could sustain the promise of detente. The 1980s seemed destined to replicate the cold war tensions of the 1950s.

However, by the beginning of the 1990s the cold war appeared finally to be over. The centralized communist control of the Soviet Union had been replaced by the new Commonwealth of Independent States. The Warsaw Pact was gone. Russian troops had been withdrawn from Afghanistan and noncommunist governments had come to power throughout eastern Europe and central Asia. The United States and the Russians had eliminated medium-range nuclear missile systems from Europe, negotiated mutual troop withdrawals from central Europe, signed a treaty to cut their strategic nuclear forces by roughly one-third, and were outbidding each other in plans to cut nuclear forces even more rapidly. At the same time, the economic and political integration of Europe was accelerating. The European Community (EC), which links Germany, France, England, Italy, and several smaller western European nations, proceeded toward the creation of a single, unified economic market in the early 1990s, and a more tightly cohesive political union by the end of the decade. The EC was also forging new economic relations with the former members of the Soviet bloc, which might eventually expand EC membership across most of eastern Europe as well.

THE END OF THE COLD WAR AND THE TRANSFORMATION OF EUROPE

The Cold War and the Soviet System

The full story of the dissolution of the Soviet empire is more detailed than can be told here, but certain key points need to be understood in order to grasp the relationship between the rapid changes in the Soviet empire and the dramatic changes in U.S. policy toward its historic adversary. It is too easy for American leaders to claim that the West "won" the cold war. Such simplistic analysis will lead to dangerous errors in future policy not only toward the Russians and eastern Europe but also toward other parts of the world.

What is most important to recognize is the relationship between the changes in the Soviet bloc and the end of the cold war. In the West it is easy to see how the reformation of the Soviet system makes possible new relations between the former adversaries. But what is less recognized is how the demise of the cold war made the transformation of the Soviet system possible. It was no accident that the rise of Russian leaders like Mikhail Gorbachev and Boris Yeltsin and the acceleration of reform coincided with the reduction of political tensions in Europe.

The transformation of the Soviet system has been driven primarily by internal dynamics that have proven beyond the ability of outsiders to fully understand. It would be a mistake to credit these changes primarily to the policies of Western governments or even indirectly to Western influence. But the thaw in East-West tensions did remove the greatest external impediment to reform in the Soviet bloc, and thereby provided a key condition that needed to be met before Soviet reform could blossom.

One must remember the principal factor that drove the Soviet Union to occupy the Warsaw Pact countries and maintain such tight control of eastern Europe for more than 40 years—the memory of two massive invasions from Germany that passed through eastern Europe on their way to the Russian heartland. The Soviets lost 20 million people, 10 percent of their population, in the war against the Nazis. They were determined that never again would these countries become a staging ground for another invasion of Soviet territory. The formation of NATO only confirmed Soviet fears that another such invasion was possible, and that the next time they would face a formidable alliance including not only Germany, but also England, France, and the United States.

As long as the cold war persisted, the Soviet Union was committed to maintaining their foothold in eastern Europe. If war were to come, eastern Europe was to serve as a buffer to absorb the new wave of western invaders. But as political relations between the Soviets and the western Europeans and the United States improved, the specter of the extension of hostile Western military forces to the Soviet European borders appeared less and less likely. As the costs of controlling eastern Europe mounted, the benefits of that control seemed to be declining. As the cold war receded, the Soviets could reevaluate the need to keep communist governments in power in the Warsaw Pact nations in order to stave off the intrusion of NATO forces.

As the 1980s began, no one could foresee the massive changes that the decade would bring to Europe. Instead, a new cold war was breaking out on the European continent. In the Carter years NATO had become alarmed about Soviet deployment of the SS-20, a new generation of medium-range missiles aimed at western European nations. In response NATO had decided to deploy its own medium-range missiles, for the first time acquiring the capability to hit Soviet territory from NATO's European bases. However, these new missiles, coupled with the truculence of the newly elected Reagan administration, raised a storm of protest in western Europe, leading to massive peace demonstrations in Germany, England, and many other NATO countries.

The Gorbachev Reforms and the End of the Cold War

The new cold war developed at the same time the Soviet Union was undergoing a succession crisis after the death of Leonid Brezhnev, who had led the Soviet government for almost a generation. After a series of interim governments, Mikhail Gorbachev emerged as the new Soviet leader. Gorbachev took the lead in breaking the cycle of escalating tensions of the new cold war. He promised major changes in the Soviet system, articulating the three slogans of *perestroika* (restructuring), *glasnost* (openness), and new thinking in foreign policy.

The rise of Gorbachev in the Soviet Union coincided with the rise of the peace movement in Europe, but it was no simple coincidence. The Soviet old guard had hoped that political opposition to the deployment of the new Euro-missiles would split the NATO alliance. But their heavy-handed tactics had not succeeded. However, Gorbachev, the reformer of the Soviet system, master media politician, and proponent of new thinking in international relations, was a much more attractive figure to western Europeans. He was much more skillful in appealing to the western Europeans' desires for peace and security. The new politics of the European peace movement and Gorbachev's reform movement in the Soviet Union made the old politics of cold war and nuclear confrontation increasingly untenable.

Gorbachev moved quickly to build his domestic and international prestige by a series of summits with western European leaders and even the old cold warrior Ronald Reagan. The first fruit of this new spirit in Europe was the Intermediate Nuclear Forces (INF) treaty abolishing medium-range nuclear missiles on the continent. The accord, signed by Reagan and Gorbachev in 1987, was the first arms control treaty actually to eliminate existing weapons systems. All U.S. and Soviet ground-based medium-range missiles, defined as missiles with a range of 300-3,300 miles, were to be destroyed; 1,752 Soviet and 859 U.S. missiles were included in the pact. All future manufacture and flight testing of such missiles were banned. There were strict provisions for onsite inspection of the process. The signing of the INF treaty was the first tangible sign that Gorbachev's new thinking could transform Europe. It institutionalized a new relationship between the Soviet Union and NATO, reversing the decades of confrontation. It set the stage for the more massive changes in Europe that were to follow.

The rise of Gorbachev and his reform movement in the Soviet Union had a ripple effect in eastern Europe. If reform was possible in the heart of the Soviet system, perhaps change was also possible in the other Warsaw Pact nations. Gorbachev's policies of *glasnost* and *perestroika* within the Soviet Union gave new legitimacy to those in other communist-controlled societies who spoke out against repression and tight party control in their countries. Gorbachev's promise of new thinking in foreign policy raised hopes that the Soviets would not just respond reflexively with tanks but were willing to consider new political arrangements in eastern Europe.

The INF treaty was followed by other signs that the new thinking of Gorbachev was real. In the spring of 1988 the Soviets sued for peace in Afghani-stan. The Soviet withdrawal from Afghanistan, which marked the first time in generations that the Soviets had made territorial concessions, was even stronger encouragement to those seeking a new order in eastern Europe.

The beginning of the end of Soviet control of eastern Europe came in Poland, where the Soviets had been struggling with the anticommunist trade union Solidarity for nearly a decade. Under the sustained pressure of massive popular resistance, the Polish government agreed to allow opposition candidates to run in a series of elections. Anticommunist forces swept to victory, and Solidarity named the first noncommunist leader of government in the history of the Warsaw Pact. The Soviets merely stood by and watched. Other eastern Europeans were watching as well. Hungary, the site of the first large-scale rebellion against Soviet occupation in 1956, was next. Again, the Soviets were spectators as a new regime rose to power in Hungary. The Communist governments of the rest of the Warsaw Pact nations quickly fell like dominoes, and noncommunists came to power in all of the former Soviet client states. The Berlin Wall fell and Germany, divided by two generations of cold war, was reunited. Except in Romania, the process was surprisingly peaceful.

Gorbachev's response to the disintegration of the Warsaw Pact was not to move Soviet troops into eastern Europe but to accelerate the pace of Soviet withdrawal from the region. Gorbachev pressed the West to match his retrenchment with mutual agreements on reductions in conventional military forces in Europe. NATO and the Warsaw Pact had been negotiating conventional force reductions since the early days of detente, but the talks had bogged down on the differing perceptions of the participants and the complexity of issues like what kinds of forces to count and how to compare the different force structures. However, Gorbachev was able to cut through these complexities with the sword of unilateral action. He simply began announcing Soviet troop reductions and challenging the West to match him with similar signs of good faith.

In February 1990 the United States and the Soviet Union agreed to sharp reductions in their troop levels in central Europe. Both sides agreed to a limit of 195,000, down from 300,000 Americans and over half a million Soviets. Later in the year the Soviets announced agreements with Hungary and Czechoslovakia to withdraw all troops from those countries.

The conventional forces agreement was followed by finalization of another long series of negotiations, the START treaty to reduce U.S. and Soviet strategic nuclear arsenals. Concluded in the summer of 1991, START cuts the number of nuclear warheads on each side. The Soviets will reduce their arsenal by roughly one-third to a total of 7,160. The United States will cut the number of its warheads by roughly one-fifth to a total of 9,500.

Arms control agreements had been part of the U.S.-Soviet relationship since the signing of the Nuclear Test Ban Treaty in 1963. The SALT process had put overall caps on the superpowers' nuclear arsenals. But the arms control agreements of recent years have a different character. For the first time, U.S. and Soviet arsenals are being reduced. The INF, conventional forces, and START treaties institutionalize the changes in American-Russian political relations. They reduce the chances of conflict between the two sides by changing the structure of forces while providing for strict onsite inspection regimes that make it highly unlikely significant cheating will go undetected. They build confidence on both sides that a new relationship is being forged which makes conflict unlikely.

The Demise of the Soviet Union and the Rise of Yeltsin

On the heels of the signing of the START treaty came another set of shocking developments in the Soviet Union. Gorbachev's original reform program had never directly addressed the most serious problem confronting the Soviet Union—the fact that it was not a union at all but an empire in which dozens of different nationalities were held together primarily by the depth and breadth of communist power over the society. In each of the republics except the Russian Republic the majority of the population was not Russian, and in many cases did not speak the Russian language.

Glasnost let loose the nationalist sentiments that had been repressed under the regimes of Stalin and Brezhnev. The changes in eastern Europe unleashed great political unrest in the 14 non-Russian republics of the Soviet Union. The three tiny Baltic states declared their independence from Moscow, openly expressing desires felt in the other republics. Gorbachev's government responded to these pressures by trying to negotiate a new constitution, or "union treaty," that would have massively decentralized the Soviet system.

However, on the eve of a meeting with most of the leaders of the republics to sign the new union treaty, hard-liners in the Communist Party, frustrated with the unraveling of Soviet power, put Gorbachev under house arrest, seized power in Moscow, and set out to reverse the reform process. But the coup plotters were quickly routed by reformers, led by Russian Republic President Boris Yeltsin's dramatic stance of resistance in occupying the Russian Republic parliament building. Gorbachev was quickly restored as head of the Soviet government.

Nevertheless, the power of the center had been further undermined by the failed coup. The center of gravity of the Soviet system shifted further in the direction of the republics. Yeltsin, president of the Russian Republic which had half of the population and two-thirds of the territory of the Soviet Union, emerged from the coup more powerful than Gorbachev. Many of the leaders of the other Soviet republics who had been negotiating with Gorbachev for a reform constitution, opted instead to make a total break with the past. When Yeltsin met with the leaders of the Ukrainian and Byelorussian Republics to form a new alliance of independent states, most of the other former Soviet republics quickly signed on and the new, loosely structured Commonwealth of Independent States (CIS) was formed to replace the Soviet Union. Under the CIS each republic would become an independent state on political, economic, and cultural matters, although military and economic cooperation would be encouraged. Mikhail Gorbachev, his hopes of a new economic and political union abandoned, resigned the now powerless Soviet presidency at the end of 1991.

The Bush Administration and the Demise of the Soviet Union

It is clear that the United States was not prepared for these massive changes. For years, ideological blinders had limited U.S. policymakers' image of the Soviet Union, overemphasizing the importance of economic factors and underemphasizing how the nationalities question shaped the nature of the Soviet regime. U.S. leaders had long wished that the Soviet Union would simply disappear from the world scene. Now that the Soviet Union was dissolving, the American reaction recalled an old Chinese proverb: "Be careful what you wish for; you just might get it."

The dream of generations of cold warriors soon was recognized to have a nightmare scenario. What if, as the Soviet Union fractured, several newly independent republics gained control over existing Soviet nuclear weapons or weapons-making technology? Would the world really be better off with several new nuclear nations rising from the ashes of the Soviet Union and quarreling over the carcass of the communist system?

The situation that was developing in Yugoslavia added plausibility to this nightmare scenario. Like the Soviet Union, Yugoslavia was a multinational state that had been held together by a Communist Party, although one that had been much less repressive than its Soviet counterpart. As the rising tide of nationalism swept eastern Europe, several of Yugoslavia's component republics, led by the second largest one, Croatia, declared their independence. The largest republic, Serbia, wanted either to maintain central control or to claim big chunks of the other republics where large numbers of Serbs lived. A full-scale war has broken out between Serbia and Croatia and most of the other republics, with thousands of casualties. Similar kinds of conflicts are possible between the republics of the Soviet Union; minor skirmishes have already occurred in or between several former Soviet republics. The chief difference is that in the former Soviet Union, rebel groups might be able to seize control of Soviet nuclear weapons based on their territory.

The Bush administration showed little foresight about the possibility, much less the dangers, of the breakup of the Soviet Union. But to its credit, once the implications of the dissolution of the Soviet Union dawned upon the Bush administration, the United States acted swiftly. For most of Bush's presidency his administration had largely stood by as the Soviet system imploded and made only modest adjustments in U.S. military policy. But alarmed at the now obvious potential for nuclear proliferation and armed conflict, the Bush administration finally seized the initiative with a bold unilateral proposal. The new U.S. plan was designed to allow Moscow to destroy or recall the very weapons the United States was most afraid would fall into the wrong hands.

The Bush initiative focused on so-called tactical or battlefield nuclear weapons, although it also had key components affecting strategic weapons. The United States would destroy all its ground-launched tactical nuclear weapons and remove all its sea-launched ones from its ships if the CIS would follow suit. The

United States would also cancel its plans to develop the MX and Midgetman mobile missile systems if the CIS would make concurrent reductions in its existing mobile, land-based systems, which were spread throughout several CIS republics and vulnerable to rebel takeovers. The United States also took its nuclear bombers off the permanent alert they had maintained for over 40 years and proposed the abolition of all multiple-warhead missile systems.

There was much to quibble with in the Bush initiative. It did not affect air-launched cruise missiles, meaning that the United States retained the option of introducing tactical nuclear weapons into any crisis situation in a matter of hours. It left largely untouched expensive and perhaps ineffective weapons systems such as the Star Wars missile defense. But despite its flaws, the Bush initiative was a revolutionary step in U.S. foreign policy thinking. After years of simply standing by as the Russians made concession after concession, the United States was finally moving the process rapidly forward by taking unilateral action to break through the barriers posed by narrow, piecemeal negotiations.

The experts were confounded by the transformation of the Soviet bloc. Few, if any, Soviet specialists had foreseen the magnitude of the changes, and virtually no one thought such rapid and peaceful change would have been possible. U.S. policy and policy doctrine could not keep up with the pace of events. Old ideologies had not prepared policymakers for the new Russia or the CIS and old ideas could not adequately describe the new world.

The one new idea generated by the Bush administration to characterize these changes was the concept of a new world order, a phrase that may or may not join "containment of communism" and "making the world safe for democracy" as a fundamental slogan symbolizing U.S. policy goals. However, even if the concept of a new world order becomes the dominant symbol of an era, it is a slogan, not a concrete guide to policy. During the cold war, most policymakers agreed with the general goal of containing communism, but there were serious disagreements about strategies for accomplishing this, particularly in the 1970s and 1980s. In the same way, the concept of a new world order is at present too vague to give explicit guidance to policy and will mean many different things to many different people.

THE RESTORATION OF THE INTERVENTIONIST STATE

George Bush's foreign policy successes in relations with the Soviet Union were matched by the successful military campaigns in Panama in the winter of 1989-1990 and in Iraq in early 1991. Following the defeat in Vietnam, the fall of the Shah and the hostage crisis in Iran, and other reversals of U.S. foreign policy, many questioned the ability of the United States to effectively use its military power to achieve its political objectives. The wisdom of the interventionist policies of the national security state was under question, as was the willingness of the American people to bear the burdens associated with prolonged military campaigns. One of the primary ideological goals of the early Reagan restoration had been to revive the ability of the United States to intervene effectively in conflicts with revolutionary forces in the Third World.

The Reagan administration's attempts to revive the interventionist state met with mixed results. The U.S. Marines sent to Lebanon were hastily withdrawn after they sustained serious casualties. The war against the Sandinistas in Nicaragua never gained political support in the United States. But Panama and Iraq were quick, decisive, and relatively painless applications of military power. In particular, the "Vietnam syndrome" appeared to have been cured by the "feel-good war" against Iraq.

Panama and Iraq marked another significant change in U.S. foreign policy. For more than 40 years the cold war had served as the principal ideological justification for almost every major foreign policy action the United States took. However, the two most important military actions of the early Bush administration did not rely primarily on anticommunism for their legitimation. Panama and Iraq show that the end of the cold war is not likely to mean the end of U.S. military operations in the Third World. The United States played an activist, interventionist role in several regions of the world before there was a Soviet Union and long before the cold war. The rationales for these operations illustrate the new forms that justifications for future U.S. intervention in Third World conflicts might take.

The Invasion of Panama

The longest and deepest history of U.S. intervention is in Latin America, particularly Central America and the Caribbean. U.S. intervention in Latin American predates the existence of the Soviet Union and will likely continue regardless of the role the Soviets choose to play in the region. At the turn of the century the United States provoked a war with Spain in order to take control of her colonies in Cuba and the Philippines. It then carved the republic of Panama out of the territory of Colombia in order to get a free hand in building the Panama Canal. Around the time of World War I the United States sent military forces into Mexico and Nicaragua in order to put down radical peasant movements. The United States set up permanent military presences in Cuba and Panama, and periodically stationed forces in Nicaragua, in order to maintain political control of these countries. However, U.S. intervention in Latin America intensified during the cold war. The United States was directly involved in military operations in Guatemala, Cuba, the Dominican Republic, Nicaragua, El Salvador, and Grenada. It also provided indirect support to military coups or other operations in Brazil, Argentina, Chile, Bolivia, Peru, and Colombia. The invasion of Panama was only the latest in a long line of similar operations.

Except for neighbors Canada and Mexico, Panama is probably the most important country for U.S. interests in the western hemisphere. The Panama

Canal is a vital economic and military asset. From the Panamanian point of view, the importance of the United States as an economic and political force can hardly be exaggerated. Panamanian resentment at the overwhelming U.S. presence periodically has led to resistance movements.

Panama has been an issue in each of the past three presidential administrations. Jimmy Carter sought to fundamentally transform the U.S.-Panamanian relationship by renegotiating the treaty governing the all-important canal. Ronald Reagan sought the help of Panamanian strongman Manuel Noriega in his campaigns against socialist regimes in Nicaragua and Cuba. During the Iran-contra investigations, allegations that Noriega and other Panamanian military figures were involved in the cocaine trade began to intensify. The Dukakis campaign alluded to George Bush's ties to Noriega, when he was director of the CIA under Gerald Ford, as part of its charges that the Reagan-Bush administration was not doing enough to stop the rising tide of cocaine on America's streets.

Manuel Noriega had become a U.S. intelligence operative early in his career. As he rose through Panamanian military intelligence to become head of the armed forces and de facto head of government, Noriega had provided the U.S. government with much intelligence about revolutionary forces in Central America. He had been a valuable ally in the contra campaign against the Sandinista government in Nicaragua. He was seen by many as providing the most useful information on the situation and was thought to have conducted sabotage operations within Nicaragua. Because Noriega was irreplaceable in the campaign against the Sandinistas, the anticommunist zealots backing the contra campaign had ignored or suppressed information linking Noriega to the cocaine trade.

However, in 1988 Noriega was indicted on drug trafficking charges. This situation presented a dilemma for George Bush both during the campaign and after he assumed the presidency. Any trial of Noriega could put on the front pages the shady deals of Republican administrations and U.S. intelligence agencies with known and suspected drug lords. But failure to act would bring charges of ineffectiveness, indifference, or even complicity in the drug trade. After a year of trying to negotiate a deal for Noriega to go into exile and attempting to dislodge him by political means within Panama, the Bush administration finally concluded that only military force could remove Noriega. At the end of 1989 the United States unleashed an invasion of Panama, seeking to capture Noriega. A 24,000-man force quickly overwhelmed Panamanian forces, many of whom had divided loyalties. Street fighting with pro-Noriega guerrilla forces continued for several days and even weeks, but most of the fighting was over quickly, a military success with few U.S. casualties. Noriega took refuge in the Vatican embassy in Panama City but surrendered to U.S. authorities a few days later.

The invasion of Panama was the turning point in the conservative campaign to restore political support for U.S. military intervention abroad. In stark contrast with the Reagan administration's contra war or commitment of Marines in

Lebanon, the Panama invasion was a large-scale military operation that achieved its mission quickly and with few casualties.

The invasion of Panama demonstrates that anticommunism is not the only ideological legitimation that can be used for U.S. military action in the Third World. It foreshadows what may be a new long term justification for American intervention in Latin America in particular: the "war" against drugs. The revulsion most Americans feel against drug traffickers can be utilized to legitimate military campaigns against forces in Latin American countries that Washington does not like, regardless of whether drug issues are the primary motivation.

The War in the Persian Gulf

Even more important in the ideological restoration of U.S. military interventionism was the war with Iraq. The invasion of Panama posed real risks. Noriega might have escaped capture, Americans might have sustained casualties over weeks and perhaps months of fighting, and the political situation in the region could have soured. But there was little doubt that the military operation would succeed or that Noriega would be toppled from power.

There was much more at stake when Iraq invaded Kuwait in the summer of 1990. The U.S. and allied military commitment was a massive operation that faced a medium-sized military power which might be able to inflict heavy casualties on the U.S. and allied forces. The flow of oil from the Persian Gulf, on which the Western alliance depends, could be jeopardized. In the tinderbox of Middle Eastern hatreds and rivalries, it was hard to predict what the long-term political effect of conflict would be.

Certainly the reality of the changes in world politics in recent years could be seen in the political alignments touched off by the Persian Gulf crisis, alignments that would have been unthinkable just a few years before. However, the continuities between the old world and the new were also apparent.

Of course, war in the Middle East was nothing new. There have been five wars between Israel and the Arabs since the Jewish state was formed after the second world war. Iraq and Iran fought a bloody war for dominance of the Persian Gulf that lasted through most of the 1980s. Coups and civil wars have also been common, the outstanding example being Lebanon, which has been racked by a civil war stretching across a generation.

Nor was Western intervention in Middle East politics anything new. The discovery of major oil deposits in the Middle East around the turn of the century only intensified the interest European powers have historically shown in the region. The British and French controlled most of the Middle East between the two world wars, and briefly seized the Suez Canal in 1956. After the second world war the United States replaced the Europeans as the leading power in the region, backing its favored regimes in Israel, Iran, Saudi Arabia, and more recently Egypt with massive arms shipments and other assistance. The United

States supported not only the Israelis but also several traditionalist monarchies trying to check the influence of Soviet-backed Pan-Arabic socialists.

The war with Iraq was the largest, but not the first, U.S. military involvement in the region. The United States sent the Marines into Lebanon in the late 1950s and the early 1980s. It sent large naval armadas to the Arabian Sea and Persian Gulf theater more than once in the last generation. The Soviet Union was also deeply involved, giving major military backing to its favored clients, including Iraq, Syria, and for many years Egypt.

Nor was aggression by the regime of Saddam Hussein anything new. Early in the 1980s Hussein had attacked Iran, hoping to capitalize on the internal divisions and the international isolation of revolutionary Iran. Hussein was backed with arms from both the West and the Soviet Union; Iran's former arms supplier, the United States, was leading an international boycott of arms to Iran. Because of Israeli opposition the United States gave Iraq little direct aid, but it encouraged its NATO allies to take up the slack. With French, German, and Soviet support Hussein's Iraq was built into a regional power. The United States briefly reversed itself on the arms embargo to Iran when it traded some small arms shipments for the release of American hostages held by pro-Iranian militants in Lebanon, but generally the United States backed Iraq as a check on the spread of Iranian-style Islamic fundamentalism. The Iran-Iraq war claimed hundreds of thousands of casualties. Iraq was never really able to strike a decisive blow against Iran, but over the course of the long war Saddam Hussein had built the largest and best-equipped army in the Arab world.

By the time Iraq attacked Kuwait in the summer of 1990, changes in the world system brought a new alignment to Middle East politics. Iraq's invasion of Kuwait was almost universally denounced outside the Islamic world, with the Soviet Union and even China lining up with the United States, Britain, and France in backing United Nations actions against Iraq. Even when the United States, Britain, and France sent massive military forces into the region, the Soviet Union did not object, much less react by assisting its former client Iraq. Middle Eastern politics was also turned upside down as Saudi Arabia, Egypt, and even Syria joined the U.S.-led forces while Israel steered clear of any military action in order not to drive a wedge between the strange alliance of the United States and Israel's Arab adversaries.

The Bush administration characterized the international response to the Iraqi invasion as a test of the new world order, arguing that if all the major world powers could cooperate to protect a small, weak nation from an aggressor, a new precedent for international cooperation would be established. Certainly there was unprecedented cooperation among the United States, its NATO allies, and the Soviet Union during the crisis. All the major powers supported U.N. sanctions to isolate Iraq economically. When sanctions did not prove immediately effective, the Bush administration was able to hold together the great powers in support of a U.N. resolution authorizing the use of force to expel Iraq from Kuwait. The United States, Britain, and France then assembled the largest and most powerful international military force the world had seen in two generations. While the Soviet Union, China, Germany, and Japan did not send fighting units, they supported or quietly acquiesced to the use of force.

Iraq appeared to possess a formidable military force, with a million men under arms, many of them combat hardened from nearly a decade of war with Iran. The United States was cautious about making a frontal assault on Iraqi ground forces, which reportedly were equipped with chemical weapons capable of inflicting heavy casualties on attacking forces. However, the actual fighting was surprisingly brief and Western casualties were unbelievably low. Iraqi casualties have been estimated at 100,000 and the devastation of the Iraqi economy will cause civilian suffering, disease, and death for years to come.

The military campaign began in January 1991 with massive bombing of Iraqi targets. The Iraqi air force chose not to fight, fleeing to the north. Iraqi ground-to-air missile defenses were largely ineffective and the U.S.-led forces were able to pound Iraqi troops and supply centers almost at will. As the United States prepared to initiate its ground war, the Iraqis, having suffered great losses from a month of the ceaseless bombing, sued for peace, promising to withdraw from Kuwait in return for a truce. But the United States spurned the offer and quickly began the ground campaign before international pressure to negotiate could mount, rapidly encircling Iraqi positions. For reasons that are not yet entirely clear, the demoralized Iraqi army offered little resistance, surrendering in large numbers without using their dreaded chemical weapons.

The Bush administration portrayed the victory over Iraq as evidence of the "new world order" at work. But the Persian Gulf crisis was not a very severe test of any new world order. First of all, it was clearly a case of unprovoked international aggression. Iraq had a troubled relationship with Kuwait, but its invasion was a totally unjustifiable use of force against a weaker state. Few cases of international conflict are so clear-cut. More commonly international conflicts build over time, with clear grievances on both sides. The conflicts between India and Pakistan, or the Arabs and Israel, or in southeast Asia have no such international consensus about good guys or villains.

The politics of the Persian Gulf crisis were also favorable for broad international cooperation. The Iraqi invasion of Kuwait struck at one of the few things on which there is real consensus among the United States, its major NATO allies, and Japan—the need to maintain the flow of oil from the Persian Gulf. The United States, its NATO partners, and Japan all have very different expectations about any new world order, but they all want to maintain their access to Middle East oil.

The crisis also came at an opportune time for the United States to enlist Russian cooperation. With all his internal troubles, the last thing Gorbachev wanted was a confrontation with the West that would undermine both his prestige as a skilled international operator and expectations of Western aid.

Even many Third World regimes that would have had serious concerns about U.S. military intervention in their region felt little sympathy for the Iraqi attempt to establish greater control over Persian Gulf oil. The oil price rises of the 1970s had badly hurt most non-oil-producing Third World nations, adding to their already burdensome foreign debt. Many Third World states that had criticized U.S. military intervention in Vietnam or more recently in Panama were silent or even supportive in the Persian Gulf case.

Negotiations on the Middle East and Other Regional Conflicts

Even as the United States seemed to be reasserting its role as a kind of global policeman in Iraq and Panama, there were countervailing tendencies in the Middle East and Central America, as well as in southern Africa and southeast Asia. There were some signs that the changes in the world system might actually bring a more peaceful world order. Reflecting their new political relationship, the United States and Russia were both terminating support for governments and rebel groups they had backed as part of their cold war power rivalry.

In the aftermath of the Persian Gulf war, the United States was able to persuade Syria, Jordan, the Palestinians, and Israel to meet for talks on the Arab-Israeli question. In the past the United States had followed the Israeli line and opposed a regional peace conference because it feared the Soviet Union would have to be included. But with the Soviet threat diminishing and Soviet cooperation in the conflict with Iraq, the Bush administration was willing to cosponsor such a conference with the Soviet Union. The war against Iraq had pushed Syria and the United States into an alliance of convenience against a common enemy, an alliance that both hoped to exploit to achieve their historic goals in the region.

Even as Central America was rocked by the conflict in Panama, the regional hot wars of the 1980s seemed to be cooling. In 1989 the Sandinistas conducted a free and fair election, and when they lost a close vote, allowed the opposition to take power peacefully. In early 1992 the leftist insurgency and the rightist government in El Salvador also agreed to a peaceful settlement of their long-standing civil war. In Africa, the white government of South Africa was in the process of abolishing the formal structures of apartheid that had denied the majority blacks' basic human rights. South Africa also withdrew its forces from the territory it had seized in South-West Africa, and ended its guerrilla conflict with Angola. And, in southeast Asia, the Cambodian factions that had been warring for more than 20 years agreed to a peaceful political settlement.

It is too early to say that all these regional settlements will last. But clearly the United States and Russia have both decided there is little to gain from bankrolling governments and guerrillas in the far corners of the world. Iraq and Panama show that the end of the cold war does not mean the end of U.S. military intervention in the Third World. But developments in the Middle East, Central America, southern Africa, and southeast Asia show that there is some hope that with the end of the cold war, there is a better chance for a more peaceful world.

FOREIGN POLICY IDEOLOGIES AND THE NEW
WORLD ORDER

The categories of thought that have shaped U.S. foreign policy for the past two generations are inadequate to characterize either the massive changes in the world in recent years or the U.S. policy response to these changes. Future foreign policy ideologies will be centered on new issues. The cold war was central to virtually every foreign policy issue in the last two generations, and thus served to simplify policy debate. The issues were tough but the framework was largely unidimensional.

The Bush administration has coined the phrase "new world order" as an alternative to "containment of communism." But the actual content of any policy based on the concept of a new world order is not yet clear. Any new philosophy about U.S. foreign policy will have to face a complex set of interrelated issues including: (1) how to deal with the changing security picture in Europe and Russia; (2) what the role of military power, and particularly of nuclear weapons, will be in any new world order; (3) how to deal with the economic challenges of the new Europe, Japan, and the rising economies of the Pacific Rim; and perhaps most centrally, (4) whether the United States will remain a dominant force in world affairs. It is too early to see clearly the clusters of positions that will emerge on these new issues. But fools rush in where wise men fear to go, so Figure 13.1 suggests one possible set of categories that might characterize debates about U.S. foreign policy as we move into the third millennium. These categories are not unrelated to the ideologies of the cold war era but represent how different ideological tendencies might respond to the challenge of new issues.

Figure 13.1
Old and New Foreign Policy Ideologies

Old Spectrum

Peace Movement	Hegemonic Flexibility	National Security	Holy War

New Spectrum

Globalism	Multilateralism	Global Interventionism	Militant Nationalism

Global Interventionism

A possible successor to the national security ideology might be called global interventionism. The national security ideology was defined by its response to Soviet power, and thus in one sense has become obsolete because the Soviet challenge is over. But as a new world emerges, certain themes from the national security ideology are sure to survive. The most important of these are a determination to maximize U.S. power, defined largely in military terms; a related tendency to see many threats to U.S. power around the world; and a inclination to unilateralism in policy action. The desire of many in Washington to maximize U.S. power and to intervene militarily around the world predates the cold war. At the turn of the century the United States took the Philippines from Spain and established protectorates in the Caribbean and Central America. American presidents took the United States into two world wars without a communist menace to justify global activism.

The communist menace is not what it once was, but global interventionism will see several new threats to U.S. power in the post-cold war world. Terrorists are still active around the world. Drug lords have entrenched themselves in many Latin American societies. Regional powers hostile to U.S. interests such as Saddam Hussein's Iraq, the Islamic fundamentalists in Iran, and even Castro's Cuba still remain.

Nor is it clear that the old threats are entirely erased. Whatever replaces the former Soviet Union, Russia will remain the second greatest military power in the world for a long time. It is not at all clear how much U.S. and Russian interests will harmonize or will conflict in the new world system. China, once the top demon of the national security state, remains communist, as yet largely untouched by collapse of the Soviet bloc.

Global interventionists will warn that the United States must keep its guard up, that global instability means new dangers as well as new opportunities. They will argue that any new order will have to be established and protected through military force. As in the past, there will be a tendency among many U.S. policymakers to define the problems the United States faces and potential solutions to those problems in military terms.

Global interventionism therefore will have two central characteristics: a desire to maintain American supremacy in the post-cold war world and a tendency to use military power to intervene unilaterally in political conflicts in the Third World. Global interventionists will try to keep the United States as the only superpower in the post-cold war world, to maintain U.S. hegemony in the global system. They will also rely primarily on unilateral action to protect U.S. interests. The invasion of Panama is an example of this kind of thinking. In Panama the United States acted alone, against the advice of most of its allies and over the objections of most of the world community, including many of the regimes in the region.

Multilateralism

The other centrist ideological tendency might center on a concept of multi-lateralism which would take a different approach to the problem of maximizing U.S. power in a changing world. Multilateralism would emphasize the use of nonmilitary as well as military forms of power, rely more on cooperation with allies and friends around the world rather than unilateral action, and accept a role for the United States that is less preeminent than in the cold war era. The INF and conventional arms control agreements in Europe, the war in the Persian Gulf, and the negotiations in the Uruguay round of the General Agreement on Tariff and Trade to remove the barriers to international trade reflect a multilateralist perspective on foreign policy.

The debate between those who define U.S. power and the threats to it primarily in military terms and those who have a more multidimensional perspective can be expected to continue even in the post-cold war world. Multilateralists can be expected to argue that while the military challenge of the Soviets has passed, the economic challenge of Europe and Japan has sharpened. Multilateralists will believe that economic power rather than military power will be the key to international influence in the new world, and therefore trade issues should join security issues at the center of U.S. foreign policy.

Multilateralists will also be more likely to believe that the post-cold war world has truly changed. Multilateralists would be more likely to think Russia is no longer a real military threat to the United States and that it should be drawn into closer cooperation with the West through trade and aid.

At a more fundamental level, multilateralists will argue that just as Soviet military power could not maintain Soviet political power, so U.S. military supremacy can no longer assure U.S. economic or political supremacy. Multi-lateralists will be more likely to believe that the days of U.S. hegemony are drawing to a close and that any new world military, economic, and political order will need broader and deeper support than the American military can provide. Multilateralism will see a posthegemonic world constructed through broad international agreements between the major powers.

Militant Nationalism

The centrist ideological tendencies that dominate U.S. policy-making always face challenges from more idealistic tendencies on both the left and the right. The right tendencies that might influence future foreign policy could be labeled militant nationalism. With the crusade against the atheistic communist menace over, a new isolationism might emerge on the right, a twenty-first century version of "American First." Like global interventionism, militant nationalism would see the world populated with hostile, anti-American forces. But militant nationalists might feel less need to intervene in this hostile world. Rather, they would desire to withdraw from it. On the trade front, militant nationalism might offer resistance to the penetration of American society by foreign goods, particularly those produced in nonwhite nations.

Globalism

Many of the developments of recent years have gone beyond the wildest dreams of peace activists opposed to the cold war and nuclear weapons. But in fact, much of the agenda of the peace movement will remain unrealized in the early years of the new world order that is emerging. A tendency that could be called globalism might emerge on the left. Globalism would emphasize that a new world requires new thinking in U.S. foreign policy, and a truly peaceful, orderly world would require new concepts of America's role in the world. Globalism would see the end of the cold war as the first step in a process of creating a new world, the beginning of a process of transformation rather than its culmination.

For example, the cold war may be over, but even after the START treaty and other arms commitments are fully implemented, there will still be tens of thousands of nuclear weapons in the U.S. and Russian arsenals, and perhaps a dozen potential nuclear powers waiting in the wings. Globalists might argue that new, truly global institutions will be needed if the threat of nuclear war is to be effectively relegated to the past. They would believe that traditional concepts of national sovereignty and maximization of national power will have to give way to global security regimes. A similar kind of reasoning could be applied to environmental issues, since ecological degradation recognizes no national boundaries.

Globalism will also point out that although the East-West conflict has subsided, the divisions between the rich nations of the North and the poor nations of the South, which have been at the root of so much conflict in the twentieth century, remain as severe as ever. Globalists might argue that for any world order to be truly new, or even to be orderly, it must be more than just a deal among the U.S., Europe, and Japan to divide the world up into spheres of influence. Globalists would want a new world order to transform North-South relations as well as East-West relations.

PART V

THE PRESIDENCY AND THE AMERICAN FUTURE

14

PRESIDENTIAL IDEOLOGIES IN THE 1990s

WHAT DIFFERENCE DO PRESIDENTIAL IDEOLOGIES MAKE?

The President as the Wizard of Oz

Does it really make any difference what presidents say or do? Are presidential ideologies a lot of smoke and mirrors which do more to obscure the realities of American politics than to chart the course for the nation's future? Is the president really a kind of Wizard of Oz, impressive when viewed from afar but really empty and ineffectual when looked at too closely?

The American people are increasingly coming to believe the "Wizard of Oz" thesis. The decline of confidence in government that began in the 1960s has accelerated in the 1990s. Ronald Reagan was able to temporarily restore some of the traditional American optimism, but in the recessionary times of the early 1990s voters have become ever more cynical about the ability of political leaders to cope with the social, economic, and foreign policy crises that face the nation.

There are certainly grounds for the low opinion Americans have of their political leadership. In order to win an American presidential election, a candidate must garner 40 million or more votes. In a people as diverse as Americans, this requires putting together a very broad and heterogeneous coalition of voters who often have very different reasons for supporting a candidate. Usually the interests of a winning presidential candidate's supporters conflict on many key issues, and expectations of what a candidate will do once in office vary considerably.

Presidential campaigns and administrations in the television age deliberately convey a series of mixed and ambiguous messages about a president's beliefs and intentions. Presidential statements often give symbolic support to policy goals but real action does not follow the rhetoric. So, for example, the Reagan and Bush administrations continued to endorse a constitutional amendment to balance the federal budget even after they had become accustomed to submitting budget plans to Congress that had imbalances well over $100 billion and they had largely abandoned any serious attempts to significantly reduce the deficit.

Presidents who have pursued a particular policy direction over time feel the pressure to combat the negative images that are associated with strong policy positions. So while Jimmy Carter had directly challenged some of the central premises of the cold war and the national security state in his first years in office, in the second half of his term Carter sought to combat the impression that he was "weak" on foreign policy by tougher talk against the Soviets, particularly after the invasion of Afghanistan.

Even Ronald Reagan, who generally showed more ideological consistency than most presidents, felt the need to combat his "negatives" in his second term. Reagan's consistent tough stand toward the Soviet Union had given him and his party the negative image of being rigid and inflexible. But then, in his second term, the most consistent of cold warriors opened up and sought agreements and accommodation with the "evil empire."

Even when presidents chart a consistent policy course and stick to their guns, the brute fact remains that the American political system is one of separated powers in which the president must share control over public policy with Congress and the judiciary. Political party loyalties can help the president influence the other branches. But in 26 of the 38 years since 1954, Republican presidents have found at least one house, and usually both houses, of Congress controlled by the opposition Democrats. The difficulties the president has in exercising policy leadership in a system of shared powers are magnified under continuous conditions of divided government.

The President as Ideological Leader

However, despite the tendencies toward immobilism and centrism in the American political system and the temptations of symbolic politics, throughout history presidents have at times exercised significant ideological and policy leadership. Exactly because the president is the symbolic center of the political system, only he can provide the kind of direction to dramatically alter prevailing public policies and philosophies.

Not all presidents serve when conditions are ripe for such leadership, and not all presidents who have the opportunity to exercise policy direction rise to the challenge. But presidential leadership is a necessary condition for significant ideological and policy change.

There have been times when presidents have given considerable ideological and policy direction to the nation. FDR set in motion the activist state as we understand it today and committed the United States to a permanent and continuous role of leadership in world affairs. Harry Truman proclaimed the doctrines of the cold war and built the institutions of the national security state. Lyndon Johnson significantly expanded the role of the activist state. Richard Nixon altered perceptions of the communist world, institutionalized a more flexible range of policies toward China and the Soviet Union, and raised the possibility of world order. Ronald Reagan reversed some of the trends set in motion in the 1960s and 1970s and restored to political respectability some ideas of earlier eras.

In each of these cases the president not only charted a new course for his own administration. He also articulated ideas and constructed institutions that kept these policies alive in succeeding administrations. His policies not only had immediate impact during his tenure, but his philosophy also set the tone and the parameters of the actions of future administrations.

Ideological Majorities and Presidential Leadership

In domestic policy there is one set of conditions that set the stage for potentially historically significant presidential policy leadership: when a president with a consistent ideology is elected when his party is at a peak in its strength in Congress. This has happened three times in the last 60 years since the Democrats have controlled Congress: in 1932-1936 under FDR, in 1964-1966 under Lyndon Johnson, and in 1980-1982 under Ronald Reagan. In each of these cases the course of domestic public policy was altered, changes that had impact for decades to come.

Presidents Eisenhower and Carter also enjoyed brief periods when their party was unusually strong in Congress. But both men were political centrists, not inclined to press an ideological agenda. Also, in both cases, although their party was numerically strong in Congress due to short-term political trends, their parties were still suffering identity crises because of historic political and policy failures. So despite political majorities in Congress, these administrations did not have the long-term impact on public policy that more ideological presidencies did.

Since ideological majorities have recurred periodically over American political history, the probability exists that a new ideological majority will emerge sometime in the next decade or two. The continuing ideological polarization of the parties also makes such an ideological majority a real possibility. In the 1940s and 1950s, when there were significant liberal and conservative wings in both parties, one would not have expected ideological consistency from an administration. A president had to try to please both wings of his party, and he faced a possible challenge on either ideological flank from the opposition.

But as in recent decades the parties have become more polarized, and thus more ideologically consistent, presidents have had to steer a different set of currents. Now they must find safe waters somewhere between the ideological wings of their party and the political center. The persistence of divided government since 1968 has masked the ideological polarization of the parties because the dominant pattern has kept Republican presidents checked by Democratic Congresses. But if short-term political factors led to significant gains in congressional elections for either party, then there would be a strong probability of formation of a new ideological majority, giving the president the opportunity to exercise strong control over domestic policy.

Divided Government and Presidential Leadership in Foreign Policy

While presidential innovation in domestic policy is linked to party government and ideological polarization, the most significant cases of presidential leadership in ideological change in foreign policy have come under conditions of divided government. Democrat Truman constructed the national security state during one of the rare periods when Republicans controlled Congress. Richard Nixon articulated the philosophy of hegemonic flexibility and opened up toward the communist world during a period when he was in ever more contentious conflict with a Democratically controlled Congress. And in his early administration George Bush has shown more leadership in moving toward a new world order than he has in dealing with the Democratically controlled Congress in domestic policy.

While two or three cases are not many to generalize on, this pattern fits the often-made observation that when presidents are checked by domestic political or policy obstacles, they tend to turn to foreign affairs as a more fertile ground for policy success. The president does have more constitutional authority in foreign affairs where he is granted such key powers as commander in chief of the armed forces, the appointment of ambassadors, and negotiations with foreign nations. The president usually has greater political autonomy, more room to maneuver in foreign policy.

There still is some expectation that politics should "stop at the water's edge," that the United States should present a unified front toward the outside world. The tradition of bipartisan foreign policy-making that was established in the heyday of the national security state is probably gone forever because the philosophical consensus supporting the national security state has dissipated. For example, Ronald Reagan was never able to get Congresses controlled by Democrats to share his perception of the threat in Nicaragua. But when the president and Congress share the same foreign policy goals, even under divided government, policy innovation is possible.

This has been particularly true when hard-line cold warrior Republican presidents have softened their stance and moved toward the policies of hegemonic flexibility that congressional Democrats have generally advocated. Presidents Nixon, Reagan, and Bush were all criticized by congressional Democrats for passing up opportunities to improve relations with the Soviet Union. But they all also enjoyed the support of Democratic Congresses when they made serious attempts to recast the relationship between the United States and the Soviet Union.

Of course, the ability of a president unable to shape the domestic agenda to turn to foreign affairs in search of policy success is limited, too. Congress also has the power to thwart presidential policy-making in international affairs. More important, policy success in the international arena is contingent on a series of events outside the president's control. Foreign leaders and foreign powers can often prove much more formidable obstacles to presidential will than congressional opponents. But even so, one can expect that under divided government, presidents will often look to foreign relations as a more likely arena for policy success.

In the early 1960s students of the presidency were struck by the contrasts between the deadlock in domestic policy that had prevailed since FDR and the seeming foreign policy successes of Presidents Truman, Eisenhower, and Kennedy. The theory was advanced that there were really two presidencies, a strong foreign affairs presidency where the executive could control policy-making and have a high expectation of success, and a weak domestic affairs presidency where the executive had to share policy-making powers with Congress and could expect to fail more often than he succeeded.

Of course, just as this theory was gaining credence, along came the administration of Lyndon Johnson, who won many historic triumphs in domestic policy but who failed even more spectacularly in Vietnam. In the years following Vietnam the bipartisan consensus over the policies of the national security state unraveled and the "two presidencies" hypothesis faded away.

But perhaps a revised version of the "two presidencies" hypothesis is worth considering. Perhaps we can expect that in the rare situations where a president can work with an ideological majority in Congress, he will be consumed with taking advantage of this unusual historical opportunity. But when a president is faced with seemingly unalterable conditions of divided government and cannot expect cooperation from Congress on domestic policy, then he is more likely to try to make his mark on foreign policy.

THE IDEOLOGICAL SIGNIFICANCE OF THE 1992
GENERAL ELECTION

This book has tried to provide a perspective from which presidential elections can be viewed. Chapter 5 in particular introduces a typology of presidential elections in this era. Each individual election presents a unique set of conditions, but during long historical periods elections tend to fall into a pattern. If one understands that pattern, then one can get insight into the dynamics of any particular election.

For example, the recession of 1991-1992 will play a central role in the upcoming election. The recession of 1991-1992 is unique in that it has been the longest running period of stagnation in the postwar period. But 1992 is certainly not the first election to be run under the shadow of a recession or economic or fiscal crisis. We know a lot about how the major parties handle the politics of recession and other economic issues.

In the same way, the riots in Los Angeles in the wake of the Rodney King beating case and the possibility of a major Supreme Court decision on abortion rights loom over the 1992 election. One cannot know for certain how these issues will play out in 1992, but one can learn a lot from looking at the stance of the major parties on social issues in recent years.

Perhaps the truly defining characteristic of the 1992 campaign will be the intensification of the fundamental crisis of legitimacy that the political system is undergoing. This book has detailed the crises of the activist state in domestic policy and the national security state in foreign policy and the attempts of the Reagan restoration to revive the legitimacy of political institutions and particular public policies. But the Republican attempts to return traditional policies and restore the old system have not solved the crisis of legitimacy. The white-hot public anger over bounced checks at the House of Representatives bank and the congressional pay raise, issues that might have seemed trivial a generation or two ago, demonstrate the breadth and depth of public loss of faith in political institutions. The final proof of this crisis in confidence is the power of the most unique aspect of the early 1992 campaign—the Perot phenomenon.

The Perot Phenomenon

The emergence of an outsider candidate like H. Ross Perot as a serious contender for president is not totally unprecedented in American politics. After the electoral successes of Jimmy Carter and Ronald Reagan, it has become a cliche of American politics to run for president as an outsider "anti-politician." In many ways the Perot campaign most closely parallels that of Dwight Eisenhower in 1952. Like Eisenhower, Perot is running as a man of proven accomplishments in a field outside of politics who is untainted by the corruption and policy failures of the career politicians.

Certainly third party and independent candidates have had impact on presidential elections throughout American history. In late spring of 1980 John Anderson was running nearly as well as Perot in the polls. Anderson received 7 percent of the popular vote in November. In 1968 George Wallace won 13 percent of the vote and more importantly, carried 5 states in the Electoral College. Third party candidates also won electoral votes in the elections of 1948 and 1924. In 1912 Theodore Roosevelt, running as the Progressive Party candidate, outpolled the Republican nominee in both popular and electoral votes. In fact, before the election of 1932 it was more common than not that a third party would pick up several percent of the vote, and third parties would often win votes in the Electoral College. The Republican Party itself was born as a dissident third party. But not since before the Civil War has an independent or third party candidate actually won the presidency.

Although there are precedents analogous to the Perot phenomenon, there has been nothing quite like it in American politics. Never before has a billionaire promising to pour virtually unlimited funds into an independent campaign been able to bypass the major parties and yet run even or ahead of the major party candidates in the spring polls. Most third candidates have been leaders of third party movements who have had strong ideologies of the right or left that represented fundamental philosophical challenges to the prevailing orthodoxies. Perot has built his popularity largely on his reputation as a "can-do" guy who can offer strong leadership. His ideas about government are largely unknown, and he has resisted being pinned down on specifics about public policy. Thus in its early stages his candidacy has been able to pull support from disaffected voters across the ideological spectrum—left, right, and center.

When the Perot phenomenon first appeared in the early spring, many experts thought that Perot was destined to fade away in the polls before November. John Anderson in 1980 and George Wallace in 1968 ran much stronger in the middle of the election season than they did in the final voting. Many citizens who are originally attracted to a relatively unknown third candidate later desert them when they learn more about them. When Perot first emerged he was a kind of political wish fulfillment into which citizens could read their own beliefs and values, a way of saying "none of the above" to the entrenched political parties. Over the course of the campaign, more will become known about Perot and at least some of his earlier supporters will be alienated by something he says or does or something about his background. Also, as the real election draws near voters are often reluctant to "waste" their vote on a third candidate who is given little chance to win the White House.

In some ways Perot is particularly vulnerable to having his bubble burst. Leaders of third party movements have a cause as well as a persona, but Perot is running largely on his leadership abilities. Widespread doubts about his character or acumen would be even more damaging to him than to the head of a political party. In addition, the picture of a billionaire pouring his personal wealth into a campaign that far outspends the established parties makes Perot vulnerable to charges of buying the election. But so far Perot has confounded the skeptics and over time has gained rather than lost support.

It is hard to predict at this point which of the major party candidates Perot will hurt more. As the campaign develops, more will be learned about Perot's philosophy. If it turns out he is a highly conservative Texas billionaire, then he will draw most of his support from ideological conservatives who otherwise would support George Bush. If Perot runs an ideologically diffuse centrist campaign, he would probably draw mostly disaffected, anti-incumbent voters who otherwise would have either supported Clinton or stayed home. There are two unlikely, but possible, scenarios where Perot would really damage Clinton. If Perot were to chose a black running mate, he could split the black vote which would otherwise go almost entirely to Clinton. And if Perot were to run far enough ahead of Clinton in the polls long enough, he could conceivably be come to seen as the real alternative to the incumbent, making potential Clinton supporters reluctant to "waste" their votes.

As Chapter 5 pointed out, the president is elected not by popular vote, but by the votes of the states in the Electoral College. If the Perot phenomenon lasts until election day, there is a real chance that no candidate would get a majority of the Electoral votes. It has been more than a century since that has happened, but the Constitution provides for such an outcome. When there is no Electoral College majority, the House of Representative chooses the next president from among the three leading contenders. Each state delegation will have one vote, so the one representative from Wyoming will have as much say in the selection as the 52 from California. The Democrats are likely to maintain control of the House in this election, although large Republican gains in the lightly populated western and central states could conceivably give them a majority of state delegations. However, if Clinton ran a poor third, far behind Perot, House Democrats might turn to Perot rather than face charges of overturning popular will.

Another scenario if there is no Electoral vote majority on election day is a deal between two of the candidates before the Electoral College meets. There are few laws or precedents binding those selected to the Electoral College to vote for the candidate to which they are pledged. Depending on the circumstances, the Bush and Perot forces might be tempted to cut a deal before the Electoral College meets to avoid a Democratic House putting Clinton into power.

The Improbability of an Ideological Majority

The analysis presented in Chapter 5 argues that certain kinds of presidential elections have greater historical significance than others—realigning elections, dealigning elections, and elections that produce ideological majorities. In the currently dealigned American system, a realigning election is a logical possibility. But such critical elections are extremely rare and are triggered by massive political or economic crises. It is unlikely that the conditions for a critical election will be found in the 1992 election unless the recession becomes much more severe.

The year 1992 might bring a reelected President Bush an ideological majority or propel a Democrat to the White House with such a majority, but that is unlikely. The Democratic majority in Congress is slightly larger than its average since 1938. The Republican congressional delegation is so small that the Republicans would have to make major gains to have any chance of putting together an ideological majority. Gains large enough to swing the ideological tides historically have not come to a party that controls the White House but only when the voters are rejecting an incumbent president's party.

The current party balance in Congress does mean that if 1992 brings a strong swing to the Democrats, a Democratic president could be elected along with an unusually large congressional majority. But there are several reasons to doubt that that will occur. Congressional Democrats have been battered with scandals in the House banking and postal systems, and are taking the heat for pay raises they voted themselves. The House of Representatives is being redistricted in this election which makes things tougher on many incumbents who have to run in new districts. In 1992 many of the Senate seats the Democrats won in close races in 1986 will be hotly contested again. Because of redistricting and certain financial incentives, several veteran Democrats are retiring, giving Republicans more chances to win districts where there are no incumbents. At the time this is being written, Bill Clinton, the Democrat's probable presidential nominee, is running poorly in the polls, meaning the head of the ticket will likely be a drag on Democratic congressional candidates. If the Perot campaign brings a large turnout of disaffected, anti-incumbent voters to the polls, Democratic members of Congress could be the big losers. It is unlikely Democrats will lose either political or ideological control of Congress, but it is also unlikely they will gain any ground in the 1992 congressional elections.

Even if there are large swings in Congress in 1992, none of the candidates is likely to run the kind of campaign that would contribute to the formation of an ideological majority. If Bush is renominated, he is likely to run as an ideological conservative, as he did in 1988, using ideological identification to try to woo independents and disaffected Democrats who feel their party has become too liberal. In the nomination phase in particular, Bush has emphasized his conservative credentials to offset the challenge of the more conservative Pat Buchanan. But like Reagan in 1984, in the general election Bush is likely to be more concerned about his reelection than about conducting a referendum on ideology.

The role that ideology will take in the Democrats' campaign will depend largely on the outcome of their nomination process. But most likely the Democrats will follow their historic strategy of downplaying ideology in favor of particularistic appeals to separate elements of their electoral coalition. Michael Dukakis was not the first Democrat to avoid the label of "liberal." He was following the time-honored strategy of such Democratic presidential winners as Jimmy Carter and John Kennedy. The only recent Democrats to run polarizing ideological campaigns were George McGovern in 1972 and, to some extent, Walter Mondale in 1984. Both these candidacies went down in flames, and the lesson was not lost on the Democratic Party.

It is hard to predict the ideological tenor of the Perot campaign. It would seem that the best electoral strategy would be to continue to remain as vague as possible on the issues in order to pick up disaffected voters from all ideological perspectives. But once subjected to the scrutiny of a presidential campaign Perot's core beliefs may come to the fore. Nobody knows exactly what they are, but it is more likely from what Perot has said and done and from his background that Perot is to the right of center than that he is to the left of center.

Issues in the 1992 Campaign

The significance of ideology in a presidential campaign depends to some degree on the strategy that the contenders employ. But regardless of campaign strategy, ideology and issues always play some role in presidential campaigns, and 1992 will be no exception.

Foreign policy will of course play a role in the 1992 campaign. The early 1990s are a crucial period for defining what any new world order will look like and what the U.S. role in such a new world order would be. All candidates can be expected to hail the end of the cold war and appeal to nationalist sentiments by proclaiming victory in that struggle. Certainly a major theme of President Bush will be the positive changes in the world during his watch and his role in bringing them about. The military successes in Iraq and Panama will also be recurring themes.

The themes that the Democrats will emphasize on foreign policy depend largely on the unfolding of world events. However, any Democratic candidate is likely to attack continued spending on expensive weapons systems now that the cold war appears to be over. All Democratic candidates can be expected to take a harder line on trade negotiations, particularly with the Japanese, than President Bush has. Perot can be expected to sound similar themes on foreign policy, probably also emphasizing his skill as a business negotiator, his work trying to find American soldiers who might have been left behind in southeast Asia, and his heralded rescue of his employees held hostage in Iran.

But in the absence of large American casualties in a long war, foreign policy has rarely dominated a presidential election. The costs of the Vietnam and Korean wars contributed to the defeats of the Democrats in 1968 and 1952, but even in those elections there were other important issues. In 1992 the Democrats, and perhaps Perot, are likely to cede President Bush the high ground on foreign policy and base their campaign on domestic issues.

Pundits generally agree that economic issues are the most important ones in most presidential campaigns, and because of the recession of 1991-1992 that is more likely to be true in 1992 than in many other elections. The last three Republicans running for reelection have won easily. But in 1932 the Republican seeking reelection was Herbert Hoover, who paid the political cost of the Great Depression. Hoover's massive loss to FDR was the only critical realigning election in this century. Economic troubles could cost George Bush the White House.

Both the Democratic candidate and Perot will make the state of the domestic economy their major issue and argue that a more activist government is needed to solve economic problems. They will point to the Bush administration's initial refusal to acknowledge the existence of the recession and its vetoes of extended unemployment compensation and other worker benefits as signs of indifference to the suffering of ordinary people. The Democrats and Perot will appeal to the groups who have not prospered in the Reagan-Bush era—industrial workers, farmers, women heading households, and the urban underclass—promising to extend more government help to these groups. The Democrats in particular will argue that the Republican administration's concept of limited government has not stopped it from helping rich bankers, but it has blocked programs to aid the unemployed and others suffering from economic deprivation.

Democrats will point to the tide of imports that put American jobs in jeopardy and argue that more activist trade and industrial policies are necessary to preserve the position of the United States in the world economy. They will argue that President Bush has spent more time on foreign policy than domestic policy, and given more help to foreigners than Americans.

Each of the contenders in the Democratic primaries made access to health care and medical cost containment key issues, with each candidate issuing his own reform plan. Health care costs have risen at something like twice the inflation rate for more than a generation, making the U.S. health care system the most costly in the world. Tens of millions of Americans have no health insurance at all, and even more have inadequate coverage. Since most people are covered through work, the number of uninsured or underinsured has climbed by millions in recent hard times. In the early primary season the Democratic candidates signaled this is an issue they intend to try to seize in the fall campaign.

Perot's views on economic issues are not well known as this is being written. Perot can certainly be expected to use his success as a businessman to argue that he has a better grasp of economic issues than professional politicians.

President Bush signaled some of the Republican campaign themes in his economic recovery plan outlined in his State of the Union message. He will run against the Washington establishment, portraying himself as the champion of limited government who has used his presidency to fight against the forces of big government. In particular, he will try to blame the Democratic Congress for any weakness in the economy, saying they have blocked his economy recovery program and generally hamstrung his efforts to limit the size of big government. At the same time he attacks Democratic "special interest" politics, he will propose aid to many specific industries and social groups. In his State of the Union message he proposed tax breaks for capital gains, the real estate industry, the health insurance industry, and families with children.

In 1992 the hopes of all candidates seem to ride largely on the state of the economy in the months before the election. If the economy is still in recession at that time, either the Democratic candidate or Perot could well move the electorate. If the economy has made a strong recovery by then, the Republicans would be expected to retain the White House.

Of course, presidents have many macroeconomic tools to stave off a recession in the short term. Nixon imposed wage and price controls to further his reelection campaign. Bush is following the 1984 Reagan strategy of borrowing heavily at home and abroad to pump up the economy in his reelection year. The Federal Reserve has given him a large boost by cutting interest rates, which should stimulate short term economic activity. The question of whether these policies will give the economy a short-term jolt is probably the single most important variable in the 1992 election.

The Bush campaign will point to the general prosperity of the Reagan-Bush era. It will argue that the Republicans' policies of tax cuts and limits on government spending have made most Americans better off. The plausibility of these claims will be determined largely by the state of the economy in late 1992.

The parties will also make their historic appeals to their constituency groups through social issues. The 1992 election will not turn on social issues alone, but they can play a key role if the election is close. The Democrats will pursue a strategy of cultural pluralism, supporting programs aiding women, various minority groups, organized labor, and so on. The Bush campaign will run a more culturally monistic campaign, targeting white Americans. Particularistic appeals will be made to evangelical Christians and conservative Catholics, but primarily through preaching the secular religion of Americanism.

The riots in Los Angeles after the Rodney King police beating verdict will be on the minds of the voters. All candidates are likely to denounce both the riots and the verdict. The Republicans, and perhaps Perot, will put more emphasis on the breakdown of law and order. The Democrats will put more emphasis on the deterioration of social and economic conditions in the cities. Attempts to play on racial tensions may be more numerous if the race is close, similar to the 1988 Republican TV ads on the crime issue that dramatized the case of Willie Horton, a black prisoner on furlough who raped a white woman.

All sides will also try to seize the issue of the crisis in the American family. Republicans will blame the decline of the family on the loss of traditional values and misguided social programs. Vicepresident Dan Quayle's attack on the unwed mother in the Murphy Brown TV show was only the opening salvo. The Democrats will point to Bush vetoes of family leave and other social legislation as evidence that Republican support for the family is rhetorical but not substantive. Democrats will try to revive the "gender gap" of the Reagan years by playing on many women's fears that a Republican-dominated Supreme Court will abolish access to legal abortions. Perot is also known to be pro-choice, but his views on other social issues are not as yet well known.

The impact of the abortion issue depends largely on whether the Supreme Court waits until after the election to issue any decision that seriously curtails abortion rights. A pre-election decision that significantly limits access to abortions would instantaneously become a central issue in the campaign. But the Supreme Court may well wait until after the election to issue any far-reaching decision, thus making it difficult for the opposition to mobilize mass support on this issue.

THE PRESIDENCY IN THE 1990s

Presidential Ideological Leadership in the Future

The concepts introduced in the early chapters of this book provide some limited basis for making predictions about the ideological and policy behavior of the Bush administration if it wins a second term and the behavior of future administrations. This section considers five general scenarios: (1) policy in a second Bush term and any Republican administration that has to govern without a large, supportive Republican congressional delegation; (2) how a future Republican president who did have an ideological majority might operate; (3) the projected behavior of a future Democratic president without an ideological majority; (4) how a future Democratic president with a large and ideologically cohesive majority might govern and (5) how an independent, anti-ideological president might try to construct a centrist, bipartisan majority.

The analysis here focuses on domestic and trade policy, since the historical analysis in this book shows that major shifts of domestic policy are dependent upon the strength of a president's party in Congress. But it also shows that foreign policy, particularly in the military and diplomatic spheres, moves primarily in response to external events. The party of the president or the size of his congressional delegation is less useful as a predictor of international security policy.

This book has argued that a large congressional delegation is a necessary but not a sufficient condition for a president to set a new ideological course in domestic policy. Eisenhower and Carter each had unusually large congressional delegations, but that alone did not translate into strong ideological leadership. In addition to its size, the congressional delegation must have ideological cohesiveness. Further, the president must have an ideological vision and the ability to communicate it.

The conduct of the candidate in the presidential campaign and in the first year after election are also crucial in setting the tone of an administration. A candidate who articulates an ideological vision in the presidential selection process is in a better position to put a program into motion upon winning election, as Ronald Reagan and, to a lesser extent, Lyndon Johnson showed. A president who wants to set a new policy course must act quickly to utilize his honeymoon period. FDR, LBJ, and Reagan all had their most significant impact on the legislative process during their first year in office.

Policy factors also shape the potential of any new president to be an ideological leader. Severe crises call for presidential leadership. Relatively calm times make ideological innovation difficult. And, of course, the quality of presidential programs is significant. Having a bad plan is worse than having no plan, and having a long agenda is not the same thing as having a coherent strategy.

The Bush Administration and Republican Successors

The past 8-10 years have demonstrated how conservative Republican presidents govern in the absence of ideological support in Congress. In its first term, facing a Congress controlled by Democrats, the Bush administration has generally chosen a politically centrist path. In economic and budgetary policy this policy centrism has meant continuation of the policies of the limited interest state. Rhetorically Bush has been more accepting of the idea of the activist state than was his predecessor, Ronald Reagan, but there have been few programmatic initiatives.

However, if short-term political movement in the 1990s produced either Republican congressional majorities or near majorities, as in 1980, the possibility exists that the Bush administration or some Republican successor would try to complete the Reagan restoration. On the domestic scene this would mean an administration that would more consistently implement budgetary and economic policies which would match the laissez-faire rhetoric of the Republican Party. A Republican president backed by a renewed conservative ideological majority in Congress could possibly attack federal spending with the same determination that the Reagan administration showed for tax cuts.

The policy behavior of Republican presidents and Republican members of Congress in the 1980s makes that seem unlikely. The interest groups that benefit from public spending wield real power in the American political system, a power an elected official must beware of. The political support for the benefits of government spending programs make such a strategy risky—too risky for the most popular Republican president since the 1920s to take the challenge. But under conditions of rising budgetary pressures and renewed political support in Congress, it might be the course chosen by a Republican president.

One area where a renewed Republican ideological majority would be more likely to make a difference is social policy, particularly judicial appointments. Since 1986 Republican judicial appointments have had to gain the approval of a Senate in which the majority of members are Democrats. Highly ideological candidates like Robert Bork have either been rejected or not even nominated because of the probability of rejection. Southern Democrats have provided the votes to confirm moderately conservative Supreme Court appointments, but if the Republicans can regain control of the Senate, they will have absolute control over the future of the judicial branch. Then more sweeping reversals of the Warren Court and other past decisions in the areas of abortion, civil rights, workers' rights, criminal justice, and government secrecy, can be expected.

Future Democratic Administrations

The policy behavior of any future Democratic president is more difficult to predict. Given the long exile of the Democrats from the White House, there is much interest in how a Democratic president would fare but few precedents from which to extrapolate.

Historically there has been more variability in the ideology and actions of Democratic administrations. This reflects the wider range of interests and philosophies within in the Democratic Party, the fact that the Democrats are more a coalition of factions than a cohesive political party. This has been even more true since the downfall of Lyndon Johnson, the last strong Democratic president. Since then, the Democrats as a party and liberalism as a philosophy have been on the defensive. The ideological inconsistencies of the Carter administration reflected this identity crisis of the Democratic Party.

A future Democratic president who wins the election by articulating a clear philosophy and direction for the country, and who is backed by numerically strong and ideologically cohesive Democratic majorities in Congress, will behave one way, particularly in his early years. A Democrat who wins the presidency by avoiding the difficult issues and who must govern with a relatively small Democratic delegation in Congress will be in a weaker political position and will have to govern differently. Considering these two idealized cases will show the range of possibilities of future Democratic administrations. The actual behavior of the next Democratic president will likely fall somewhere in between these two scenarios.

A weak Democratic president is more likely to try to stick to the political center. His administration will show more contradictory movement on public policy. It will move toward the left at one time, back to the center at another, toward the left on one issue, but toward the center on another. The Carter administration is a recent model for the probable behavior of a weak Democratic president.

In domestic policy, any Democratic administration will talk more about the positive role of government, activist trade policies, and the ideals of social justice. But a weak Democratic president will not be able to put significantly greater amounts of resources toward these goals. Historically the practice of Democratic presidents has been to preach social justice but to engage in the practices of the social security state. Democratic administrations often do expand government protection to interest groups who have not traditionally benefited from the programs of the limited interest state, but with more regard for political clout than for social justice.

However, the fiscal crisis makes the historic Democratic pattern of expansive interest group politics difficult. Under a weak Democratic president, groups that have been shut out during the Reagan-Bush years could expect some slight increases in funds for their programs but few bold or dramatic initiatives. Like the Carter administration, a weak Democratic administration might show a much more culturally pluralistic dimension in its appointments to executive and judicial positions, with more women and minorities in prominent positions. In the main the search would be for policy initiatives that were strong on media appeal but made few commitments of government money.

The policy behavior of a Democratic president who ran a campaign exhibiting strong philosophical convictions and was backed by an ideological majority in Congress would be different from that of a politically weak Democratic president. These conditions would allow a future president to take more bold policy initiatives. Both the general themes of any future Democratic administration and the differences between the probable approaches of a weak versus a strong Democratic president can be illustrated by analyzing two key issues: industrial policy and social welfare policy.

The one policy arena where it is almost certain that a new Democratic administration would take initiatives is in the international competitiveness of the U.S. economy. With the globalization of the world economy and the rising U.S. trade deficit, international trade and industrial policy has assumed a new importance in American politics and in the agenda of the Democratic party. In the 1988 primary election candidates like Richard Gephardt, Albert Gore, and others criticized the Reagan administration severely for allowing the U.S. trade balance to deteriorate.

Any new Democratic president would likely be more activist in using government to try to meet the needs of the United States in a competitive global economy. The next Democratic administration will continue to talk free trade, but it will also take a tougher position on trade negotiations. It will also talk about fair trade, taking the stance that the United States should keep its markets open only for nations whose own domestic markets are open to U.S. goods.

A new Democratic administration would likely seek to develop a coordinated industrial policy to plan a U.S. strategy for competition in the international marketplace. It would try to induce greater cooperation among business, labor, science, and government to develop competitive products. This strategy could be called the corporate planning state. The model would be Japan's Ministry of International Trade and Industry or, more likely, the northern European model of corporatism—active cooperation of business, labor, and government to achieve economic planning goals. In the American context it is reminiscent of FDR's attempt to induce such cooperation to achieve economic recovery established in the early New Deal, and the more successful tripartite planning for military production during and following World War II.

In a weak Democratic administration the concepts of the corporate planning state and fair trade would be largely symbolic. There would be much rhetoric and some policy movement, but little change in the domestic political economy or in trade patterns. A weak Democratic president would not be in a political position to challenge the power of strong economic institutions that prefer the status quo.

However, a strong Democratic administration might choose to create new governmental and economic structures that significantly reshape corporate America. The crises of the Great Depression and World War II led FDR to reform the institutions of U.S. capitalism. The crisis of permanent budget and trade deficits, combined with the deterioration of America's industrial capacity and its central cities, could spur a comparable restructuring of corporate America by a future Democratic administration.

Historically, Democratic administrations have had an agenda of activist programs for social justice. Administrations like Franklin Roosevelt's and Lyndon Johnson's had both the will and the power to enact many new programs. Even Democratic presidents who did not have such strong congressional backing, like Carter, Kennedy, and Truman, have given lip service to the idea of using the activist state to seek social justice even when they lacked the political or financial resources to do much programmatically.

A new Democratic administration can be expected to talk about doing more to combat poverty, particularly emphasizing programs for the working poor and for single parents and their children. Democrats will promise more funds for education, child care, job training, and eradication of the drug traffic. They will talk about new initiatives for housing and urban development, national health care, the environment, and workers' rights on the job and democracy in the workplace.

The new wrinkle will be that many of these programs will be justified not only in the name of social justice but also as ways to attack America's international trade problems. Programs for education, job training, drugs, and even national health care will be sold as ways of making the United States more competitive again. Concern for workers' rights and workplace democracy will be advocated as ways of making workers more involved in their jobs and raising productivity. Old agendas will be recycled in new packages.

In the area of social justice, the most important difference between a strong and a weak Democratic president would be the ability to generate new resources for new programs. A weak Democratic president will be forced to work within the fiscal constraints set by the Reagan-Bush era. A strong Democratic president backed by an ideologically cohesive majority in Congress will be able to generate new resources from a number of possible sources.

A strong Democratic president will be able to get congressional backing to reprogram federal spending to meet a new agenda. He will be able to squeeze a bigger peace dividend out of the Pentagon. He will be able to generate interest group support for deeper cuts in ineffective, poorly designed programs in return for newly designed, more effective approaches. He will be willing to take the political flak for a tax increase if fiscal conditions warrant, particularly if it is part of a tax reform package. The political sting of a tax increase might be lessened if it were done quickly upon taking office. A new administration might be successful in blaming a tax increase on the fiscal "mess" it inherited from the outgoing Republicans, just as Ronald Reagan blamed the pain of early Reaganomics on Jimmy Carter.

In any forecast about future Democratic administrations, one must always keep in mind the difference between saying and doing, between rhetoric and reality. Talk about the corporate planning state and social justice has always been a part of Democratic Party rhetoric. However, the political reality has been that all too often Democratic administrations have been unwilling or unable to set priorities.

In the past, Democratic programmatic initiatives have often been shaped more by the politics of interest group factions within the Democratic Party than by ideals of government planning or social justice. The mentality has been more "something for labor, something for women, something for minorities, something for education". rather than determining what are the most effective means of meeting goals. Republican presidents have always preached laissez-faire philosophy but more often rewarded the dominant interest groups in their political coalition through the policies of the limited interest state. The most likely outcome of a future Democratic administration is not an effective corporate planning state or real social democracy, but an expansion of interest group politics toward the social security state.

An Independent President and the Potential for a Centrist, Bipartisan Majority

The polls in spring of 1992 force one to consider an historically unprecedented scenario—the election of an independent presidential candidate not tied to either political party. If Ross Perot or any future independent turns out to be an ideological conservative, his behavior in office would likely be similar to that of Republican presidents. He will oscillate between confrontation and cooperation with a less conservative Congress. An independent conservative might feel more inclined toward confrontation than the head of the Republican Party, and thus might feel inclined to pursue his beliefs, whatever they were, more consistently. If an independent, conservative president believed strongly in a pure laissez-faire economy, he would certainly face many confrontations with Congress. If a conservative independent were comfortable with the close relationship between powerful interests and the government, he would be able to cooperate more closely with Congress in the practices of the limited interest state. An independent liberal president would face similar choices between pursuing a pure ideological line and cooperating with Congress.

An independent president who was an ideological centrist would be likely to try a different strategy of governing. Particularly during his honeymoon period, he might try to construct a bipartisan majority using the centrist, moderate elements of both the major parties. It is likely a centrist independent would be attracted to some form of the corporate planning state. Depending on the form it took, an independent president offering a legislative package to encourage cooperation between business, labor, and government could conceivably draw support from significant parts of both major parties.

Although there is no precedent for such a strategy in twentieth century American politics, it is possible that both major parties would be so chastened by the election of an independent candidate that they would be reluctant to challenge him politically, at least in his first few years in office. A politically skillful independent president could use such an opportunity to rally the leaders of both parties in a kind of grand coalition of national salvation. Leaders of both parties might be willing to make hard political choices on issues like the federal deficit if they could later blame the impact on an independent president, and possibly spare their party the electoral consequences.

However, such an outcome for an independent presidency is unlikely. The more likely outcome is that he would be unable to win the cooperation of either major party and would become the target of both. While the voters often respond to political amateurs, politics in late twentieth century American requires professional political skills. Jimmy Carter showed that a relative political amateur can make a good candidate but not necessarily a good president. A complete political amateur might conceivably design a successful national campaign, but he is unlikely to be able to govern the country effectively.

15

PRESIDENTIAL IDEOLOGIES AND THE FUTURE OF AMERICA

ECONOMIC POLICY IDEOLOGIES AND THE AMERICAN FUTURE

The Contradictions of the Limited Interest State

This book has examined the ideas that have guided the actions of American presidential administrations in the last half a century. It has chronicled both the important changes and the significant continuities in the policy philosophies of presidents in this period. This chapter goes beyond description of presidential philosophies to take up the question of whether the dominant presidential ideologies are adequate to the public policy challenges of the 1990s and the beginning of the next century.

For the last 50 years domestic policy has been dominated by the ideology and policy practices of the limited interest state. The limited interest state is characterized by a basic contradiction. On the one hand, it preaches the philosophy of limited government and limited interference in private economic markets. But on the other hand, it is open to the penetration of many interest groups that are able to shape public budgets and public law to reap vast benefits from public policy.

The limited interest state was well suited to the domestic policy-making environment in the 1940s and 1950s, when the United States was the dominant economic power in the world and demands for social justice were only beginning to awaken in the groups historically excluded from the center of American economic and social life. Under these conditions the limited interest state was a stable compromise between the idea of the limited state and the demands of the more powerful interest groups in American society.

But since the 1960s the contradictory demands on government have intensified. On the one hand, a whole new range of social interests has become politically activated—blacks, Hispanics, women, environmentalists, consumers, and so on. Their demands are less easily met without conflicting with the interests of groups already incorporated in the state structure, and without increasing public expenditures. At the same time, the globalization of the world economy and the decline of the U.S. economy in the world have made it much more difficult for government to use public budgets and economic policy tools to attack domestic problems without aggravating America's problems in the international economy.

The Policy Failures of the Limited Interest State

The limited interest state has proven unable to cope with four crucial interrelated issues: (1) the chronic fiscal crisis, (2) the declining position of the United States in the world economy, (3) the problems of poverty and the underclass, and (4) the growing economic and social insecurity of middle-class Americans. By the 1980s the contradictions of the limited interest state had become so acute that they produced what can be called the chronic fiscal crisis, the perennial budget and trade deficits that have dominated economic policy-making in the Reagan-Bush era. The limited interest state has proven inadequate as a solution to the domestic and international policy challenges the United States faces in the late twentieth century. Even after a decade of ideologically conservative Republican presidents rhetorically committed to cutting federal spending, the government spends the same fraction of national income as it did at the beginning of the 1980s.

It is largely inaccurate for Republican presidents to place blame solely on Democratic Congresses for this situation. It is true that Congress has more power over budgets than the president, and that Congress has voted to fund many programs recent presidents have wanted to cut. There is plenty of blame to go around, and congressional Democrats share a large portion of it.

But on the other hand, Republican presidents have wanted to spend more in many areas where Democrats have been more frugal. Republican members of Congress have often not been willing to back cuts recommended by Republican presidents and have even supported many of the increases in spending Congress has voted. Many of the cuts Republican presidents have proposed in recent years are largely symbolic because administrations know that Congress has refused to make similar cuts in previous years. Support for the spending programs of the limited interest state comes from both parties. Republican administrations may reduce the scope of federal programs but not the amount of federal spending.

The changing global military situation has raised hopes that a "peace dividend" might be the solution to the fiscal crisis. Certainly significant cuts in military spending would ease fiscal pressures. The Pentagon directly accounts for roughly a quarter of the federal budget. When military spending not on the

Pentagon's ledger is added in, such as its share of the national debt or military aid to key allies, the figure for all military spending is actually much higher. However, the size of the peace dividend is still in doubt. The Pentagon's budget is nearly $300 billion, whereas the fiscal 1991 deficit was $268 billion. Thus, under 1991 conditions a 10 percent cut in military spending would equal roughly a 10 percent cut in the deficit, a 20 percent cut for the military would bring roughly a 20 percent cut in the deficit, and so on. Clearly, even by Washington standards those are big bucks. But even a large peace dividend will not make the fiscal crisis go away.

Related to the inability of the limited interest state to solve the current fiscal crisis is its inability to respond to the growing international economic challenge the United States faces. While recent administrations have preached free trade, they have also granted trade protection to key industries hard hit by foreign competition. If an industry has enough clout in Washington, it can expect government protection; if not, then it must practice free trade. But in the long run the status of the United States in the world economy will be determined not by policies of free trade or protection but by the productivity and competitiveness of the U.S. economy. The limited interest state has proven unable to deal with these dimensions of the trade issue and is unlikely to be able to do so in the future.

The first reflex of the limited interest state is to protect powerful industries that are suffering losses, to "rescue losers" in the international competition. The limited interest state was able to cushion the inevitable decline of the U.S. steel, auto, and textile industries. But developing a forward-looking industrial policy similar to those of Japan's Ministry of International Trade and Industry or its European equivalents is beyond the ability of the limited interest state. For example, while the Reagan administration preached free trade and members of Congress pressured for protection of particular industries in their districts, the Japanese subsidized the development of a new generation of high-definition television that not only could renew their dominance in the sales of television sets into the early twenty-first century, but also could give them control of certain key segments of the computer industry. But the American limited interest state reflects the current power structure; it cannot plan for the future.

The limited interest state is not able to deal with another key element in the trade picture—upgrading the skills of the American work force. As the United States struggles to cope with international competition, one of the key factors in its success or failure will be the productivity of its workers. The perpetuation of the urban social underclass with few or no useful job skills, or even the ability to read or write, is a permanent drag on the ability of the United States to compete internationally. In addition, many workers who have been a productive part of the labor force or women reentering the job market find their job skills obsolete and need to be trained with new skills for the changing marketplace.

But because it reflects the concerns of the current power structure, the limited interest state has given little attention to the key issue of the capabilities of the

American work force. While the limited interest state protects the interests of politically strong industries, the broader interests of workers are not represented. As the number of manufacturing jobs has shrunk, organized labor has declined as a force in the American political system. Because of labor's historical ties to the Democratic Party it has had little influence in conservative Republican administrations. Organized minority and women's groups have even less clout in conservative Republican councils. While corporate interests receive protection, and therefore some workers indirectly are assisted, activist strategies for improving America's trade position by improving the skills of its workers are beyond the scope of today's limited interest state.

The limited interest state is also oblivious to issues of social justice and economic security. Its spending patterns are driven by existing power structures, not by any higher values of social justice or equity. The budget cuts that did pass during the Reagan restoration disproportionately targeted poverty programs, assistance to politically weak and isolated groups, and programs that benefited groups outside the Republican electoral coalition.

While the grand rhetorical flourishes of the 1960s about abolishing poverty were more symbolic than real, by the 1980s and 1990s even such rhetoric was disappearing from American political discourse. As the inner cities were deluged by the tides of crime, unemployment, functional illiteracy, drugs, gangs, and AIDS, supporters of social programs were reduced to trying to protect existing programs from the budget ax. The idea of any large-scale national quest for social justice was discredited intellectually and seemed out of touch with the realities of the fiscal crisis.

But a much wider range of American families and workers than just the underclass have had their lives become harsher and more insecure in recent years. The number of women who have had to raise children with no man in the house and little or no financial support from the father has skyrocketed. The number of workers who have been forced to change jobs and the frequency of such job changes have risen sharply. The number of workers who have had to change their occupation or who must relocate to a different region of the country in order to find work also has risen. The number of Americans working at part-time or low-wage jobs with few or no health benefits is increasing. In most families where there are two adults in the household, both need to work to ensure a regular income flow, access to health benefits, and a moderate life style.

Alternatives to the Limited Interest State

The fact that the limited interest state suffers from inherent contradictions or has failed to meet certain crucial policy tests does not mean that it will necessarily be replaced by something better. American society has survived through more than two centuries despite manifold policy failures in Washington. The American people can live under a rising burden of debt. They can find ways to cope with a nation less insulated from foreign economic penetration. They can close their eyes to the suffering of the underclass and ignore the uncertain future their families face. But the policy failures and basic contradictions of the limited interest state raise the possibility that if short-term political forces produce ideological majorities of either the right or the left, domestic policy could shift as it did in the 1930s, the 1960s, or the early 1980s. If the weak economic performance of recent years continues indefinitely or gets worse, this not only will likely produce movement against whichever political party gets stuck with the blame, it will also intensify immensely the budgetary pressures of the fiscal crisis, perhaps forcing some significant policy movement.

There are two basic types of ideological alternatives to the current limited interest state. The first is the laissez-faire ideology, which would make significant cuts not only in the scope, but also in the size, of government. The second alternative would be more activist government. However, there are different forms of activist government. This book has identified three different forms of activist government which might guide future policy: (1) the social security state, (2) a corporate planning state, and (3) a social democratic state.

Laissez-Faire

A truly laissez-faire ideology might be attractive as a short-term solution to the fiscal crisis. Dramatic cuts in programs would temporarily solve the budget squeeze. But laissez-faire policies would not be likely to solve the problems of the decline of the U.S. economy, social injustice, or the growing insecurity of the middle class. Nor is it likely that they would be able to sustain political support.

Unless significant gains were made in either improving the U.S. trade position or incorporating Americans whose capacity is currently underutilized into the job market, the fiscal gains from massive spending cuts would prove illusory. The free trade doctrine advocated by the laissez-faire philosophy is one of the major causes of the current trade deficit and U.S. economic decline, and it is a prescription for future disaster. As long as there are significant barriers to U.S. access to the markets of the Japanese and other Pacific Rim exporting nations, and to a lesser extent to European markets, it would be folly for the United States to pursue a pure free trade policy. As long as trade with some of its most important partners is on a tilted playing field, the United States will continue to run a large trade deficit.

Laissez-faire doctrine holds that the benefits of free trade are so great that a nation should practice this policy even if its trade partners do not. Certainly there are benefits to free trade, particularly if it is practiced by all major players. But even if Asian and European economies were to liberalize and open themselves to more imports from the United States, free trade would not be an unmixed boon. Certainly such a opening will not come unless the United States shows that it is willing to selectively restrict access to its markets of trading partners who do not open theirs.

Laissez-faire doctrine also cannot deal with the permanent social underclass or the rising insecurity of the middle class. Most members of the urban underclass lack the skills to compete in a marketplace that no longer values muscle power, but only skilled labor. Pure economic competition will have particularly deleterious effects on families headed by a single adult, who will find it even more difficult to balance the demands of the workplace with those of the family.

Nor can conservative appeals to traditional family values solve social problems, particularly in the absence of other social policies. It is true that the economic problems of the underclass and the insecurity of the middle class are closely linked to the deterioration of the family unit. But a program of pure market economics coupled with exhortations about family values is no solution to these problems. As Jesus taught, the values of the marketplace and the values of community are in fact in conflict. Every study shows that men who never take any responsibility for their children or abandon the family unit are better off economically. It is a brute economic and social fact that poor people with few job skills make poor risks for marriage, particularly poor women with children who must be supported or poor males enmeshed in gangs and the criminal justice system. Adults unable or unwilling to economically support or properly raise their children are a key element of American social problems, but simple appeals to traditional family values will not put Humpty-Dumpty back together again.

Activist State Policies

The ideological alternative to the limited state is the activist state. Of the variants of more activist state responses to U.S. economic problems, the one least likely to solve the problems facing the country is the one that historically has proven most politically attractive—the social security state. The extension of government benefits to an ever wider range of social groups was reasonable public policy in the 1950s, when the United States was the overarching economic power in the world, when social programs were a relatively small component of a national budget that spent a relatively small proportion of national economic output, and when the number of interest groups making claims on the national government was relative small. But it is no solution to the fiscal crisis of the 1990s to extend government benefits to every interest group that presses for government aid.

A variant of activist government that is gaining credence within the Democratic Party and even in some Republican circles is the concept of a corporate planning state. Models for the corporate planning state are the highly successful Japanese and German political economies where government, business, and to some extent labor cooperate in devising strategies in key industries. The corporate planning state at least has the possibility of coping relatively effectively with the fiscal crisis and of easing, if not eliminating, both the decline of the U.S.

position in the world economy and the social problems the nation faces. The mere mechanism of greater government, business, and labor coordination would be no guarantee of success. Corporate planning could produce ineffective policies. It could prove to be a new version of the limited interest state that would only give new sanction to existing power relations and programmatic priorities. Or it could prove to be a new move toward a social security state, simply extending broader and deeper protection to industries that are unable to meet international competition and further entrenching programs favored by narrow interest groups in the federal budget.

Certainly as Soviet Leninism has collapsed, the idea of government planning has taken another beating in the American ideological system. But the Japanese, Korean, German, and French experiences prove that thoughtful corporate planning can work to improve a nation's fiscal and trade positions. Government support for key technologies, coupled with broad-based education and training to develop an appropriately skilled work force, can make an economy more, not less, competitive. A corporate planning state could build political support for the tough budget choices that will have to be made to ease the fiscal crisis. When the alternative is simply the budget ax, interest groups fight hard to defend programs that benefit their members even if they are poorly designed. From the point of view of an interest group, a poorly designed program is better than none. But interest group support might be mobilized for the redesign of programs if it were perceived as part of a larger effort by the government to restructure industries while getting its fiscal house in order.

Even if a corporate planning ideology were relatively successful in coping with the fiscal crisis and in beginning the process of making U.S. industry more competitive internationally, these accomplishments would not solve fundamental issues of social justice and economic insecurity. The South Korean political economy may be admired for its economic growth and stability, but it is hardly a model of social justice or of elemental fairness to workers, women, or those outside the power structure. An American corporate planning state could serve to mute political opposition to massive layoffs, reductions of job benefits and protections, union-busting, and flight of capital to cheap labor markets overseas in the private economy and large-scale social program cuts in the public sector.

The only way to ensure that a corporate planning state would protect the interests of ordinary workers and work to incorporate the underclass into the economic system would be to ensure that planning structures and mechanisms were democratic, that they reflected the needs of workers, women, and minorities as well as corporate shareholders. While a corporate planning state could conceivably improve the nation's fiscal condition, only a social democratic state has the potential to simultaneously attack the nation's economic problems and move the country toward social justice and economic security. Again, simply incorporating workers into more broadly based public and private policy-making processes would be no guarantee of policy success. The more broadly based such institutions would be, the more difficult it would be to come to any consensus on basic issues. But it would be a minimal condition for keeping issues of social justice and the needs of ordinary Americans in front of such institutions.

This is a study of presidential ideologies, and so it is beyond the scope of this work to explore in detail an agenda for future domestic or foreign policy. But the history of domestic policy demonstrates that certain forms of the activist state are almost certain to fail to meet the challenges the nation faces. Other forms of the activist state provide the potential, if not any guarantee, that more successful policy responses can be developed.

THE CHALLENGE OF A NEW WORLD ORDER

New Thinking for a New World

The parameters of ideological debate about domestic economic policy have remained remarkably stable over the past half of a century. New concepts like supply-side economics and the war on poverty have emerged, but the range of programmatic initiatives can be reasonably captured by the categories in this book. But foreign policy ideologies have proven to be more volatile, shifting dramatically in the post-World War II period and again in recent years. Rather than pretend the tentative characterization of future foreign policy debate offered in Chapter 13 can be assumed to prove precisely accurate, I will present my conclusions about foreign policy on an issue-by-issue basis.

Like the limited interest state in domestic policy, the national security state that dominated U.S. foreign policy in the postwar period was unable to deal with several new developments. It could not protect Americans from the specter of nuclear holocaust; it led to the costly and disastrous intervention in Vietnam; and it could not cope with the declining position of the United States in the world economy. Since the national security state was based on perceptions of a Soviet military threat, the recent unraveling of the Soviet system has probably dealt a death blow to this ideology as a consistent philosophy of governance. But several problems of foreign policy posed by the national security ideology still plague policymakers trying to cope with a new world system, albeit in different form.

The late 1980s and early 1990s brought renewed hope that the cold war could finally be laid to rest and a new, peaceful world order could be constructed in its place. Certainly the map of Europe was being transformed, and relations between the United States and Russia were better than at any time since the second world war. President Bush, Russian President Yeltsin, the major European leaders, and many other world leaders have expressed noble sentiments about working for a more peaceful world.

Certainly a new world is emerging. But whether that new world will have a truly peaceful, stable order is not at all clear. The creation of a new, peaceful world order requires more than sentiment. It requires new international behavior on the part of the great powers. On the American side it requires a foreign policy that recognizes what is needed to fashion a sustainable structure of peace and how historical U.S. policies must change in order to make such a world possible. Most of all, it requires new thinking about the goals and instruments of foreign policy. A new world cannot be constructed with old thinking. A new world order will require new ideas about (1) the effect of the pursuit of U.S. power on world peace, (2) relations among the United States, Russia, and other European nations, (3) the relationship between nuclear arms and national security, and (4) the practice of U.S. intervention in conflicts in the Third World.

New Thinking About World Order and U.S. Power

A peaceful world order will not emerge simply because the old structure of forces in Europe is changing. Instead, a new world order must be created by a series of actions and policies by the leading powers that put maintenance of peace before the power stakes of each nation. Perhaps the final sign that the United States is ready truly to contribute to the development of a peaceful world order will be when its foreign policy begins to consistently value the maintenance of world peace more highly than the pursuit of U.S. power.

In the postwar era policymakers have tended to fuse together the values of U.S. power and world peace. U.S. power was thought to be the only check to communist aggression, and thus whatever furthered U.S. power furthered world peace. Like the General Motors executive who said, "What is good for General Motors is good for the country," policymakers acted as if they believed, "What is good for American power is good for world peace." Of course, what is good for General Motors is not always good for the country, and what is good for U.S. power is not always good for world order.

There has been much talk in recent years about the globalization of the U.S. economy and the need to develop new policies to meet this challenge. But thinking in global terms is even more important for progress in political relations. There will be times in the near future when the short-term U.S. power interests will conflict with the requirements of a new world order—when pursuing narrow U.S. interests will conflict with the requisites of world peace. It is then that the degree of U.S. commitment to a new world order will be revealed.

New Thinking About U.S.-Russian Relations and the New Europe

New thinking has begun to be applied to U.S.-Russian relations. But before truly new thinking about this relationship can fully develop, some old ghosts must be exorcised. The cold war itself needs to be thoroughly reexamined and reinterpreted. The issue of the origins of the cold war is an old and contentious debate in American foreign policy circles, but it is worth returning to for at least two reasons. First, the collapse of the Soviet bloc reveals startling new evidence about the historic weakness of the Soviet position. Writing about the disintegration of the Warsaw Pact in *Time* magazine, Strobe Talbot subtly caught one of the generally ignored implications of the fall of the Soviet empire with the clever line "The Soviet threat isn't what it used to be, and it never was." The menace of the Soviet Union was at the heart of the doctrines and policies of the national security state. But the complete disintegration of the Soviet bloc demonstrates that in fact the Soviets were never ten feet tall.

Even more important, the reinterpretation of the wisdom of the policies of the national security state has huge implications for the direction of future U.S. foreign policy. If the militaristic policies of the national security state were successful in turning back what was a serious Soviet threat of world conquest and domination, as President Bush stated in his 1992 State of the Union message, this validates future confrontational policies against Russia and other potential foes.

But if the whole cold war was an unnecessary game of chicken on the precipice of nuclear annihilation based on misperception and ultranationalism, its history clearly has different lessons to teach us about future U.S. policy. If the national security state won a stunning victory over an evil empire that was the principal threat to world peace and security, then future policy should simply modify old thinking to reflect the decline of the old adversary. But if the cold war was a massive miscalculation, a foreign policy Topsy that grew out of control, then the kind of foreign policy doctrines that produced this colossal mistake need to be replaced.

Clearly, relations between the United States and Russia are set on a new course that is not likely to be reversed in the short term. But can this era of good feeling be sustained long enough to truly transform political and military relations? Certainly in the past the United States has miscalculated badly in its dealings with the Russians, miscalculations that seriously undermined the development of good policy. For years it wildly overestimated the Soviet threat. Then, when the Soviet bloc was crumbling, the United States failed to realize the implications of the total breakup of the Soviet state. For more than forty years the obsession of U.S. foreign policy was to negate Soviet power, and thus the United States encouraged the break up of the Soviet Union. American policymakers did not see, until it was too late, the threat to world peace posed by a totally independent and nuclear armed Ukraine and/or Kazakhstan on the borders of an ever weaker and more unstable, but still nuclear, Russia. When the implications of the total collapse of the Soviet Union dawned on policymakers, the United States had to rapidly revise its entire nuclear doctrine. Suddenly U.S. policy aimed to maintain some kind of Russian control over nuclear weapons remaining in the republics.

A similar miscalculation of U.S. interests regarding Russia is certainly possible in the future. Since almost no one foresaw the events in the East in recent years, it is unlikely anyone can accurately predict the even more cloudy future. But it is at least possible that serious military conflicts will develop between Russia and some of the former Soviet republics. No one can be sure that Yugoslavia is not the model for the future of most of eastern Europe. Future U.S. policymakers may be tempted to simplistically interpret Russian behavior in such conflicts as a revival of Russian imperialism. Old stereotypes of the predatory Russian bear have not been completely exorcised.

In the West the debate about how to deal with the new Russia and eastern Europe has focused almost entirely on the potential of economic aid to help the reform process. But the economic future of Russian and eastern Europe is primarily in the hands of the people themselves. The kind of outside aid that would have a significant impact on these economies would be of a scale that would engender economic dependency and nationalist resentment at outside interference and control, particularly in the case of the chauvinistic Russians. Outside aid can marginally strengthen the hand of reformers, but too much intervention in the Russian and eastern European economies is likely to be counterproductive in both economic and political terms.

However, there is one set of policies that could significantly strengthen the political hand of the reformers against the reactionaries and at the same time give real long-term help to the Russian economy—relieving the military pressure on the Russians. The Russian army remains the biggest threat to reform movements both in the Russian Republic and in other former Soviet republics. Following the failed coup, the Communist Party has been routed, but the army remains a relatively strong and cohesive force in Russia. It has also been a massive loser in the changes in the past decade. It has lost the buffer zones in eastern Europe and the eastern Soviet republics that protected Mother Russia from another invasion from the west. It has lost many of its nuclear weapons. It has lost the ability to conscript young men from the non-Russian republics. It has lost its privileged place in the command economy, and thus its guaranteed access to material resources and the best Russian technical minds. In sum, the military must cope with a radically weaker strategic position with only a fraction of the resources it once commanded, facing the organization of potentially hostile armies in what used to be its home territory.

Yet in the chaos that is contemporary Russia, the army remains one of the few institutions at least potentially capable of being a force for stability in deepening crisis. The last antireformist coup was led by Communist Party functionaries who did not have the will or the ability to coerce their opponents as in the days of Stalin. But any new antireformist coup could well be led by a desperate Russian army. It could also engender more popular support from a Russian people feeling ever more vulnerable to hostile forces at their borders and alien powers around the world. U.S. and NATO policies have a direct effect on the power of the military in the new Russian political equation. Western complacency about its newly improved strategic situation and slowness to alter its historic military position fosters the feeling that reform has only made Russia weaker and more vulnerable. However, Western recognition of the new strategic realities and change in its military doctrines and deployments help to create the alternative perception that the reformers have been successful in removing the threat of Western military action against Russia by transforming the external environment.

Relieving the military pressure on the Russians will also have beneficial long-term effects on the Russian economy. From its inception the Soviet economy was directed more to defending the Soviet system from a hostile world than to producing goods for consumers. As much as a quarter of all Soviet production went to the military, and almost all scientific and engineering talent was devoted to military rather than civilian use. The high technical level developed by the Soviet system could yield great dividends if converted to civilian use. But that is dependent on the external and internal political situation.

For almost three years the Bush administration simply watched as the Soviet system collapsed and the Russian military withdrew from country after country and then republic after republic, feeling the United States did not need to make any significant reciprocal responses. But finally in 1991 Bush, spurred by fears of newly independent republics gaining control over Soviet nuclear weapons, finally began to act rather than just react. However, it is apparent that U.S. foreign policy doctrine and behavior have not caught up with the changes in the former Soviet Union, much less developed policies adequate for the unpredictability of future events.

Because of the many European nations involved and the possibility for more changes in the map of Europe, the exact form of new military doctrines and deployments is impossible to specify. But two principles stand out. First, NATO should play an ever diminishing role in Europe, its security and political activities being increasingly replaced by European-wide institutions such as the Conference on Security and Cooperation in Europe. NATO should continue to reduce its permanent force levels and should not admit any former territories of the Warsaw Pact into its military structure. Whether or not a formal shell of NATO is preserved makes little difference, for Western nations will continue to coordinate their military policies both inside and outside of Europe. But NATO as a massive military force in Europe should recede from the scene.

The second principle is that Western nations and NATO members in particular should refrain from military intervention in any conflicts that arise in eastern Europe, such as the one now occurring in Yugoslavia, unless such action also has the support of Russia, Ukraine, and most other states in eastern Europe. The Balkans, as southeastern Europe was called in the first half of the century, historically was very politically unstable, with ethnic tensions between the different peoples of the region causing many conflicts. World War I began when the major powers intervened in Balkan politics.

Today ethnic strife has already broken out into full-scale civil war in Yugoslavia, and other ethnic conflicts could follow, perhaps even between former Soviet republics and Russia. NATO countries might be tempted to send military forces in response to calls from help from local combatants. But Western intervention in the conflicts in eastern Europe would run the risks of making this volatile region once again a staging ground for great power rivalry and of reviving reactionary Russian nationalism, fearful of the extension of Western military power ever closer to the Russian homeland. Western European nations and perhaps even the United States can play a mediating role in such conflict if the parties will listen, but sending NATO forces into eastern Europe would be a tragic mistake, guaranteed to strengthen the hand of Russian reactionaries and militarists.

New Thinking About National Security and Arms Control

The United States also needs to rethink its historic conception of national security and the role that nuclear weapons play in its foreign policy. This process of rethinking has already begun, but it still has a long way to go. The national security state defined national security almost exclusively in terms of the possession of military power. For nearly half a century U.S. presidents built up conventional and military forces, only to find the nation ever more vulnerable to complete annihilation.

The changes in presidential conceptions of national security can be seen by comparing early Reagan administration statements about the evil empire with President Bush's historic unilateral cuts in nuclear arsenals. Increasingly U.S. foreign policy has become based on the principle that the best way to avoid war is for all powers to feel that their basic security interests are protected. In the nuclear age national security is mutual security; national means alone cannot provide real security.

Related to the idea of mutual security is the concept of minimal deterrence. Perhaps the most bizarre distortion of policy doctrine in the nuclear age was the belief that the United States must have the capacity to annihilate an adversary completely in order to effectively deter war. As Americans came to face the fact that they, too, would face annihilation in a nuclear war, policymakers slowly began to recognize that in nuclear arms, less is better. But a coherent doctrine about how much is enough has yet to emerge. A candidate for such a doctrine would be the idea of minimal deterrence. The United States should seek to reach the minimum nuclear force that can sustain deterrence, not the maximum capability it can afford. Arms reduction treaties should serve the principle of minimal deterrence. Agreements have already begun to target weapons systems most useful in a potential first strike for the greatest reductions. As first-strike capabilities are reduced, fewer and fewer total weapons will be necessary to assure a survivable deterrent. As the most destabilizing first-strike weapons are eliminated, the justification for new acquisitions in order to ensure a survivable force will also be eliminated. Small, survivable nuclear forces will make everyone more secure.

While the general idea of mutual security has gained widespread acceptance on a philosophical level, it has not truly altered the way U.S. policymakers think about the use of military power. Most foreign policymakers have come to recognize in principle that national militaries cannot ensure national security, but the process of erasing the equation of national security with the possession and use of military power has not really taken hold at the operational level. In the Persian Gulf, Panama, and elsewhere policymakers still reflexively turn to the military to solve their policy crises. Even in the arms reduction process U.S. policies still often seem aimed more at gaining some military advantage than at maximizing mutual security. Truly redefining the idea of national security requires completely redefining American beliefs about the role of military power.

Certainly from the perspective of the cold war, the movement of recent arms reductions is breathtaking. But it is a measure of just how distorted cold war thinking was that after the most breathtaking arms reductions in human history, both the United States and Russia retain the ability to virtually erase human life from the planet. The biggest test of arms reduction will be if the nuclear powers ever reach the point where further reductions will actually have a meaningful impact on their ability to inflict genocide on their enemies. It is worth noting what the historic arms cuts of recent years have not yet done. They have not dealt effectively with the issue of modernization, the race to develop new technologies of destruction. They have not dealt directly with the issue of the current nuclear capacity of western European and other nations. They have not dealt directly with the problem of proliferation of nuclear weapons beyond the few current nuclear powers. Most important, new thinking about arms reduction has not really replaced the tendency to maximize national advantage in arms competition. Doctrines based on maximizing national advantage need to be replaced with new doctrines of minimal deterrence and maximizing gains in mutual security.

Stopping development of new weapons systems and putting limits on modernization of existing systems is crucial to bringing an end to nuclear competition. Early arms control negotiations did little to stop the arms race because both sides built up to the limits set, and speeded up development of systems not specifically controlled by the agreements. Arms reduction treaties will have a similar perverse effect if at the same time that obsolete or politically contentious weapons systems are being destroyed, new and more threatening systems are being developed to take their place. Reductions of existing systems need to be matched by a freeze on the deployment of new systems if they are going to effectively increase security.

Recent arms reduction agreements have been largely U.S.-Russian affairs. But there are at least five other nuclear powers and several nations trying to join the club. Other Third World regimes may find chemical or biological weapons a cheaper, less technological demanding form of mass destruction. If an arms reduction regime is to be truly effective, eventually it will have to incorporate other nuclear powers and include other weapons of mass destruction. For decades the United States and the Soviet Union set the wrong example that nuclear weapons translate into real political power, and thus encouraged other nations to seek their own nuclear capacity. Now the United States and Russia are setting a new course, but it is no longer just a U.S.-Russian issue.

The United States and Russia are not going to reduce their arms below a certain threshold if Britain, France, China, India, Pakistan, Israel, or any other powers are building beyond that threshold. Certainly Russia will at some point balk at future reductions if Britain's and France's weapons are not counted in Western totals. Bringing Britain and France into the equation could help establish a process by which non-European nuclear powers could also be accommodated. This is an even more difficult issue than those arms controllers have faced in the past, and there is no magic solution. But it has to be tackled if the threat of genocide is to be reduced, rather than multiplied, in the twenty-first century.

The Future of U.S. Interventionism in the Third World

If a truly new world order is to be created, the United States needs to transform its relationship not only with the Russians but also with the Third World. While relations with the Russians have been moving forward, in its attitude toward the Third World the United States seems to be returning to the policies characteristic of the worst days of the cold war. Following the collapse of Soviet power, many U.S. policies toward the Third World seem to be attempts to reestablish American hegemony, to prove that the United States is the only superpower left. The chronic poverty and political instability in the Third World sow the seeds of both internal conflict and discord with the richer American and western European societies. Too often the United States reflexively responds to these conflicts largely with military force. Yet a truly peaceful world order will require more than following the old policies toward the Third World more aggressively now that the Soviets no longer check U.S. power.

Far from being the harbingers of a new world order, the invasion of Panama and the war with Iraq harkened back more to the days when the United States aspired to be the policeman of the world. These actions were successful in achieving their military objectives, and because they were cheap and easy victories, they were popular with broad segments of the American public. But that does not mean they are models of desirable policies that should be emulated in the future.

In the 1950s the United States achieved several cheap and easy victories in the Third World that only led to future disaster. CIA paramilitary operations were successful in ousting governments the United States did not like in Iran and Guatemala. A show of force with the Marines kept a friendly government in power in Lebanon. U.S. economic and military support for pro-Western forces kept communists from gaining control of most of Indochina when French colonial rule was overthrown. The very success of these operations engendered a certain arrogance in Washington, a belief that indirect and controlled interventions in Third World nations could easily produce favorable results. This hubris, as Senator William Fulbright later called it, led the United States to some costly miscalculations in the 1960s. A similar operation to overthrow Fidel Castro ended in public humiliation at the Bay of Pigs in 1961 and exacerbated the conditions that led to the Cuban missile crisis the following year.

U.S. intervention in Indochina led, through step-by-step escalation, to the debacle in Vietnam. Many commentators have celebrated the fact that the U.S. victory in Iraq has finally put to rest the "Vietnam syndrome." But in fact the war with Iraq and the invasion of Panama have actually inflamed the real "Vietnam syndrome," the tendency of the United States to take sides in a wide range of conflicts in the Third World. It was not only in Vietnam where these cheap and easy victories later proved very costly. For example, the hostage crises in Iran and Lebanon resulted when pro-Western governments which had been propped up by the United States were later overthrown and the revolutionaries did not forget whose side the United States had been on. Just as the "successful" Third World interventions of the 1950s engendered a hubris in U.S. policymakers in the 1960s, so the victories in Iraq and Panama, and the restoration of domestic political support for military operations in the Third World, may lead to future disasters.

There are two regions of the world in particular where the probability of future U.S. interventions is high and the possibility for disaster is very real: Latin America and the Islamic world. The preceding pages tell many stories of U.S. intervention in Latin American affairs. U.S. intervention in Latin America predates the existence of the Soviet Union and will likely continue regardless of the role the Russians choose to play in the region. History tells us that U.S. intervention in Latin America is almost a certainty, but the Latin American debt crisis means that instability may come in countries much larger and harder to control than Nicaragua or Panama, countries like Argentina or Brazil.

The Reagan and Bush administrations have liked to point to events in Latin America as successes in their foreign policies. The Sandinistas have been driven from power in Nicaragua, as have Manuel Noriega in Panama and the radical government in Grenada. In the 1980s many Latin American countries moved from military governments to elected ones, including Brazil, Argentina, and Chile.

But many Latin American nations are deeply mired in debt to foreign banks, teetering on the brink of severe economic and political crises. Brazil and Mexico owe over $100 billion in total debt, Argentina over $60 billion, and several other Latin American countries owe in the tens of billions. Countries like Colombia, Peru, and Bolivia have economies largely dependent on the cocaine trade to keep afloat. The veneer of elective institutions has not fundamentally changed the oligarchical nature of most Latin American societies, solved the problems of dependent development, or significantly improved the lives of the impoverished masses.

When Latin American economic crises become political crises, the tendency has been for the United States to use military force to put down radical insurgencies. The huge cocaine-smuggling operations from South American countries into the United States are another potential cause of serious conflict. As Manuel Noriega proved, Latin American drug lords make a convenient scapegoat for the growth of crime and gangs and the deteriorating social conditions in many U.S. cities. Historically, the direct costs to the U.S. of intervention in Latin America have usually been low because they have mostly been conducted in small countries that did not have the population or resources to effectively resist the colossus of the North. However, for more than a decade a serious economic and political crisis has been building in the larger Latin American countries like Argentina, Brazil, and Mexico. The burden of foreign debt has weighed ever more heavily in these countries, leading to the possibility of political upheaval and even civil war. Given its historic attitude toward the region and the revived faith in military solutions recent successes have engendered, The United States may be tempted to intervene in a conflict it cannot control.

The other area where the United States is likely to intervene despite great risks is the Islamic world, which can be envisioned as a belt that runs from Algeria and Libya in northern Africa across the Middle East, much of southern Asia, and Soviet central Asia, all the way to Indonesia and the Philippines in the Pacific. The war with Iraq was the largest, but not the first, major American intervention in the Islamic world. In the postwar period the United States has supported Israel in five wars and numerous other conflicts against its Arab neighbors. It has also intervened in civil wars and coups in Algeria, Libya, Egypt, Lebanon, Jordan, Iran, Afghanistan, Pakistan, Bangladesh, Indonesia, and the Philippines, among others. In many ways the fanatic Islamic terrorist has replaced the cunning Soviet Communist as the stereotypical devil of U.S. foreign policy.

The Islamic world is far from homogeneous, and many different kinds of conflict occur there. But Islam plays a pivotal role in some of the most unstable regions of the world. It is at the heart of the conflict between Arabs and Israelis. It is the crux of the conflict between Pakistan and India. It was Islamic revolutionaries who took Americans hostage in Iran and Lebanon. Islamic revolutionaries have replaced communists as the leaders of the armed opposition in Indonesia and may soon do so in the Philippines. It has also been Islamic revolutionaries who have opposed the Soviet-backed regime in Afghanistan. Most of the non-Russian peoples in Soviet Asia have Islamic roots, so Islam will play a growing role in several formerly Soviet republics.

Conflicts in the Islamic world have often cut across classic cold war lines. Historically the United States has more often fought Islamic forces opposed to its interests, but it has also supported Islamic forces fighting Soviet-backed regimes. Thus the United States led the forces fighting Islamic Iraq and has backed Israel in its wars against the Arabs. The United States has bombed Libya, sent Marines into Lebanon, and conducted paramilitary operations in Iran. It has supported the Shah of Iran and numerous other pro-Western governments against their Islamic opponents. It has portrayed Libya's Qaddafi, the Iranian mullahs, and more recently Iraq's Saddam Hussein as mad dog fanatics who are beyond the bounds of all reason. Yet at the same time the United States has supported the same kind of Islamic revolutionaries against the pro-Soviet regime in Afghanistan. It has continued close military cooperation with Pakistan even as Islamic fundamentalists stand on the threshold of power in that country.

So far the United States has been lucky enough to intervene frequently in the Islamic world without getting bogged down in a Vietnam or Afghanistan type of conflict. But that luck may not run indefinitely. Whether it is in the Middle East, the conflicts between India and Pakistan, or counterinsurgency against Islamic revolutionaries in Indonesia and the Philippines, the United States is taking several risks of being drawn into a major shooting war which will not end as quickly and easily as the war against Iraq.

The old adversary that defined U.S. foreign policy for half a century is fading from the picture. But even during the cold war the major wars the United States has been involved in—Korea, Vietnam, and Iraq—were not directly against the Soviets but were fought against Third World regimes. As East-West conflicts recede, North-South issues will gain increasing importance. It is certain that poverty and political instability will produce continuing conflicts within the Third World. In many such cases the U.S. will be tempted to intervene. But any new world order will not really be very peaceful if the United States is locked in perpetual hostilities with a series of Third World nations.

The New Global Economy

In the post-cold war world, economic issues will become ever more prominent in global relations. It will take a new set of policies for the United States to deal effectively with the challenges of an integrated European market and the rise of Japan and other east Asian economies. Certainly the United States has taken a beating in international economic competition in recent years. Perennial trade surpluses have given way to perennial trade deficits in the range of $100 billion. America's economic problems are primarily home grown, but they are made worse by trade policies designed during American economic ascendance.

The U.S.-led postwar free trade regime is clearly under serious stress. Paradoxically, the very successes of the General Agreement on Tariffs and Trade have put its survival into question. The increasing volume of world trade has put more and more industries in more and more countries under serious threat from international competitors and thus has heightened protectionist pressures. The extension of a common market across western Europe has made possible coordinated European policies to keep out non-European goods. In the Pacific, the Japanese and several other Asian economies have effectively penetrated relatively open Western markets but have structured their own economies on a different model, restricting outsiders' access to their growing markets.

While the general concept of free trade is still strong in the American ideological system, some of the historic policies pursued under free trade doctrine are under attack. As long as the trade deficit approaches $100 billion, advocates of fair trade will be ever more convincing in arguing that access to U.S. markets should be reduced for those nations which do not allow U.S. firms comparable access to their markets.

There are dangers both to the overall international trading system and to political relations with particular nations in taking a hard trade line. In the current Structural Impediments Initiative trade talks with Japan, the United States may have gone too far in demanding that the Japanese restructure their highly successful economy just to please U.S. exporters. Too harsh a stance will only strengthen the growing perception that the United States is just out to bash Japan and other nonwhite competitors. There is no iron law of necessity that Japan or other Asian economies conform to the U.S. model of economic organization. But there is also no iron law that the U.S. market be wide open to nations that do not reciprocate by keeping their markets open.

The trade deficit has had some salutary effects on U.S. economic policy. It certainly has spurred rethinking of the role of government in economic development and the drag placed on the American economy by an unskilled, underutilized underclass. It may lead Americans to learn from other models of economic organization. Trade problems may even serve to sensitize Americans to the problems Third World nations face in a global economic system shaped by foreign powers. But the United States still has not really learned the hard economic lessons that the trade deficit will eventually force it to face. Economic policies shaped in the era of U.S. hegemony will only hasten the American decline.

CONCLUSION

As it prepares to enter a new century, the United States faces several serious challenges to its world economic and political position. Meeting these challenges effectively requires effective leadership, leadership that at least in part must come from the president. As this book has tried to document, leadership is not just providing inspirational images that make people feel good about themselves. Real leadership requires making tough policy choices. It requires new ideas to respond to a changing world. It requires a consistent philosophy of the role of government that meets the critical issues of the times. It remains an open question whether the American political system can produce presidents that can provide effective ideological and policy leadership for the challenges of the next century.

BIBLIOGRAPHY

REFERENCE DOCUMENTS

Congressional Budget Office. *Report to the Senate and House on the Budget* (Washington, DC: U.S. Government Printing Office, annual).

Congressional Quarterly Almanac (Washington, DC: Congressional Quarterly, annual).

Council of Economic Advisers. *The Economic Report of the President* (Washington, DC: U.S. Government Printing Office, annual).

Inaugural Addresses of the Presidents (Washington, DC: U.S. Government Printing Office, 1989).

Israel, Fred L., ed. *State of the Union Messages of the Presidents* (New York: Chelsea House-Hector, 1966).

Johnson, Donald Bruce, and Kirk H. Porter, eds. *National Party Platforms* (Urbana: University of Illinois Press, 1972).

_____. *National Party Platforms of 1980* (Urbana: University of Illinois Press, 1982).

National Urban League. *The State of Black America* (New York: National Urban League, annual).

Office of Management and Budget. *The U.S. Budget* (Washington, DC: U.S. Government Printing Office, annual).

_____. *The U.S. Budget in Brief* (Washington, DC: U.S. Government Printing Office, annual).

Podell, Janet, and Steven Anzovin, eds. *Speeches of the American Presidents* (New York: H. W. Wilson, 1988).

Presidential Elections Since 1796 (Washington, DC: Congressional Quarterly, 1991).

Public Papers of the Presidents (Washington, DC: U.S. Government Printing Office, annual).

Rauch, Basil, ed. *The Roosevelt Reader* (New York: Rinehart, 1957).

Roosevelt, Franklin D. *Nothing to Fear*, B. D. Zevin, ed. (Boston: Houghton Mifflin, 1946).

U.S. Census Bureau. *The Statistical Abstract of the United States* (Washington, DC: U.S. Government Printing Office, annual).

World Almanac and Book of Facts (New York: Pharoh Books, 1992).

COMPARATIVE STUDIES OF THE PRESIDENCY

Burns, James MacGregor. *The Crosswinds of Freedom* (New York: Knopf, 1989).

Edwards, George C. III. *At the Margins* (New Haven: Yale University Press, 1989).

Edwards, George C. III, and Stephen Wayne. *Presidential Leadership* (New York: St. Martin's Press, 1985).

Kellerman, Barbara. *The Political Presidency* (New York: Oxford University Press, 1984).

Lowi, Theodore. *The Personal Presidency* (Ithaca, NY: Cornell University Press, 1985).

McQuaid, Dennis. *Big Business and Presidential Power* (New York: Morrow, 1982).

Neustadt, Richard. *Presidential Power* (New York: The Free Press, 1990).

Palmer, John L., ed. *Perspectives on the Reagan Years* (Washington, DC: Urban Institute Press, 1986).

Palmer, John L. and Isabel V. Sawhill, eds. *The Reagan Record* (Washington, DC: Urban Institute Press, 1984).

IDEOLOGICAL DYNAMICS

Edelman, Murray. *The Symbolic Uses of Politics* (Urbana: University of Illinois Press, 1964).

Erickson, Paul D. *Reagan Speaks* (New York: New York University Press, 1985).

Furniss, Norman, and Timothy Tilton. *The Case for the Welfare State* (Bloomington: Indiana University Press, 1977).

Goldwater, Barry. *The Conscience of a Conservative* (Shepherdsville, KY: Victor Publishing, 1960).

Higgs, Robert. *Crisis and Leviathan* (New York: Oxford University Press, 1987).
Hinkley, Barbara. *The Symbolic Presidency* (New York: Routledge, 1990).
Lowi, Theodore. *The End of Liberalism* (New York: Norton, 1979).
Stockman, David. *The Triumph of Politics* (New York: Harper Row, 1986).
Thompson, Kenneth W. *The President and the Public Philosophy* (Baton Rouge: Louisiana State University Press, 1981).

IDEOLOGIES ABOUT FOREIGN POLICY

Eagleton, Thomas. *War and Presidential Power* (New York: Liveright, 1974).
Goldwater, Barry. *Why Not Victory?* (New York: McGraw Hill, 1962).
Kennedy, Paul. *The Rise and Fall of Great Powers* (New York: Random House, 1987).
Mills, C. Wright. *The Causes of World War III* (New York: Simon and Schuster, 1958).
Schlesinger, Arthur. *The Imperial Presidency* (Boston: Houghton Mifflin, 1973).

PRESIDENTIAL IDEOLOGIES AND PARTY POLITICS

Burnham, Walter Dean. *Critical Elections and the Mainsprings of American Politics* (New York: Norton, 1970).
Burns, James MacGregor. *Deadlock of Democracy* (Englewood Cliffs, NJ: Prentice Hall, 1963).
Chubb, John E., and Paul E. Petersen, eds. *New Directions in American Politics* (Washington, DC: Brookings Institution, 1985).
Clubb, Jerome M., William H. Flanigan, and Nancy Zingale. *Partisan Realignment* (Boulder, CO: Westview Press, 1990).
Downs, Anthony. *An Economic Theory of Democracy* (New York: Harper, 1965).
Key, V. O. "A Theory of Critical Elections," *Journal of Politics 17* (February, 1955).
Phillips, Kevin P. *The Emerging Republican Majority* (New Rochelle, NY: Arlington House, 1969).
_____. *The Politics of Rich and Poor* (New York: Random House, 1990).
Sundquist, James L. *Dynamics of the Party System* (Washington, DC: Brookings Institution, 1983).
_____. *Politics and Policy* (Washington, DC: Brookings Institution, 1968).
Watson, Richard. *The Presidential Contest* (New York: John Wiley, 1984).

INDEX

ABOUT THE AUTHOR

DENNIS FLORIG holds degrees from American University and the University of Maryland, and a Ph.D. in Political Science from Stanford University. He has taught at several American universities. Presently, he is associated with the International Education, Research, and Analysis Corporation in Tokyo.